Teacher Training

 A REFERENCE HANDBOOK

Other Titles in
ABC-CLIO's
CONTEMPORARY EDUCATION ISSUES
Series

African American Education, Cynthia L. Jackson
The Assessment Debate, Valerie J. Janesick
Charter Schools, Danny Weil
Migrant Education, Judith A. Gouwens
Special Education, Arlene Sacks
Student Rights, Patricia H. Hinchey

FORTHCOMING

Bilingual Education, Rosa Castro Feinberg
Educational Leadership, Pat Williams-Boyd
School Vouchers and Privatization, Danny Weil

CONTEMPORARY EDUCATION ISSUES

Teacher Training

●✦ A REFERENCE HANDBOOK

Dave Pushkin

A B C ● C L I O

Santa Barbara, California • Denver, Colorado • Oxford, England

Library of Congress Cataloging-in-Publication Data

Pushkin, Dave.
    Teacher training : a reference handbook / Dave Pushkin.
      p. cm. — (Contemporary education issues)
Includes bibliographical references and index.
    ISBN 1-57607-357-2 (hardcover : alk. paper); 1-57607-752-7 (e-book)
    1. Teachers—Training of—United States—Handbooks, manuals, etc. 2.
Teacher educators—United States—Handbooks, manuals, etc. 3.
Universities and colleges—United States—Curricula—Handbooks, manuals,
etc. I. Title. II. Series
    LB2165.P87 2001
    370'.71'173—dc21

                                        2001005058

This book is also available on the World Wide Web as an e-book.
Visit www.abc-clio.com for details.

07 06 05 04 03 02 01   10 9 8 7 6 5 4 3 2 1

ABC-CLIO, Inc.
130 Cremona Drive, P.O. Box 1911
Santa Barbara, California 93116-1911

This book is printed on acid-free paper ∞.
Manufactured in the United States of America

► Contents

◆◆ Series Editor's Preface

The Contemporary Education Issues series is dedicated to providing readers with an up-to-date exploration of the central issues in education today. Books in the series will examine such controversial topics as home schooling, charter schools, privatization of public schools, Native American education, African American education, literacy, curriculum development, and many others. The series is national in scope and is intended to encourage research by anyone interested in the field.

Because education is undergoing radical if not revolutionary change, the series is particularly concerned with how contemporary controversies in education affect both the organization of schools and the content and delivery of curriculum. Authors will endeavor to provide a balanced understanding of the issues and their effects on teachers, students, parents, administrators, and policymakers. The aim of the Contemporary Education Issues series is to publish excellent research on today's educational concerns by some of the finest scholar/practitioners in the field while pointing to new directions. The series promises to offer important analyses of some of the most controversial issues facing society today.

Danny Weil
Series Editor

❧ Preface

This is not a typical "reference book." Although this book is part of a reference handbook series, it is perhaps helpful for you, the reader, to consider this a *point-of-reference book*. What do I mean by this? What I mean is that this book takes a somewhat critical and experiential reflective look at the teaching profession, from academic preparation to professional advancement. This book does not intend to provide an encyclopedic presentation of the profession; it seeks to raise a broader and deeper awareness about the profession.

Unlike the typical reference book or encyclopedia, this book delves heavily into the scholarly literature, and provides you, the reader, with a considerable number of references for further reading. I firmly believe, as an educator, it is my moral and intellectual obligation to set an example for you in terms of thorough examination of the literature. As a potential student of the teaching profession, it is your own moral and intellectual obligation to explore as much of the literature as possible. Do not rely on just one source, for no single source is the gospel.

It is important to understand and appreciate that my book is not the sole authoritative voice about the teaching profession; it is not *any* authoritative voice, for that matter. In fact, my book is but a small, single voice in a very large world where many voices are expressed and heard. To even consider my book authoritative is a gross overstatement, albeit rather flattering. Please keep in mind, there is no uniform consensus about the teaching profession, as it is advocated from various philosophical perspectives.

My book primarily seeks to raise your consciousness about the teaching profession from a particular perspective, that of considering teachers' *epistemologies* and *ontologies*. As you read on in Chapter 1, you will see what I mean by these terms and why I consider them important to the teaching profession at all stages. By no means do I have grand answers to the ultimate questions about this profession, nor do I have easy solutions to relevant problems.

Quite frankly, we have enough people offering answers before the question is fully understood or articulated. It is sad but true, from my perspective, that our American culture expects quick answers and easy solutions; but what exactly are we answering and solving? After 19 years in education, I am still trying to identify the "problem" and ask the "question." I make no promises to fill this void by the end of my book. However, I (as well as contributing authors) do have thoughts to offer and encourage you to consider them as you seek to learn about the teaching profession.

This point-of-reference book delves into several aspects about teacher education and the teaching profession. In Chapter 1, I present an essence of what the teaching profession had become by the end of the twentieth century. In Chapter 2, I present a brief chronology of how teacher education has evolved since the days of the so-called normal schools. In Chapter 3, I take a more in-depth look at the academic process of teacher education, and I build this theme further in Chapter 5 in terms of teacher-certification policies.

Chapters 4 and 7, respectively, are written by two of my former graduate students, Tovia Rosenfeld and Rebecca Fabiano. Both received their master's degrees in secondary education from CUNY–Brooklyn College in 1999 and teach in New York City public high schools. Tovia's chapter will look at the student teaching experience from the perspectives of both the student teacher and the mentor teacher. Rebecca's chapter will look at teaching outside one's field of certification and why this is a potentially critical issue in education.

These chapters complement my Chapters 6 and 8, where I examine the processes of teacher recruitment and hiring, as well as the phenomenon of the probationary period (prior to tenure). These two chapters ultimately set the stage for Chapters 9 and 10, where I examine professional development (e.g., graduate education and professional advancement) and professional disillusionment (e.g., burnout).

Finally, Chapters 11, 12, and 13 will provide a retrospective about teacher education and the teaching profession as well as useful supplemental reference information. Hopefully, this book, in its composite, will provide you, the reader, with a wealth of food for thought as you seek to understand more of what teaching is about, and perhaps it will challenge you to think differently about education. In fact, this book is dedicated to all of you who care enough about the teaching profession and the education of classroom teachers to read this book.

Many thanks to many people for their assistance in the writing and publishing of this book. First, I give great thanks to Dr. Danny Weil for recruiting me to write this book. His countless hours of support and guidance and of being both mensch and devil's advocate helped me immeasurably. I am not only a better writer and thinker because of Danny, I am, hopefully, a better person.

Second, I give great thanks to Tovia Rosenfeld and Rebecca Fabiano for their wonderful chapter contributions. Not only were they wonderful graduate students a few years ago, they are fantastic and caring high school educators. With all my Brooklyn pride, I thank them and love them both for their continuous efforts to help improve education.

Finally, I give great thanks to people past and present with ABC-CLIO Publishers (Marie Ellen Larcada, Alicia Merritt, Allison Miller, Vince Burns, and Kathy Delfosse) for their facilitation of the book writing and publishing process.

Chapter One

⊷ The "Dime a Dozen" Teacher?

How does one coin a phrase like *"Dime a Dozen Teacher"*? Are teachers perceived as a "dime a dozen"? The inspiration for this term comes from near the end of Act II of Arthur Miller's play *Death of a Salesman*. In this scene, the protagonist, Willy Loman, is trying to console his eldest son, Biff, and cajole him into becoming a businessman and following through on a career choice he is not meant for. Biff tells his father of his epiphany, of realizing, as he ran down 11 flights of stairs after a job interview, that he did not want to be something he loathed. The scene heatedly continues:

> BIFF *(continuing, trying to make Willy face him):* Why am I trying to become what I don't want to be? What am I doing in an office, making a contemptuous, begging fool of myself, when all I want is out there, waiting for me the minute I say I know who I am! Why can't I say that, Willy?
>
> WILLY *(pulling away with hatred, threateningly):* The door of your life is wide open!
>
> BIFF: Pop! I'm a dime a dozen, and so are you!
>
> WILLY *(wildly):* I AM NOT A DIME A DOZEN! I AM WILLY LOMAN, AND YOU ARE BIFF LOMAN!
>
> BIFF *(in emotional fury):* I am not a leader of men, Willy, and neither are you. You were never anything but a hard-working drummer who landed in the ash can like all the rest of them! I'm one dollar an hour, Willy!

We all know how the rest of this scene plays out. A son bares his soul to his father of his human frailties while his father is unaccepting of his son's or his own limitations in a great big world. According to Sylvan Barnet, Morton Berman, and William Burto (1989), Arthur Miller's play sought to document the frustration of man as if the common man was a tragic figure. However, Barnet, Berman, and Burton considered Willy Loman more pathetic than tragic, a victim of his own desire to live with

1

bourgeois values in a system that ultimately chewed him up and spat him out.

Throughout his personal demise, Willy struggled to reclaim his identity as a uniquely special contributor to the system, indispensable and infinitely valuable, while all around him the reality he had lost touch with viewed him as irrelevant. Once Willy lost touch with reality, he lost his skill, pride, dignity, and finally his life. Never before had I encountered a theatrical figure so sad and disturbing. Never before had any one phrase struck such a nerve in me as an educator as did "dime a dozen," especially since I first encountered this play some years before I became an educator myself.

Our plight as educators is not much different from Willy Loman's. As we continuously struggle to prove our individual worth in peer reviews, supervisory evaluations, school systems and academic communities, and a sociopolitically driven economy, a systematic agenda deems us interchangeable spare parts in a complex dehumanized and decontextualized machine. The individual is a threat to structure; conformity and obedience are needed to remind us how much bigger the system is than any of us individually. In our world of predigested teacher-proof curricula and standardized pedagogical practices, the system reminds us how replaceable and disposable teachers are.

> More and more, the conservative reforms of the last fifteen years have turned teachers into semiskilled functionaries. . . . Indeed, teachers are supervised and evaluated not on the basis of notions of competence and creativity but on their adherence to format, that is, their compliance. . . . [They] become executors of managerial plans. . . . it is not surprising that teachers lose a sense of meaning. . . . some of the best and brightest teachers leave the field after only a few years. (Kincheloe 1999, 11)

THE IMAGE OF TEACHERS

How did we reach this point in our profession? Consider the insights of the late comedian Steve Allen (1998) in his book *"DUMBTH": The Lost Art of Thinking*. Allen first cites an article by W. Timothy Weaver (1979), then an associate professor of education at Boston University. Weaver wrote of the decline in Scholastic Aptitude Test (SAT) scores among high school seniors since 1963. However, most noteworthy was how much poorer (by approximately 10 percent) high school seniors planning for a career in education scored compared to all other seniors.

Allen also shares a story from Pinellas County, Florida (one of many places I have taught), where, as of 1976, teachers took an application examination for employment. According to Allen, *"some of the teachers scored lower in math and reading than the school system's eighth graders"* (33).

Last, Allen notes findings by organizations like Associated Scientists and the American Institute of Physics. For example, as of 1997, 51 percent of the mathematics teachers in the United States had never themselves taken a single mathematics course in college, and 46 percent of California's high school math teachers lacked even a math minor. Furthermore, only 18 percent of this nation's high school physics teachers had actual degrees in physics.

On a personal level, I take slight exception to the alarmist tone of Allen's last statistic, since I happened to be one of the 82 percent teaching high school physics without a physics degree. However, I did hold two degrees in chemistry, was a physical biochemist, and took many advanced courses in physical chemistry, which includes applied physics content. This background qualified me for certification as a high school chemistry and physics teacher more than 15 years ago, and I also took graduate-level physics courses during my doctoral studies in curriculum and instruction. After graduating with my Ph.D. in curriculum and instruction, I worked as a chemistry or physics professor for four years before finally settling into my permanent life as an education professor. So when such data is presented as being cause for alarm, we should at least take it with a grain of salt. Yes, our nation's high school physics teachers should ideally hold degrees in the subject area, but the qualifications of these teachers are not as bleak as perhaps characterized. There are indeed exceptions!

Was Allen alone in his views? Hardly. Consider this insight from Arthur Levine, president of Teachers College, Columbia University:

> A growing number of states are becoming more selective about who can enter the teaching profession. After a decade and a half of research showing clearly that teacher-certification requirements are too lenient and that too many teachers are unprepared to educate their students, raising the bar is imperative. But higher standards are very likely to mean shrinking numbers of teachers, since a smaller proportion of candidates will be able to meet the higher standards. (*New York Times* editorial, April 7, 1999)

Levine's sentiments are further reinforced by Leon Botstein, president of New York's Bard College:

> No amount of effort to improve the quality of our schools will succeed
> unless we end up with better teachers. Yet, despite glimmers of re-
> newed interest . . . the most gifted and talented college students are not
> choosing teaching as a career. (*New York Times* editorial, July 26, 1999)

Botstein noted that teaching is no longer viewed as the respectable white-collar profession it was prior to World War II, especially among children of immigrants. Being a "schoolteacher" no longer carries prestige and pride. Salaries are poor, and the education bureaucracy does not treat its teachers as professionals. Teachers have little control over curricular or pedagogical practices. It hardly seems a profession worth entering.

Furthermore, Botstein noted that "fewer than 65 percent of new teachers have either a major or minor in the subject matter they teach. Nearly a third of all teachers today teach subjects in which they have no formal training." Again, sadly, he pointed to physics as a primary example of this ill of education, as if physics were the ultimate barometer to education's wellness. This, of course, should not be a great surprise, considering that physics was the centerpiece for post-Sputnik curricular reform in the early 1960s and its rallying point after the publication of *A Nation at Risk* in 1983 (e.g., Pushkin 2001c).

According to Frances FitzGerald (1980), teachers of the nineteenth century were poorly educated and poorly paid. Apparently little has changed, according to Botstein, during the twentieth. The harshest point Botstein made is that teachers are characterized as academically and intellectually weaker than other college graduates, in terms of both entrance qualifications and graduation credentials. This is certainly a topic of considerable discussion, especially with respect to qualified teacher shortages (e.g., Friedman 2000; Ingersoll 1999).

The numbing litany continues. Columnist Acel Moore ("In the Face of Frustration, Some Teachers Call It Quits," *Philadelphia Inquirer*, June 29, 2000) wrote of a 23-year-veteran teacher retiring from a West Philadelphia school, not necessarily due to an early retirement package but due to burnout. This teacher, Ann, left the profession she loves because, in her own words, "I no longer feel that I can, as an individual classroom teacher, make a difference." What drove Ann from the classroom? The aging facilities, the inadequate resources, the apathy of parents, the disruptive children, and exacerbating socioeconomic and home environment factors. But these words perhaps ring chillingly in the face of what Levine and Botstein argue: "I am stressed out and burned out from being a baby-sitter, a social worker, and a police officer. These are things that we were not trained to do."

How do university leaders rationalize their contention that teachers need to learn more content and subject matter when schools today pose more challenges for teachers than those of mere content? Even if math teachers were degreed in mathematics and if more physics teachers had majored or minored in physics, how would that address behavioral problems, emotionally disturbed children, apathetic parents, and decaying school buildings? How would requiring teachers to have degrees in their content areas attract better-qualified teachers, as Levine and Botstein call for? In what ways would such degrees make teachers better qualified and suited for classrooms?

The short-term answers to these questions seem very unsatisfactory and incomplete. First, let us consider that schools are, for better or worse, viewed in terms of educational or academic accountability; they are judged by students' performance on assessment tests. As long as testing remains high on the priority list, content competency will continue to outweigh psychosocial issues on a genuine level. As long as test scores improve and the passing rates on such tests improve, our educational leaders can continue to deem educational reform successful.

Second, let us not forget that school systems continue to invest in behavior specialists, crisis management counselors, and campus police officers. In theory, perhaps having all these professional resources outside the classrooms but within the schools increases the time-on-task for classroom learning. However, the emotional frustrations that children, young and old, bring into the classroom undermine the efficiency our technocratic leaders desire.

Third, contrary to what Levine and Botstein contend, simply raising the academic standards or starting salaries for teachers does not solve the "problem." In fact, part of the "problem" with education, and the teaching profession, is that we really have not clearly identified the "problem." At best, what we continue to see are disturbing manifestations of a deeper, more abstract "problem," which we still struggle to comprehend on a concrete level. As I tried to subtly note in my Preface, American education has many Arthur Levines and Leon Botsteins, quick to offer their answers and solutions, even though we are really not sure what they are answering or solving.

Last, as we reconsider the plight of Ann, the teacher Acel Moore wrote about, we should realize there is only so much a teacher can put up with before he or she gives up, regardless of experience, qualifications, or salary. Just as Popeye used to say, *I've stands all I can stands, and I can't stands no more!* Teachers, many of them well qualified, reach a breaking point. I myself threw in the towel after ten years as a high school chemistry and physics teacher in the Tampa Bay region of

Florida. I certainly had the content credentials, and my students performed very well on tests as well as beyond in college. And my salary was relatively acceptable. But I was no longer able to cope with the physical and budgetary limitations of my school, nor was I willing to tolerate the myopia of my administration (Pushkin 1998c). There were many more reasons than this for leaving the public school system, but these at least were the primary reasons.

Whether genetics has a role or not is debatable, but my younger sister also recently left the public school system (from the very same region, and in fact, from my original school district) after ten years as a high school English teacher. Her reasons were very similar to mine, although she considered the parents and students more apathetic than I had eight years earlier. And she also had strong credentials: a bachelor's degree in journalism and a master's in English education. And her salary was pretty good, too. But enough was enough, and after ten years she is back to her first love, working for a newspaper.

Ann from Philadelphia, my sister in Tampa Bay, and I are not alone. I have met many teachers, from many different geographic areas, who have thrown in the towel or who are about to. We have been paid rather well and had good qualifications but reached a tolerance limit. Our reasons vary, as well as our number of years of experience, but we have said enough is enough.

TEACHING AS VIEWED BY THE MEDIA

Let us reflect on the debate over how we can attract better-qualified teachers while I share with you a sampling of the print media's views on the state of education. During the past two years, I made a habit of clipping articles, commentaries, editorials, and letters to the editor from the *New York Times, New York Daily News, Record* (Bergen County, New Jersey), *Philadelphia Inquirer,* and *USA TODAY.* Here's some of what I found in these newspapers:

On June 5, 1999, the *New York Daily News,* on its front page, ran an exclusive story, "F for CUNY," telling of Mayor Rudy Giuliani's task force report on the City University system. Not only did the task force blister the City University of New York (CUNY) for the quality of its students; it blamed CUNY for perpetuating the failure of New York City's public schools. The article stated, "New York City public schools have flooded City University with high school graduates ill-prepared for college work, helping to turn CUNY into a second-rate institution."

The article further noted that CUNY students required remedial assistance at a disproportionately higher rate than the national norm. However, the most damning indictment was that "CUNY also must take responsibility for what goes on in public schools, because it graduates 25 percent to 30 percent of city public school teachers." Noting that New York City schools will recruit 40,000 teachers in the next five years, the article concluded there "is strong evidence . . . CUNY teachers are not as well prepared as they should be." The implication was that potentially 10,000–15,000 of New York City's new generation of public school teachers will be incompetent to teach, adding to a teacher force already presumed incompetent, courtesy of CUNY.

CUNY, the educational system that graduated such noteworthy people as former mayor Edward Koch, retired general Colin Powell, composer Ira Gershwin, activist Shirley Chisholm, medical pioneer Jonas Salk, and comedian Jerry Seinfeld, was under attack from multiple directions: Mayor Giuliani, his task force, Governor George Pataki, and the New York State Board of Regents. There was a call for more-stringent admissions standards and graduation requirements. However, the most sensitive issue, and most bluntly attacked, was CUNY's relationship with the public school system. CUNY was said to admit poorly educated students from public high schools, educate them dysfunctionally and substandardly, and then graduate them to teach in some of the poorest public schools in New York City, creating a new generation of ill-qualified CUNY students and prospective teachers.

Around the same time, articles and editorials also appeared vilifying the teachers, products of CUNY, who would write to parents letters in need of spelling and grammar corrections. Teachers were called incompetent and illiterate. One misstep by a teacher immediately fed a media frenzy, as parents raced to newspapers with stories, bypassing the teacher in the process.

Only a week before the article appeared in the *New York Daily News,* Governor Pataki had named Herman Badillo, lawyer, politician, and CUNY alumnus, chairman of the CUNY Board of Trustees (*New York Times,* May 31, 1999). Among Badillo's major areas of concern were a perceived weak curriculum and grade inflation. Badillo considered graduation requirements too low. However, this only reinforced Arthur Levine's concern that raising the bar of expectations would decrease the number of candidates for teacher education programs. How did Badillo expect to balance this decrease against the demand for 40,000 new teachers over the next five years? One cannot find 40,000 highly qualified teachers from a pool already considered contaminated. One cannot draw from other academic or geographic pools when presumptions of incompetence prevail. One cannot draw from other geographic pools if similar shortages are presumed there. One cannot draw from other pools if one's own reputation for dysfunction is well known.

Everyone seems to have an opinion on education and teachers; sometimes these opinions are contradictory. In the July 16, 1999, *Record,* a local resident wrote in a letter to the editor that college-level education courses are mostly taught by people with little or no current classroom experience. This person continued, "Just because one has a doctorate in education does not mean one is qualified to teach prospective teachers how to teach." The solution, as this person viewed it, was to have retired teachers who only hold a master's degree pass on "their demonstrated expertise." In other words, professors of education are the problem, so replace them with people who truly know what the profession is about.

Never mind that this letter could very well be defending the type of teacher Levine, Botstein, and Giuliani's task force talked about in their assessments. This letter took the position that the teachers are the real experts of education, more so than the professors of teacher education. As a former classroom teacher and now an education professor, I view such a generalized position with concern, for it represents a lack of understanding of the academic and professional requirements of becoming an education professor.

More importantly, what this letter writer fails to realize is that many retired teachers may have indeed passed on their expertise, but not as teacher education professors. They may have represented the teacher establishment in schools that potentially influenced future generations of teachers, good or bad. They may have served as master teachers or mentors to student teachers or department chairs. A veteran teacher has as much potential authoritarian influence as a professor or school administrator. That influence can be either good or bad.

Only a few days after this letter appeared in the *Record,* another local resident, a former teacher, wrote to the *New York Times* that there seemed to be "too much philosophizing and almost no talk about the how-to part of teaching children" during the ten years the writer worked as a public school teacher. This person criticized colleagues for ignoring the "nuts and bolts of classroom work" in favor of "educational fads," only to eventually give up and leave teaching when a greener pasture was offered. This letter was in response to an editorial (*New York Times,* July 19, 1999) critical of Indiana's teacher certification test. The test asked questions regarding the use of overhead projectors as opposed to questions about John Dewey. This letter in rebuttal clearly presented the sentiment that questions on the use of overhead projectors were much more important and relevant to classroom practice than questions about John Dewey.

But the printed stories kept coming. In the July 21, 1999, *New York Times,* we read that Congress and President Bill Clinton battled over a two-billion-dollar bill for teacher training and recruitment. President Clinton sought to reduce class sizes and hire 100,000 additional teachers nationwide. His congressional opponents did not want state and local school systems to be forced to hire teachers simply for the sake of numbers, arguing that the quality of teachers makes more difference than the quantity of teachers. That same day, the *New York Times* reported that a recently released report, "Better Teachers, Better Schools," by the Thomas B. Fordham Foundation, a conservative think tank, contended that some of the plans by federal and state governments to improve public school education would actually worsen things.

On October 20, 1999, *USA TODAY* reported that elementary school teachers would be facing tougher licensing exams by 2002, requiring more thorough knowledge of specific subject areas as well as creative classroom practices. Bob Chase, chairman of the National Council for the Accreditation of Teacher Education (NCATE) executive board and president of the National Education Association, was quoted as saying, "It will change the perception of teaching from a job that anyone can do on a walk-in basis to that of a profession with a base of knowledge behind that licensed teachers know and apply."

On October 25, 1999, *USA TODAY* further reinforced the ideas that teachers are unprepared for their profession and that college presidents need to lead the way in teacher education reforms. Furthermore, much as Botstein had, a task force called for an end to the practice of training teachers in colleges of education and even to the existence of degree programs or academic departments and majors in education.

On November 14, 1999, the *New York Times* reported that New York City schools had failed to reduce overcrowded classrooms, despite hiring over 800 new teachers with federal assistance funds and a total of 7,200 new teachers for the 1999/2000 school year.

On November 16, 1999, *USA TODAY* reported findings from the Thomas B. Fordham Foundation noting that most states continued to fail in their efforts to improve their teaching force. A follow-up article on January 6, 2000, reported that only five states had genuinely embraced school accountability reforms.

On November 21, 1999, an editorial by the *New York Daily News* revisits its "F for CUNY" campaign with a "groomed to fail" theme:

> The revelation that nearly one-third of city teachers failed state certification tests at least once is deeply disturbing. But it is not surprising. After all, more than 45 percent of those teachers were products of New

York City schools, from grade school through college. As were *their* teachers.

On June 25, 2000, the *New York Daily News* reported on an eighth-grade science teacher who had failed the state license exams at least 12 times during his six-year teaching career. The New York City Board of Education had recently removed him from the classroom until he could pass the exams. This teacher was a product of the CUNY system.

The article noted that approximately 15 percent of New York City teachers hold at least a bachelor's degree yet do not hold a state teaching license, either because they failed state exams or because they did not have all teacher education course work for certification. The article further noted that approximately one-third of New York City teachers fail the general Liberal Arts and Sciences knowledge exam at least once. Sadly, while the state's certification office wants to stress the importance of the exam in terms of competence and certification, the teacher in question was quoted as saying, "The test has nothing to do with teaching. The real thing is in front of 30 to 35 kids. That's when you are really tested."

A BLEAK PICTURE?

So what is the image of teachers? If we were to consider all of what we've read in these various commentaries and articles, we might suspect the following:

- Teachers were poor students in school and college.
- Teachers are poorly educated.
- Teachers are poorly paid.
- Teachers are incompetent.
- Teachers are illiterate.
- Teachers do not know anything.
- Teachers perpetuate ignorance.
- Teachers are warm bodies in classrooms.
- Teachers cannot teach, but somebody can.

I began this chapter asking if teachers were a "dime a dozen." Based on what we have read so far—that teachers are poorly educated at all levels, are hired in massive quantities regardless of their qualifications or competence, and do not always last long in the profession but are apparently readily replaced—one must wonder if the answer is yes.

Do I believe teachers are a "dime a dozen"? No, I do not. However, society seems to see teachers as if they were generic apples from a tree. Pick one, any one; they are all alike. If we do not like one, we can toss it away and get another off the tree. If we use up the apples from one tree, there is bound to be another tree nearby. If not, we will see new apples growing from the trees next year.

Joe Kincheloe and Shirley Steinberg (1998) note that too many teachers work in an anti-intellectual world, presuming it is a professional world. Unfortunately, these teachers may fail to realize what the reality is until too late. They do not recognize that doing as they are told to please their system's authority essentially de-professionalizes them. They lose their edge, their creative-thinking skills, and eventually their desire to make an intellectual difference; this cumulative loss, in turn, leads to a loss of individual self-identity.

Sadly, they are shocked to find that those outside the teaching profession already recognize this about them. They become demoralized; they either leave the profession or remain for lack of any sense of an alternative for fulfillment, as if they are incapable of anything else. Some young aspiring teachers see the proverbial handwriting on the wall early enough and escape before they enter, fearing they might become what they see and abhor. To them, leaving the profession before ever entering is a preventive form of self-preservation (e.g., Pushkin 2001b).

THE PREPARATION OF TEACHERS

Perhaps no other people intrigue me more with regards to higher education than aspiring and practicing educators (a more professional term than "teachers"). Educators represent a broad spectrum of higher education, in terms of both educational status and purpose. Educators often become professionals through undergraduate programs and return for professional development in graduate programs. In many respects, higher education is a dominating influence on an educator, from the beginning to, potentially, the end of his or her career.

When society, politicians, and the media all point a finger at educators, blaming them for the inadequacies of society's youth and of our schools, we may overlook where they come from. They are products of our institutions of higher education (colleges and universities). To what degree must higher education accept blame, and to what degree has higher education influenced the profession of education? This is perhaps a difficult question to pose, since considerable finger pointing has been aimed at institutions like CUNY. However, we should also keep in mind that CUNY does not operate in a vacuum; it is governed by city and state legislatures.

When educators are said to fail or to be incompetent or to lack healthy perspectives, what might have contributed to their inadequacy? Even though a "blame game" serves little purpose, by no means would institutions like CUNY be absolved; higher education needs to continuously reexamine itself. In fact, institutes of higher education might very well be major contributors to educators' failure, be it due to ill-defined perspectives on teaching and learning or to contrived efforts to suppress critical and independent thinking. Any educational setting potentially influences the professional development of educators and is worthy of critical examination; higher education is no less subject to such examination than school systems are. However, we cannot disregard the external influences on an educational setting. Just as all institutions of education need to take a closer look at themselves, *everyone* connected with education (directly or indirectly) needs to take that same closer look.

There are those who advocate educators being *transformative intellectuals* (e.g., Freire 1985; Giroux 1988; Kincheloe 1999, 2000). Teaching becomes an emancipatory process that makes learners knowledgeable and vocal citizens within a hopeful democratic society. Unfortunately, as both Giroux (1988) and Kincheloe (1999, 2000) note, conditions must be established that enable learners to become such citizens. Likewise, educational settings require conditions that allow educators to become transformative intellectuals without fear of reprisals, retribution, ostracization, or censure. Does higher education allow its own faculty to be transformative intellectuals or promote the cultivation of transformative intellectualism among its students? Even more critically, we need to ask whether those governing or influencing higher education sanction transformative intellectualism.

There is perhaps an inherent contradiction at play. One cannot decree educational reform, seeking "results," and yet repudiate ways of thinking that challenge the mainstream (e.g., Kincheloe 1992). In fact, Allen (1998) found it rather odd that in an era when consciousness-raising is relatively popular, genuine thinking, the prerequisite of consciousness-raising, is viewed with disdain.

If educators are said to lack command of content knowledge, why is that? Perhaps this is an issue of incompetent learning on their part during training or of poor content teaching by the institution. Or the institution might fail to place enough value on knowledge beyond its course syllabi. We need to bring the *epistemological* and *ontological* views of higher education into question. We also need to bring the pedagogical and curricular practices of higher-education faculty into question. We even need to wonder how much appreciation for knowledge educators have been exposed to during *their* years as learners.

According to Patricia H. Hinchey, "Surviving high school involves primarily remembering and regurgitating, plus mastering a few other polite behaviors" (1995, 39). Essentially, not causing any trouble leads to academic reward, and students expect this to be consistent throughout their entire education, especially during college. Such a perspective surely did not develop by accident. American society tends to be driven by a "tell people what they want to hear" philosophy, whether we are talking about students, teachers, professors, administrators, policymakers, legislators, taxpayers, or all of the above. People want to be pleased; people want to be rewarded. However, people do not necessarily understand the *value* of rewards, living in a "want it now" world of instant gratification. Somehow, education has forgotten the long-term nature of thinking and learning, consequently influencing the process of teaching, and perhaps the teaching profession.

Not too long ago, I saw a cartoon in the editorial section of one of my newspapers. It depicted a teacher shoveling content into a child's empty head. The teacher was exhorting the child to keep taking in the knowledge because accountability testing was approaching. How sad it is to think that after decades of educational reform, we still see education, teaching, and learning reduced to testing. How could we expect educators to have a strong command of content knowledge if they only recognize it as *testable knowledge* (e.g., Kincheloe 1991, 1993; Pushkin 2001a, 2001c)? Again, the long-term nature of thinking and learning has been somewhat forgotten in our "want it now" world. Unless a reward is immediate and tangible, the things we genuinely intellectually value are deemed irrelevant. If educators, administrators, policymakers, and legislators deem things irrelevant, we should not be surprised when our students, who may become educators themselves someday, deem the same things irrelevant.

If educators are said to have limited pedagogical practices, why is that? Perhaps they have personally rejected alternative practices or are genuinely unfamiliar with alternative practices. Maybe they simply practice, by default, what is most common and familiar from their studies at the institution. Although some contend that school systems are the dominant influences on educators' classroom practices, we cannot discount the degree of influence higher-education faculty have. This concern primarily focuses on secondary-level educators, who often perceive themselves in terms of their subject matter rather than as educators. They consider themselves to be teachers of content rather than educators of learners. Where did this view come from? Generally, the source is the professors of their content area. These professors see themselves as experts in the content area, not as teachers or educators. Teaching is simply something they *have* to do. Science professors are notorious for this perspective (e.g., Pushkin 1999, 2000, 2001b).

For example, when I was a chemistry professor and would introduce myself in public, people would always ask, "What do you do for a living?" I would always reply, "I'm a professor." "Oh," they would respond, "what do you teach?" Only then would I tell them, "I teach chemistry at such-and-such university." As for my colleagues, they usually proclaimed, "I'm a Chemist" (note the capital *C*). Not "I'm a chemistry professor" or "I'm a chemistry teacher" or "I teach chemistry"; they saw themselves in terms of their academic degree, not their profession. When young aspiring high school science teachers hear this kind of identification often enough, it is not overly surprising when they adopt the same mode of self-identity.

Is this such a big deal? On a very subtle, yet fundamental level, yes. When I was a physics professor, a colleague told me, *"Teaching is like a conversation, and some learning should take place as a result of that conversation. There really is no such thing as 'bad' teaching; teaching can be 'good,' or it can be inconsequential"* (Pushkin 1995, 171). So, teaching is either good or, at worst, benign? University-level pedagogy is either inspirational or follows a "no harm, no foul" philosophy? If students survive the ordeal and succeed, perhaps it is due to the professor, but if students do not survive and flounder, the professor is somehow absolved from blame (e.g., Pushkin 2001b; Tobias and Tomizuka 1992). This is quite a disturbing hypothesis, considering how influential professors can be.

If educators are said to be inflexible and resistant to change, why is that? Perhaps this reflects one level within the academic hierarchy rebelling against authority; more likely, it is a manifestation of the rigidity associated with a profession where dichotomous thinking is the norm, not the exception. What is the source of dualistic hegemony among educators? Where do we need to focus examination of policy and practice? Perhaps there is an inherent culture within education reflective of a dominant paradigm.

Thomas Kuhn (1962) educated us to the concepts of paradigms and paradigm shifts. What I find most intriguing is that Kuhn estimated that it takes approximately 75 years for a paradigm shift to occur completely. The reasons are self-evident, since views of the world can be very resistant toward change. However, when we consider that those who actively seek to challenge the dominant paradigm are often punished (e.g., Kincheloe 1992), we begin to realize that those privileged within the academic hierarchy are almost militantly inflexible (e.g., Freire 1973; Pushkin 2001b). Self-preservation and protection of privilege essentially drive the inherent culture I inquire about.

Both Michael Fullan (1993) and Peter Senge (1990) referred to educational systems as conservative, and not necessarily in terms of philosophical views. In science, we learn about conservation principles, which hold that the total amount of some entity remains constant despite its transformations. This is what Fullan and Senge meant. In other words, no matter how many changes an educational system undergoes, it will eventually return to what it originally was. So when we ask why change is so difficult in academia and education, we need to keep in mind (1) nature almost deems this inevitable, and (2) people in power like to keep things the way they are, so power is retained.

How do different institutions of higher education design their teacher education programs? I will specifically address this question in Chapter 3. However, within the context of paradigms and resistance to change, there are a few thoughts to consider now.

First, in the sciences, do different disciplines give any consideration to interdisciplinary content? Are university science faculty sensitive to the ways their curricula parallel or contradict the curricula that learners were exposed to prior to college? Are they sensitive to how their curricula meet the needs of science-teacher certification, both in terms of subject specificity and general science?

As noted earlier, if science faculty see themselves only as scientists, and not as educators of science, the odds are high that they will not demonstrate much sensitivity to the curricular and pedagogical issues critically relevant to science-teacher training. Unless these faculty view science through an interdisciplinary lens in their scientific research, they cannot optimistically be expected to view science content this way. First, they do not know any different. Second, they rarely hold teaching in high regard. This combination minimizes the chances for meaningful and progressive science-teacher training.

What about the faculty of schools of education? What are they sensitive to or cognizant of? As teacher-certification requirements evolve, either for elementary- or secondary-level teaching, have teacher education curricula shifted more emphasis to content, methods, or foundations? As pressures to require more content knowledge grow, what do schools of education sacrifice? What are the implications?

I wonder if new teachers leave higher education with a sufficient degree of perspective about education, or if they simply master methodological and mechanical skills. When new teachers write lesson plans, I wonder if they fully understand why they have written them. I wonder if they understand the cognitive goals of their lessons. I wonder if they have any degree of capacity to become transformative intellectuals. I wonder what they can (or will) encourage young minds to think and reflect about, or how they will challenge them to be good citizens. Perhaps they will simply facilitate the coverage of disjointed, disconnected, and decontextualized content for the sake of accountability and assessment and leave me nothing else to wonder about.

So many issues to think about. These will be primarily addressed in Chapters 3, 4, 5, and 9. However, we can tentatively address these issues by reflecting back on earlier parts of this chapter. We can reflect back on both Arthur Levine's and Leon Botstein's editorials. We can reflect back on the string of newspaper articles about the CUNY system. We can reflect back on the letters written to the editors of the *New York Times* and *Record*. The tentative response is pessimism. As Kincheloe and Steinberg (1998) note, the more accountability dominates education, the more standardized, technocratic, and formulaic teacher education becomes, all for the sake of a simplified rubric to quantify the quality of teaching and learning. It is rather unrealistic to quantify quality. It implies teaching is generic, foolproof, and absolute.

In other words, it may be naive wishfulness to hope that new teachers will come from higher education with any meaningful perspective or insights regarding pedagogical practice, curricula, and learning. They may simply perpetuate the status quo and never dare to be transformative. They may come from higher education with virtually zero appreciation for knowledge and the process of knowledge acquisition. They may come from higher education with the belief that knowledge is merely a commodity for accountability and assessment. They may consider curricular materials, pedagogical practices, learning activities, and modes of assessment to be completely noninfluential with regards to teaching and learning. If this is the perspective they bring from their higher-education experiences, we must sadly presume new teachers will perpetuate the ills we already observe in schools. As Hinchey (1999) suggests, these teachers may never consider themselves possible contributors to students' lack of learning. As long as they practice the appropriate recipe for teaching, they are absolved of any wrongdoing. This is disturbing, but frighteningly possible.

Whether we are referring to teachers' presumed incompetence, lack of pedagogical skills, or limited content knowledge, something seems amiss with the process of teacher education. Regardless of how well equipped for higher education aspiring educators are upon matriculation, higher education, in colleges of education and arts and sciences, seems to do little to transform them into professionals. We know students can somehow master content for the sake of assessment in spite of themselves (e.g., Pushkin 1998a, 1998b), and we know novice teachers somehow manage to teach adequately according to positivistic modes of supervision (e.g., Kincheloe 1993).

But for all those evidences of teachers who satisfactorily make the grade, why do not all teachers succeed in the profession? Why do they manage to progress through the process of teacher education classes and student teaching yet fail certification exams or fail to connect with their students? Perhaps educators are trained under one very old paradigm and confront a different, very new, unfamiliar paradigm in the professional context. The ability to bridge those paradigms does not require traditional academic or mechanical skills; it requires philosophical perspective and insight, something inadequately taught or cultivated in higher education. What educators lack more than anything else appears to be an epistemological and ontological baseline, not through any fault of their own but, as Kincheloe and Steinberg (1998) contend, through the fault of higher education.

TEACHER EPISTEMOLOGIES AND ONTOLOGIES

Allen (1998) believed schools do not teach us how to think; they teach us *what* to think. I might go one step further and say schools do not teach us to think at all. If schools teach us what to think, then what is there to think about? It has already been thought for us.

As I noted earlier in this chapter, educators are urged to be transformative intellectuals whose teaching should be a reflective, metacognitive practice. But in order to become a transformative intellectual, an educator needs to come to terms with his or her own beliefs about education, the profession of education (teaching), and the nature of knowledge. In short, consciousness-raising for an educator means establishing one's own epistemological and ontological views, not waiting for someone else to dispense them.

For a reference point, I examined two recent years' worth (1998–2000) of the *Journal of Science Teacher Education* and the *Journal of Research in Science Teaching*. I identified several articles that either directly or (more typically) indirectly addressed science-teacher epistemologies and ontologies, and I highly recommend them for further reading (see Chapter 13). It is interesting to note that a number of these articles primarily addressed science teachers' beliefs in the context of their supposed lack of content knowledge or knowledge of their learners. Very few articles considered philosophical beliefs regarding the purpose and meaning of teaching curricula. In fact, very few of these articles specifically used the terms "epistemology" or "ontology."

Perhaps an examination of these terms is necessary. Many dictionaries define "epistemology" as a philosophy of knowledge. I take a slightly different perspective, primarily because of the way I define the word "ontology." Although some dictionaries define "ontology" as a philosophy or belief about being or reality, I take a postmodern view and tentatively define "ontology" as a *philosophy of knowledge.*

Why? Both Reinders Duit and David Treagust (1998) and Stella Vosniadou and William F. Brewer (1992) describe "ontological belief" in terms of categorizing the world. I interpret this to mean a philosophical recognition of what constitutes knowledge. Earlier in this chapter I raised the issue of content knowledge being recognized only as *testable knowledge.* If knowledge is only recognized according to assessment, of what ultimate value is it? Is learning merely for the sake of assessment and short-term competency (e.g., Kincheloe 1993; Pushkin 1998a, 1998b)? It should not be!

For instance, consider a high school biology teacher discussing the nitrogen cycle with students. The teacher, in most cases, would primarily rely on the view of a course-adopted textbook; the textbook's position is viewed as authoritative. But what if that teacher taught in an urban setting, where pollution and concrete were more dominant images for children than soybean plants? What if he or she taught in a rural school setting to students who were the children of farmers and who understood plants and soil more "practically"? One would hope this teacher could adapt to the educational context.

This reflects what Lee Shulman (1986) referred to as pedagogical content knowledge (PCK). Successful classroom teachers not only need to have "knowledge," or understanding of their subject matter, they also need to understand pedagogical practice, their students, and their educational context. This is a subtle yet fundamental point overlooked by Arthur Levine and Leon Botstein. Teachers can understand their subject matter well and still not be successful; without an understanding of the process of education on a holistic level, learning seems essentially incomplete.

What constitutes knowledge? The words of the science book? Perhaps the "less scientific" perspective is trustworthy. Perhaps both views are essentially equivalent. Recent scholarly writing is dedicated to this debate (again, please see Chapter 13). My point is that we need to reflect on what we acknowledge and respect and what we dismiss as knowledge, as well as the criteria we use to make such distinctions. Is one person's knowledge another's irrelevant nonsense? Is the chemist's view of diffusion more trustworthy than a biologist's or physicist's (e.g., Pushkin 2001b)? Is only one view "the Truth" and all others inferior fallacy, or is "truth" contextual? These are questions we struggle with as we identify our ontologies.

Is there a worldview of information, subcategorizing it as knowledge or triviality? In essence, what do we deem "reality" and what do we deem, for lack of a better word, "fantasy"? If knowledge is contextual (e.g., Kincheloe 1991, 1993; Kincheloe, Steinberg, and Tippins 1992), reality should also be contextual. This is the significance of ontological beliefs or views. They are individual and contextual; no one view is worthier than another at mere face value. This is not to say one view cannot be correct, but certain conditions need to be met. This is no different from the way we view scientific laws and boundary conditions. Within a discipline of knowledge, there can be a correct view, a "truth." However, in philosophical terms, the correctness of a view is personalized and contextualized.

If an ontological view represents the way one recognizes knowledge, what does an epistemological view represent? Because one's ontology relates to questions of *what* knowledge is, it stands to reason that an epistemology relates to questions of *how* knowledge is. In other words, how is knowledge defined? How is it acquired? How is it evaluated? How is it shared?

Ultimately, we might be able to consider ontological views the philosophical underpinning to curricula, theory, and policy and epistemological views the philosophical underpinning to pedagogy, practice, and modus operandi. Not only may both views go hand in hand; one may support or justify the other (e.g., Elliott 1998; Goodson 1993). This can manifest in various ways: course enrollments, book choices, modes of assessment, expectations of faculty, decisions to reward or to punish.

From a curricular perspective, educators need to understand and appreciate how knowledge is constructed, not in terms of constructivism or other learning theories and philosophies but in terms of arbitration of knowledge exchange. In other words, who decides on the curriculum content, the mode of assessment, and the textbooks? Where are educators in this process? Have they any say? Who ultimately possesses the power and control over knowledge in schools? We can certainly raise such questions, for example, about the place of science teachers in Kansas in the debate over whether and how to teach the theory of evolution (e.g., Pushkin 2001c).

When educators are accused of having inadequate command of content knowledge, whose knowledge is being referred to? How was that knowledge constructed, and who determined the assessment of that knowledge? How was it shared with learners? In the sciences, for example, it is an all-too-frequent practice to restrict the knowledge presented to learners; oversimplifying and limiting the context of content potentially denies learners the opportunity to think critically and independently (e.g., Pushkin 1998c, 1999, 2000, 2001b). One red-flag concept is diffusion. For all the commonality between the ways biologists, biochemists, and physicists view this concept, somehow pure chemists have such a limited view that they consider all other views wrong and theirs the only correct one (Pushkin 2001b).

If new educators were to graduate from college with the above learning experiences, what kind of perspective would they have about knowledge? We can only imagine the cognitive conflicts they might have if certified to teach more than one high school science subject. I was certified to teach high school biology, chemistry, physics, and math, and I actually taught each subject during the same academic year a few times. What should I have done? Teach my biology students one thing but tell them it was wrong in chemistry class, then tell them it was wrong again in physics class? This certainly would not say much for my competence with science content. This is one of the reasons why the National Science Education Standards have emphasized interdisciplinary curricula, so that content knowledge may be viewed more broadly (e.g., Pushkin 2001a, 2001c).

Unfortunately, this is not the way science content is taught in higher education. More often than not, biology, chemistry, and physics departments are separate fiefdoms, disconnected from each other and promoting their own individual agendas. If these departments were only educating aspiring like scientists, this might be tolerable. However, the reality is that biology departments are not exclusively educating future molecular biologists and medical students; nor are chemistry and physics departments exclusively educating future polymer chemists or nuclear physicists. Many introductory (general) science courses enroll future educators. Aspiring elementary teachers are usually required to take science courses in college, perhaps even courses from each major discipline (biology, chemistry, physics, and earth/space science or geology). Aspiring high school teachers are expected more and more to major in one of those disciplines and minor in another.

It is difficult to expect educators to have enlightened perspectives about content knowledge when myopic curricula and pedagogies shape academic experiences. As noted by Kincheloe (1992) and Kincheloe and Steinberg (1998), educators may not know any better; it is not necessarily their fault, for they are simply doing what they are told. They have been acculturated by a narrow ontological view, and they perpetuate it in their future practice. The odds are great that very few if any faculty in higher education, particularly in the sciences, influenced aspiring educators to look at content knowledge critically or contextually. Therefore, high school biology, chemistry, physics, and earth/space science educators have disconnected and myopic views about their own and each others' content knowledge, and elementary educators are even worse off because of the hodgepodge way they took science in college.

So when we point an accusatory finger at classroom educators regarding their command of content knowledge, other accusatory fingers need to be pointed at higher-education faculty and their curricula, school systems and their mandated curricula, authors of teacher-certification tests, and authors of K–12 and higher-education curricula. In many ways, educators are products of all these dimensions; the odds are great against any cohesion among these different dimensions. Sadly, the result is educators who lack an understanding of content knowledge because no one has given them a fair opportunity to cultivate a philosophical appreciation for what content knowledge means. This ultimately manifests what Kincheloe, Steinberg, and Tippins (1992) referred to as *cognitive illness.*

From a pedagogical perspective, educators again need to understand and appreciate how knowledge is acquired, shared, and assessed, not in terms of pedagogical theories but in terms of power relationships, personal meaning, and knowledge regulation. If they do not, then knowledge and education have no personal meaning or value (Kincheloe 1999). This not only perpetuates cognitive illness among learners, it continues onto subsequent generations of learners, since the original learners potentially become educators.

Lev Vygotsky's concept of mediation is not exclusively limited to K–12 learning contexts. The authority figure in a classroom, even a university lecture hall, has enormous influence on learners. A professor can be just as nurturing a facilitator as those we find in elementary classrooms or can be a hegemonic gatekeeper, stifling students' desire to think and learn (e.g., Pushkin 2001b). Consequently, students learn to be de-skilled and passive and to rely on others to make decisions for them. They never develop minds of their own; if they do, it is in spite of their classroom experiences (Kincheloe 1999).

University faculty do not necessarily give students their money's worth, leaving them feeling unfulfilled at the end of learning experiences (e.g., Pushkin 1999, 2001b). Rarely do university faculty encourage students to look beyond factoids and textbook glossaries for deeper and broader meanings. Rarely do they encourage students to challenge themselves beyond the boundaries of the syllabus.

But more importantly, rarely do university faculty engage students in active discussion or debate about the validity of knowledge;

they merely dictate it as gospel. What message does this send to aspiring educators, who may not have the sophistication to discriminate between positive and negative teaching/learning experiences? Potentially, they graduate from college and, with diploma and certificate in hand, enter K–12 classrooms as facilitators of knowledge, equal members of the learning community, insensitive to students' zones of proximal development. Perhaps they enter as authoritarians, dispensing knowledge as sacred, absolute, and unquestionable. Will their students work cooperatively and collaboratively, or will they be set against each other in academic competition? Will they have an active voice in the classroom, or will only one voice matter? In other words, if new educators are unfamiliar with a culture of transformative intellectualism, we are asking a lot in expecting them to have any capacity or inclination to create such a culture in their own classrooms.

CONCLUSION

"You were never anything but a hard-working drummer who landed in the ash can like all the rest of them." What a sad realization Biff Loman came to regarding his father in the world of business, and yet this is a potential realization we all must come to terms with as educators. We are supposed to be a vibrant and unique profession, and yet in many respects, this is not how society views us. This is not how the politicians view us. This is not how state bureaus of education view us. This is not how universities view us.

If we are to be vibrant, professional, transformative intellectuals, who will be our role models? Our former schoolteachers? Maybe some of them were dynamic and challenging; maybe some of them were mechanical and hegemonic. Maybe some of them influenced us to become educators for the right reasons, and maybe some of them influenced our career choice for the wrong reasons.

What about our university professors? The same questions and speculations arise. Were our professors positive or negative influences? Which professors most often taught us? How did they, if at all, celebrate knowledge and the process of acquiring it? What did they inspire us to do with knowledge?

If teachers are a "dime a dozen" in American education, who is to blame? Anyone, everyone, or no one? When we think of how we are educated to become educators, and how we are certified to be educators, and how we are evaluated as educators, it is difficult not to wonder if we are indeed a "dime a dozen." We are taught curricula that discount our professional aspirations. We are taught and assessed in ways that discount our professional aspirations. We are certified in ways that often contradict our curricular and pedagogical experiences. We are evaluated in ways that discount our professional contexts. We are often in professional contexts without adequate preparation or perspective. And we are in a profession with minimal understanding or appreciation of why we are in it.

How do we not end up in that ash can described by Biff Loman? We need to collectively work more and more toward the ideal of transformative intellectualism. It needs to begin here, with us, now. We need to dig deep within ourselves and know who we really are, what we think and believe, why we are the way we are. In essence, we need to deconstruct ourselves to our most fundamental views and rebuild ourselves to appropriately and honestly reflect those views.

We need to take this ideal to our schools of education and schools of arts and sciences. We need to take a risk and advocate this cultural, intellectual revolution throughout our universities, among the faculty—whether in education, the sciences, the language arts, or other parts of the academic institution—and among our university leaders. We need to advocate it among our bureaus of education, our politicians, our school systems, and the media.

Education is more than a profession; it is a cultural phenomenon, an intellectual extension of our democracy. Somehow we have lost those ideals about education, if we ever had them to begin with. Somehow teachers, unknowingly, are becoming a "dime a dozen," and we need to reverse the trend. It is time for a paradigm shift regarding the way we view educators, educate educators, be educators, and evaluate educators. As long as the current paradigm of education remains in place, the more teachers risk becoming a "dime a dozen" rather than transformative intellectuals.

REFERENCES

Allen, S. 1998. *"DUMBTH": The Lost Art of Thinking.* Amherst, NY: Prometheus Books.

Barnet, S., M. Berman, and W. Burto. 1989. *Types of Drama: Plays and Essays.* 5th ed. Glenview, IL: Scott, Foresman, and Company.

Duit, R., and D. Treagust. 1998. "Learning in Science: From Behaviourism towards Social Constructivism and Beyond." Pp. 3–25 in *International Handbook of Science Education.* Edited by B. J. Fraser and K. G. Tobin. London: Kluwer Academic Publishers.

Elliott, J. 1998. *The Curriculum Experiment: Meeting the Challenge of Social Change.* Buckingham, UK: Open University Press.

FitzGerald, F. 1980. *America Revised.* New York: Vintage.

Freire, P. 1985. *The Politics of Education: Culture, Power, and Liberation.* New York: Bergin and Garvey.

———. 1973. *Education for Critical Consciousness.* New York: Continuum.

Friedman, S. J. 2000. "How Much of a Problem? A Reply to Ingersoll's 'The Problem of Underqualified Teachers in American Secondary Schools.'" *Educational Researcher* 29, no. 5: 18–20.

Fullan, M. 1993. *Change Forces: Probing the Depths of Educational Reform.* London: Falmer Press.

Giroux, H. 1988. *Teachers as Intellectuals: Toward a Critical Pedagogy of Learning.* Boston: Bergin and Garvey.

Goodson, I. 1993. *School Subjects and Curriculum Change.* London: Falmer Press.

Hinchey, P. H. 1999. "Emotion: Educational Psychology's Pound of Flesh." Pp. 128–145 in *The Post-Formal Reader: Cognition and Education.* Edited by J. Kincheloe, S. Steinberg, and P. H. Hinchey. New York: Falmer Press.

———. 1995. "The Human Cost of Teacher Education Reform." *Education Week* 25, no. 9: 39.

Ingersoll, R. M. 1999. "The Problem of Underqualified Teachers in American Secondary Schools." *Educational Researcher* 28, no. 2: 26–37.

Kincheloe, J. L. 2000. "Making Critical Thinking Critical." Pp. 23–40 in *Perspectives in Critical Thinking: Essays by Teachers in Theory and Practice.* Edited by D. Weil and H. K. Anderson. New York: Peter Lang.

———. 1999. "Trouble Ahead, Trouble Behind: Grounding the Post-Formal Critique of Educational Psychology." Pp. 1–54 in *The Post-Formal Reader: Cognition and Education.* Edited by J. Kincheloe, S. Steinberg, and P. H. Hinchey. New York: Falmer Press.

———. 1993. *Toward a Critical Politics of Teacher Thinking: Mapping the Postmodern.* Westport, CT: Bergin and Garvey.

———. 1992. "Education Reform: What Have Been the Effects of the Attempts To Improve Education over the Last Decade?" Pp. 227–232 in *Thirteen Questions: Reframing Education's Conversation.* Edited by J. L. Kincheloe and S. R. Steinberg. New York: Peter Lang.

———. 1991. *Teachers as Researchers: Qualitative Inquiry as a Path to Empowerment.* London: Falmer Press.

Kincheloe, J. L., and S. R. Steinberg. 1998. "Lesson Plans from the Outer Limits: Unauthorized Methods." Pp. 1–23 in *Unauthorized Methods: Strategies for Critical Teaching.* Edited by J. L. Kincheloe and S. R. Steinberg. New York: Routledge.

Kincheloe, J. L., S. R. Steinberg, and D. J. Tippins. 1992. *The Stigma of Genius: Einstein and beyond Modern Education.* Durango, CO: Hollowbrook Publishing.

Kuhn, T. 1962. *The Structure of Scientific Revolutions.* Chicago: University of Chicago Press.

Pushkin, D. B. 2001a. "The Atheoretical Nature of the National Science Education Standards? There's More Theory Than We Think. A Response to Thomas Shiland." *Science Education,* in press.

———. 2001b. "Cookbook Classrooms; Cognitive Capitulation." In *(Post) Modern Science (Education).* Edited by J. Weaver, P. Appelbaum, and M. Morris. New York: Peter Lang. In press.

———. 2001c. "To Standardize, or Too Standardized: What Becomes of Our Curriculum?" In *The Encyclopedia of Educational Standards.* Edited by J. Kincheloe and D. Weil. Santa Barbara, CA: ABC-CLIO Publishers. In press.

———. 2000. "Critical Thinking in Science: How Do We Recognize It? Do We Foster It?" Pp. 211–220 in *Perspectives in Critical Thinking: Essays by Teachers in Theory and Practice.* Edited by D. Weil and H. K. Anderson. New York: Peter Lang.

———. 1999. "Post-Formal Thinking and Science Education: How and Why Do We Understand Concepts and Solve Problems?" Pp. 449–467 in *The Post-Formal Reader: Cognition and Education.* Edited by J. Kincheloe, S. Steinberg, and P. H. Hinchey. New York: Falmer Press.

———. 1998a. "Introductory Students, Conceptual Understanding, and Algorithmic Success." *Journal of Chemical Education* 75, no. 7: 809–810.

———. 1998b. "Is Learning Just a Matter of Tricks? So Why Are We Educating?" *Journal of College Science Teaching* 28, no. 2: 92–93.

———. 1998c. "Teacher Says; Simon Says: Dualism in Science Learning. Pp. 185–198 in *Unauthorized Methods: Strategies for Critical Teaching.* Edited by J. Kincheloe and S. Steinberg. New York: Routledge.

———. 1995. "The Influence of a Computer-Interfaced Calorimetry Demonstration on General Physics Students' Conceptual Views of Entropy and Their Metaphoric Explanations of the Second Law of Thermodynamics." Ph.D. diss., Penn State University.

Senge, P. 1990. *The Fifth Discipline: The Art and Practice of the Learning Organization.* New York: Doubleday.

Shulman, L. S. 1986. "Those Who Understand: Knowledge Growth in Teaching." *Educational Researcher* 15, no. 2: 4–14.

Tobias, S., and C. T. Tomizuka. 1992. *Breaking the Science Barrier: How to Explore and Understand the Sciences.* New York: The College Board.

Vosniadou, S., and W. F. Brewer. 1992. "Mental Models of the Earth: A Study of Conceptual Change in Childhood." *Cognitive Psychology* 24: 535–585.

Weaver, W. T. 1979. "In Search of Quality: The Need for Talent in Teaching." *Phi Delta Kappan* 61, no. 1: 29–46.

Chapter Two

✦ The Evolution of Teacher Education (Chronology)

1700s

There were two competing establishments of American education. The first establishment essentially reflected the traditional, classical curriculum endorsed in Europe. This classical curriculum primarily emphasized Latin, Greek, literature, and history. Such a curriculum was intended for privileged families and was taught by men.

The second establishment was known as the American academies. The Philadelphia Academy, established by Benjamin Franklin, was among the most prominent. The academies emphasized a "practical" curriculum, which included surveying, navigation, agriculture, and accounting. This curriculum was to serve the practical needs of men and women as the nineteenth century approached. Although academies were open to all members of society, the teachers were predominantly male. Academies remained very important and a vibrant part of American education for older children until the 1850s. By the 1880s, the academies were essentially replaced by the rapidly growing concept of public high schools.

1830s

The formation of independent, so-called normal schools for teacher education coincided with the development by Horace Mann of the first public (grammar) schools in Massachusetts. At this time, more women were gradually entering the teaching profession than men. Although the goal was to construct and maintain respected academic programs, it was constantly countered by a prevailing sexist and classist attitude toward teaching.

This prevalent attitude was exacerbated by rapidly expanding curricula in the academies. Just prior to the 1830s, many new subjects were added, such as algebra, astronomy, botany, and chemistry. Even

the classical curriculum diversified to include U.S. history, English literature and grammar, intellectual philosophy, and debating. However,
teachers were only superficially prepared to teach such a variety of
courses during their university training.

1860s

For compulsory education (i.e., grammar and elementary schools,
grades K–8), teaching gradually became a female-dominated profession. There was considerable resistance to allowing women to teach, for
it meant they were members of the American workforce. However, this
reality was warranted by the economic and political times. Men served
as soldiers during the Civil War. The industrial revolution was in
progress. Child labor laws were initiated. The waves of immigration
from Europe began.

Consequently, the available source of schoolteachers was single
women needing to support themselves. This, however, led to the stereotype of teachers as "marms" or "spinsters," for schoolteachers were expected to be celibate; to be otherwise would, it was said, "send a wrong
social and moral message" to children, especially at the elementary
level. Fewer and fewer men became schoolteachers because of the ef-
feminate stigma attached to the profession.

In terms of curriculum, two major developments were standardized testing (originated in 1845 by the Boston school system) and bilingual education. In 1865, the New York State Board of Regents began what
is now known as "Regents Exams," which children had to pass before they
could be promoted or graduated. Bilingual education was finally gaining
strength and support in public schools by the middle of the decade. Its
roots were established in the early part of the nineteenth century in German, French, and Scandinavian parochial schools. Unfortunately, what
support there was for bilingual education had fizzled by 1890.

1890s

Up to this point, normal schools served as potential (albeit underuti-
lized) feeder schools for four-year universities, especially for people
pursuing careers in secondary-school education versus elementary- or
grammar-school education. Normal schools were essentially two-year
institutions that overlapped high school and first-year college curricula
(perhaps a precursor to junior colleges). In fact, normal schools were

considered glorified versions of the academies of the 1700s rather than institutions of higher education.

As four-year colleges still offered primarily liberal arts education, normal school administrators hoped their graduates would eventually continue their education. Colleges and universities allowed normal school graduates to matriculate as juniors, thus enabling them to earn their bachelors' degrees within two years. This was fairly rare; normal school graduates typically went directly into jobs in elementary schools. In essence, normal schools and four-year colleges were in direct competition rather than in cooperative relationships.

Additionally, some colleges (e.g., Swarthmore, Bucknell, Franklin and Marshall) explored the possibility of becoming a normal school, but their administrators were averse to offering what they called "subcollegiate teacher training." It should be noted, however, that these same colleges did begin to offer graduate-level education courses, as well as a master of arts degree program. These master's degree programs were short-lived, eventually fading from colleges by 1910.

However, it was the colonial-era and land-grant universities that began to offer undergraduate teacher education programs just prior to the end of the decade. These programs, however, primarily consisted of lectures on contemporary textbooks on the history of education, the science and art of teaching, and additional course work in school subjects. In 1893, Columbia University's Teachers College offered the first Ph.D. program in education. This degree required course work in educational psychology, history of education, and philosophy of education, graduate course work in a department outside education, and research toward a dissertation. The primary purpose of this degree program was to better train university faculty, especially those who would teach aspiring schoolteachers.

Meanwhile, in schools, the curriculum began to evolve from a classically based one to one based on more contemporary and practical subjects. Although the emphasis was still considered liberal education, to parallel the liberal arts emphasis of colleges and universities, school curricula became more balanced. Beyond the traditional humanities, history, and language courses, the curriculum now included more mathematics and sciences. The major focus of this new curriculum was high schools; it was motivated by the entrance expectations of high school graduates as they matriculated to universities. In fact, by the end of this decade, there were four general curricular theories in competition:

- ➡ classical humanism (i.e., liberal arts), primarily advocated by Charles Eliot, president of Harvard University

→ child centering (e.g., child development), primarily advocated by eminent psychologist G. Stanley Hall of Clark University

→ social efficiency (i.e., preparation for adult life), primarily advocated by John Franklin Bobbitt of the University of Chicago

→ social reconstructionism (e.g., societal equity), primarily advocated by Harold Rugg of Teachers College, Columbia University

1900–1909

Increasing sensitivity (or concern) arose regarding teachers, their marital status, gender roles, and sexual orientation. This began a six-decade-long debate regarding the social norms for teachers, including such issues as human sexuality, marriage, procreation, employment, mental health, and homosexuality/lesbianism, a debate that became highly charged between 1945 and 1964, the Baby Boom era as well as the height of the Cold War era.

By this time, males had almost completely abandoned normal schools in favor of the liberal arts universities (even though many normal schools were coeducational). For the most part, normal schools were two-year institutions designed to prepare teachers for K–8 classrooms, where a bachelor's degree was not required. The majority of these teachers were females or males coming from lower-class families. High school education was still noncompulsory; generally only children from middle- and upper-class families attended. Men predominated among the high school faculty for several reasons: (1) A bachelor's degree from the universities was required to teach, (2) the opportunity existed to advance into an administrative position, (3) salaries were higher compared to those of the elementary schools, and (4) there was greater respect for content specialization.

However, it should be noted that more than 80 percent of the teaching workforce had virtually no formal specialized training for classroom teaching. Pedagogical training was still a relatively abstract concept, teacher education programs were still rare, and many schoolteachers still lacked even a high school diploma (ironically, the Scholastic Aptitude Test was first established in 1900). Not only did teacher-certification requirements vary from state to state, they varied from county to county. It was assumed that teachers had a basic knowledge of grammar school content and enough sense to use corporal punishment as needed.

1910–1919

As the balance of demography tilted heavily toward female teachers at the elementary level, school systems appealed for an increase in the male presence. During the prior decade, the number of male classroom teachers in the United States had declined by 24 percent. For example, in 1911, New York City educators appealed for more male teachers to offset the "effeminism of boys" due to a very dominant female presence in schools. To make teaching seem more attractive to men, school systems began to create "masculine niches," such as administration, coaching, vocational education, manual trades, mathematics, and science.

This initiative strongly reflected a socialist critique that public schools failed to benefit children for future adult roles in a society increasingly economically inequitable. However, economics was not the only issue of the socialist critique. For perhaps the first time in American education, genuine debate focused on the social and intellectual needs of children of skilled and unskilled laborers, working-class children, migrant children, immigrant children, women, and ethnic and racial minorities.

In fact, it was during this decade that immigration and language became hotly debated issues in public education. By 1917, all funding for bilingual public schools was discontinued, and by 1919, 15 states had made it illegal to teach a class in a foreign language. Such legislation sought to homogenize everyone into an English-speaking culture, just as the notion of America as a "Melting Pot" expected all immigrants to blend together into one type of American.

However, within this socialist critique there were contrasting schools of thought. One school of thought advocated social functionalism, in which society was a system of interrelated forces that combine to produce social stability. Although some consider Marxism a form of functionalism, conservatism is the political system most commonly viewed as functionalist. Social functionalism viewed social phenomena in terms of a social totality that included definitive boundaries of normal/acceptable behavior for a social order. Advocates of functionalism essentially saw individuals as productive citizens contributing to society as a whole. As for subject matter taught in schools, functionalists questioned its ultimate usefulness toward societal preservation.

On the other hand, another school of thought, social reductionism, sought simple, elemental, and individualistic explanations to complex phenomena. Advocates of reductionism essentially saw individuals as members of society with needs. Until individuals' needs were met, they would neither be able nor inspired to be full citizens in a pluralistic and democratic society. In other words, citizenry should not be one-sided.

In terms of curriculum, functionalists advocated a practical subject-based curriculum, while reductionists advocated a liberal arts curriculum. The contrasting views debate the merits of preparing growing children for an occupation and economic self-sufficiency versus social responsibility and morality. Essentially, the role of school faced a dichotomy. Should schools prepare children for the workforce, or should they prepare children to be thoughtful adults?

Much of this dichotomy was driven by the previous decade's social-hygiene movement, in which gender-appropriate behaviors and concerns of social deviance were major themes. Exacerbating this movement was the almost universal embracing of the concept of the academic major at colleges and universities at the beginning of this decade. With normal schools competing for male students against a "superior" curriculum at the four-year institutions, teacher education faced many more challenges than just social conventions.

1920s

Normal schools were legislatively authorized to offer four-year bachelor's degree programs in education and thus became what were known as state teachers colleges. This coincided with higher education's evolved view that teacher education (pedagogy) was a professional field of study, as were medicine, law, engineering, and agriculture, during the latter part of the previous decade. However, education was viewed as a "newer" or "junior" profession compared to medicine or law. Pedagogy was viewed as an extension of the liberal arts curriculum, with strong connections to philosophy, psychology, and sociology.

Of course, those who recognized pedagogy did have some misgivings, as university faculty were essentially forced to interact with people (aspiring schoolteachers) they deemed inferior. Furthermore, university faculty feared the upward extension of teacher-certification laws toward their own practices and credentials. Meanwhile, public (state) universities were beginning to offer undergraduate degrees in education; this trend continued during the next five decades. However, this trend never developed among private universities (as opposed to private liberal arts colleges).

Early in this decade, Harvard University's Graduate School of Education offered a program leading to an Ed.D. (doctorate of education) degree in competition to Columbia's Ph.D. program. Admission to doctoral candidacy in Harvard's program required an advanced working knowledge of biology, psychology, and social sciences. Doctoral students studied the social theory of education, history of education, and educational psychology. Furthermore, students conducted research leading to a dissertation as the culmination of their degree.

It was during this decade that schools were strongly influenced by John Dewey's humanistic curriculum movement. It should be noted that Dewey's version of humanism was somewhat different from Eliot's version. School subjects, quite distinctive in the classical liberal arts education, were no longer as distinctive. The mode of instruction for these subjects was known as the Project Method.

The schoolteacher was expected to take on a warm, nurturing, and facilitating role, fostering emotional relationships with children and serving as a resource center. Teachers were encouraged to create opportunities for children to deal with their effective concerns (e.g., beliefs, values, goals, fears, and relationships). Classroom practice was minimally structured and activity/problem-based, guided by Gestalt psychology and human development principles, as teachers provided children with opportunities for alternative behavior to be evaluated for consequences. Errors were considered to be good learning experiences, not necessarily criteria for academic assessment.

Education was supposed to be confluent and holistic, providing children with integrated learning experiences relative to their interests and goals (i.e., it was child centered). In many respects, Dewey can be considered the first constructivist. Dewey's curriculum movement was in many ways a hybridization of all four competing curriculum theories from the 1890s.

1930s

As American school curricula evolved from a humanist paradigm to one reflecting the social reconstructionist movement, teachers were encouraged to continue to be nurturing facilitators but to be less passive. Teachers were encouraged to be more socially conscious and politically active, empowering themselves as well as their students within a democratic society. Teachers were especially encouraged to be part of the policy-making process, regardless of their level of teaching, gender, social status, or educational training.

Social reconstructionism, advocated by Harold Rugg, encouraged teachers to share the responsibility of curriculum development and construction, empowering them to be better informed of educational goals. Rugg's theory focused concern about values for which schools should work. Curriculum should raise social consciousness and discontent, inspiring citizenship action. Rugg's theory primarily advocated productive citizenry and progressive democratic pedagogy.

For all subject areas in the school curriculum, despite the fact that there were no universal objectives or content, teachers were expected to confront students with societal problems that related their personal goals to local, national, and world purposes. Students were encouraged to cooperate with their community and its resources, always considering the economic and political implications of their actions. As children learned to act upon problems, as opposed to merely studying them, teachers served as conduits between them and adults in their communities.

Social reconstructionism carried into the next decade in a variety of ways. At the elementary level, learning activities were group oriented to encourage collaboration and negotiation. At the secondary level, societal problems were integrated into the curriculum. For example, science focused on health-related issues, grammar skills were developed by reading newspapers, and mathematics was applied to economic issues.

Additionally, it was during this decade that education societies (e.g., Phi Delta Kappa and the National Education Association) began to endorse hiring married women as schoolteachers and actively recruiting men to teach. Married women were considered excellent candidates to enrich children's lives because of their understanding of family life. Furthermore, married women represented a turn away from the expectation of celibacy, a move that was expected to improve the morale of many young teachers desiring a family and career. However, pregnant women were considered ineligible to teach (a common policy for several decades), for pregnancy directly reflected sexuality; this was especially considered inappropriate for elementary classrooms. On the other hand, the male presence in schools was endorsed for the image of masculinity, authority, and discipline.

Responding to Harvard's Ed.D. program, Columbia University's Teachers College offered their Ed.D. in 1934 (in addition to their Ph.D.). Students in both of Teachers College's doctoral programs took the same courses; only the scope of dissertation research differed. In many respects, this began the distinction between professional practitioners of education and scholars of education. Such a distinction eventually fueled the debate regarding the qualifications of professors of teacher education.

1940s

American education was becoming more technocratic and oriented toward academic subjects. Curricula and pedagogy reflected a high degree of behaviorism (versus cognitivism), and teachers were extensively trained in behavior-modification techniques. Mastery learning (that is, a learner "masters" one thing before moving on to the next) was the prevalent classroom teaching model, and teachers were discouraged from broadening their roles within the education system beyond their specific content duties.

The social reconstructionist movement of previous decades lost strength and support. Although the Great Depression of the previous decade lent credence to Rugg's advocacy, World War II quickly turned perspectives in a new direction. Perhaps the most significant motivator for a new direction was a distinct drain of science talent to the armed forces. Ralph Tyler of the University of Chicago proposed what was known as the "Technical Rationalism Model" of curriculum, asking the following questions:

- What educational purposes should schools seek to attain?
- What educational experiences can be provided that are likely to attain these purposes?
- How can educational experiences be effectively organized?
- How can attainment of purposes be assessed?

Schooling essentially became a form of vocational training, especially at the high school level, as employment was still more common than higher education after graduation from high school. Ironically, the motivation for Tyler's curriculum movement came from a perception that schools were not preparing students well enough to conquer the science curriculum at universities; consequently, many university science students felt inadequately prepared for employment as professional scientists. Although a finger of blame was pointed at the quality of instruction in universities, much more blame was directed at high school teachers.

Meanwhile, achievement testing was becoming more and more common at all levels of schooling. Furthermore, recommendations were made for teachers to become content specialists in order to have sufficient expertise to teach assessment-related subject matter. However, it would be another two decades before teachers commonly pursued bachelor's degrees in specific subject areas.

For science-teacher preparation, colleges were urged to offer better courses in education, better grounding in subject matter, more emphasis on basic principles of science content, and more practical work versus theoretical studies. The rationale was that if high school science teachers knew their basic science principles better and knew how to teach them better, they would produce better-qualified students for the college level, which would ultimately produce better employees for the scientific workforce. Consequently, these demands and expectations essentially transformed classroom practice from child centered to teacher centered.

1950s

As the Cold War began, the U.S. Congress and various state legislatures subjected public school systems to investigation. The McCarthyism of the decade did not spare schoolteachers. However, in addition to investigating political loyalties (i.e., whether teachers were soft on communism), schoolteachers were continuously scrutinized on their sexual orientations (i.e., whether they were homosexual). Both "red scare" and "gay scare" inquiries (or inquisitions, for all intents and purposes) continued well into the next decade.

Meanwhile, the Technical Rationalism Model of curriculum was still a part of schooling. Each subject area had a distinct pedagogical objective (which included assessment). In mathematics, the central theme was student mastery of computational skills. In science, the emphasis was on intellectual training within the disciplines (i.e., more rigor on principles and the nature of each branch of science). In English, heavy emphasis was placed on the reading of literature. In social studies, varied curriculum programs were used; however, there seemed to be universal overlap between social literacy and demonstrating social processes. Foreign languages were offered again, not only in high schools but in elementary schools as well. Even the teaching of fine arts underwent some evolution, combining a focus on creativity skills with integration of historical aspects of artwork.

A new mode of education evolved during this decade. The concept of middle schools was initiated. Middle schools were to be transitional structures during a child's schooling. Rather than traditional grammar schools (grades K–8) and high schools (9–12), middle schools would divide grammar schools into new elementary/primary schools (K–5) and middle/intermediate schools (6–8). In due time, middle schools were replaced by junior high schools, creating a system of schooling that grouped grades into K–6, 7–9, and 10–12. However, a couple of decades later, the middle school model returned to create a system that grouped grades into K–4, 5–8, and 9–12. The primary rationale for middle schools and junior high schools was based on child-development and socialization principles. Ironically, as school structures evolved, teacher-certification programs did not keep pace. Even today, teacher-certification programs specifically for middle school teachers are rare, and certification requirements often reflect a merging of elementary and secondary-level teacher education courses. Such structural divisions within school systems, in combination with advocacy for new "gifted and talented" education programs (especially in mathematics and science), essentially laid the foundation for the practice of ability tracking students within schools.

1960s

Two seminal events from the 1950s heavily influenced this decade of American education. First was the desegregation of public schools, a consequence of the landmark 1954 U.S. Supreme Court decision in *Brown vs. Board of Education*. Second was the Soviet Union's 1957 launching of Sputnik, the first man-made satellite.

As a consequence of *Brown vs. Board of Education*, a number of conflicting events took place with regards to education during this decade. On one hand, President Lyndon B. Johnson signed the 1964 Civil Rights Act. On the other hand, bilingual education deteriorated into the practice of letting children "sink or swim," as immigrant children were expected to take classes taught only in English and to develop English-only mastery. Foreign languages were offered considerably less than in the 1950s. Meanwhile, English as a subject area dealt more sensitively with multiculturalism and racial/ethnic identities. Although the English curriculum focused on social democracy for the disadvantaged and disenfranchised, pedagogical practices effectively created disenfranchisement.

American educators began to become interested in Paulo Freire's adult-literacy movement in São Paulo, Brazil, despite the opposition he faced from his own government. Meanwhile, schools in the United States began to develop intervention programs to help at-risk, low-income, elementary-level children (e.g., Head Start). Unfortunately, while American education systems sought to wage war on poverty and illiteracy, American education was potentially contributing to these societal ills.

In response to Sputnik's launching, a number of curriculum reforms took place (led primarily by Harvard psychology professor Jerome Bruner), most notably in science and mathematics. In science, a greater focus on the disciplines (e.g., biology, chemistry, and physics) took place, with curriculum packages (e.g., BSCS Biology, ChemStudy, and PSSC Physics) prioritizing abstract problem solving. To "think like the experts" was a primary objective for learners. Essentially, university professors seeking a new generation of intellectual clones designed these science-curriculum packages; high school science teachers were merely proxies for professors, expected to transmit content as professors intended. Unfortunately, these reforms were relatively unused and unsuccessful, as teachers' need to learn how to use the curriculum packages was grossly overlooked. This failure by professors to fully appreciate teachers' roles and reference points greatly undermined an effort to boost the American scientific brain force.

In mathematics, Sputnik inspired a new mode of content and thought process (e.g., new math). Although intriguing and intellectually stimulating, the post-Sputnik approaches to mathematics suffered a quicker rebellion than did new approaches to science. Considerable frustration rose among children and parents who could solve problems intuitively yet could never apply the novel algorithms correctly. This frustration eventually turned toward teachers, who ultimately discarded the new curriculum in an effort to find peace within their instruction of content.

Social studies underwent radical changes during this decade. In response to multiple world influences—such as the Civil Rights movement, the women's rights movement, the Cold War, the Vietnam conflict and subsequent antiwar protests, and assassinations—the curriculum went into total disarray, seeking new focal points for civics, history, and government/political science.

Even reading instruction was about to undergo a philosophical shift. As the decade drew to a close, the concept/philosophy of Whole Language, generally dominant in American schools since the early 1900s when it was advocated by John Dewey and Col. Francis Parker (head of the Cook County, Illinois, Normal School), was replaced by the psycholinguistic model. In Whole Language, directed reading activity, from books relevant to children rather than from reading textbooks, placed priority on context-based (inferential) reading-comprehension skills. However, the argument against Whole Language (sometimes seen as including phonics, although others viewed phonics as a distinct contradiction of Whole Language) targeted its lack of focus on actual how-to reading skills.

However, while certain subject areas underwent either total reform, deconstruction, or elimination, two new dimensions were added to school curricula. In response to President John F. Kennedy's advocacy of physical fitness, physical education classes were added to school curricula. Additionally, art appreciation became a new curricular focal point. The arts were no longer viewed solely in terms of creativity; historical and sociopolitical aspects were also considered relevant to classical artwork.

As school curricula underwent reform, so too did teacher education, albeit maybe not on a philosophical basis. Maintaining a Technical Rationalism paradigm, teacher education programs of the 1960s (and 1970s) were primarily behavioristic in curricula and pedagogical training. During this decade, debates began regarding the merits and long-term professional benefits of teacher education programs. In fact, in 1965 the first center for research and development on teacher education was begun and federally funded at the University of Texas–Austin.

Most notably, teachers were expected to be more knowledgeable in specific subject matter, intensifying a scrutinization of teachers that had begun in the 1940s. There was increasing demand for all teachers to hold at least a four-year, bachelor's degree from an accredited college or university. Teacher education programs were encouraged to provide more depth in areas of subject specialization yet maintain sufficient breadth beyond one academic subject. There was also debate as to whether teacher education should be an extension of liberal arts education, its own entity of professional studies, or a combination of both.

1970s

The requirement that a teacher have a bachelor's degree finally became uniform in the United States when school populations stabilized both in terms of students enrolled and teachers needed. Normal schools were completely phased out and replaced by teachers colleges and schools of education. At this time, the number of classroom teachers holding graduate (master's and specialist) degrees began to increase.

The behaviorist domination of teacher education programs continued. For example, the 1970s saw the genuine beginnings of educational objectives (i.e., outcomes-based education); this was reinforced by a series of newly published "teach to the test" manuals. Learning was still viewed as a general reaction to stimuli. It was recommended that school subject matters undergo even stronger divisions than during the previous two decades.

Yet the ultimate (and most controversial) application of behaviorism was a very popular teaching/supervision model "developed" by Madeline Hunter at the University of California–Los Angeles. This model was known for its "seven essential steps," although Hunter herself did not create a seven-step lesson plan model. She suggested various elements that might be considered in planning for effective instruction. Her theory, unfortunately, was translated differently into practice.

In practice, these elements were subsequently compiled by others as the "Seven Step Lesson Plan," taught in teacher education courses, and used as a checklist of items required for each lesson. This application was contrary to Hunter's intent, and its misuse is largely responsible for objections to "direct instruction" and to her system of clinical supervision. Used as she intended, the steps were considered to make a useful structure for the development of many lesson plans, including nonbehavioral ones. According to Hunter, not all elements belonged in every lesson, although they would occur in a typical unit plan composed of several lessons. This essentially became the crux for teacher educators and supervisors. From a pragmatic administrative perspective, how does one evaluate an entire *unit* of instruction, and to what extent does it differ from an *individual lesson?*

Apparently, teacher educators and supervisors could not make the distinction. This seven-step approach was used in thousands of teacher education programs and school districts for the better part of three decades. Prospective teachers were instructed to follow those seven steps in *every* lesson, regardless of content area or educational context. What Hunter may very well have intended for comprehensive, long-term teaching and learning was applied with only short-term considerations.

These steps were

- *Objectives*. Teachers should have a clear idea of what they are supposed to be teaching and what, specifically, students should be able to demonstrate as a result of the teaching. This was based on Benjamin Bloom's Taxonomy of Educational Objectives.
- *Standards*. Teachers need to know what standards of performance specifically connect lessons with accountability assessment. Students should be informed about these standards, so they appreciate the importance of what is being taught.
- *Anticipatory Set*. This is sometimes called a "hook" to grab students' attention, as teachers try to relate the experiences of their students to the objectives of the lesson.
- *Teaching/Presentation*. This has three parts (input, modeling, and check for understanding). Input is teachers' provi-

sion of information needed for students to gain expected knowledge through multiple modes (e.g., lecture, film, tape, video, or pictures). Teachers then model by showing students examples of what is expected as an end product of their work. In checking for understanding, teachers determine whether students "get it" before proceeding.

- *Guided Practice.* Teachers provide an opportunity for each student to demonstrate a grasp of new learning by working through an activity or exercise under direct supervision. Teachers move around their classrooms to determine the level of mastery and to provide individual remediation as needed.
- *Closure.* Teachers make statements or take actions that are designed to bring a lesson presentation to an appropriate conclusion. Closure is used to cue students to their arrival at an important point in a lesson or the end of a lesson or to help organize student learning. Essentially, it is an act of reviewing and clarifying the key points of a lesson, tying them together into a coherent whole, and ensuring their utility in application by securing them in the student's conceptual network.
- *Independent Practice.* Once pupils have mastered the content or skill, it is time to provide for reinforcement practice, provided on a repeating schedule so learning is not forgotten. This is typically in the form of homework or group or individual work in class (or out of class projects).

By having a "one size fits all" protocol for teaching, teachers could be considered interchangeable clones, and school administrators would not struggle to ensure accountability. In fact, accountability was hardly accountability; it was essentially conformity to a predetermined, standardized, and generic rubric or recipe. Failure to completely adhere to or comply with the seven-step model had to be deemed failure during teacher observations. Conformity was equated with competence; this raised the stakes intensely regarding teacher performance evaluations and job security. At a time when a call for social consciousness, protection of living standards, unionization, democracy, and self-autonomy was on the rise, teacher education and the teaching profession contradicted these goals in essentially every possible dimension.

However, from a learning perspective, this method of instruction was contrived and subtly coercive. At best, it represented the cognitive apprenticeship Dewey once objected to. In fact, the modeling/teacher/

guided practice/independent practice aspect reinforced the technical/rationalism intellectual cloning envisioned by post-Sputnik science and mathematics reformers: *Monkey watch the expert. . . . See what the expert did? Monkey do with the expert . . . good. Monkey show the expert . . . very good. Now monkey can do all by yourself!* On the other hand, the objectives/anticipatory set/closure aspect reinforced an almost Orwellian logic in which students were essentially told what knowledge was of ultimate importance, why it should be important, how they should embrace it, and what consequences would be for learning or not learning. Although there may be very positive aspects to be distilled from this mode of pedagogy, two troubling questions lingered. First, were children ever asked about the importance or relevance of knowledge? Second, were all class lessons supposed to end "happily ever after," neat and tidy, like a half-hour television show?

Ironically, universities began to develop their own centers for teaching and learning; the first was developed at Stanford University. These centers were developed by college of education faculty, primarily to serve and assist faculty from other departments not as "enlightened" about pedagogical practices. Although there is still debate as to the ultimate impact these centers had on university-wide pedagogical reform, they undeniably exposed the hypocrisy within teacher education.

Meanwhile, the social-consciousness movements of the previous decade continued (e.g., reintroduction of foreign languages in the school curriculum, albeit primarily for high schools), and by the end of this decade a considerable amount of backlash against homosexuality had evolved. The social and political conservatives who created a "gay scare" in the 1950s were back with a vengeance. Not only were gay rights and gay communities threatened, American public schools once again experienced inquiries into the morality of its teachers. In fact, suspicion of homosexuality was still considered sufficient grounds for terminating educators and revocation of licensure/certification. Sadly, this policy generally still exists in most states today.

A considerable amount of litigation took place during this decade, especially with regards to bilingual education. In 1974, the U.S. Supreme Court ruled that the San Francisco school system did not have appropriate ESL (English as a second language) resources for immigrant children, deciding that the school system violated not only the 1964 Civil Rights Act but the Fourteenth Amendment of the U.S. Constitution, which essentially ensures the right to a public education, even if children are illegal aliens or of limited English proficiency. The Court ruled that all language-minority children had the right to be tested in their primary/native language in addition to English. Consequently, the

U.S. Congress passed the Equal Educational Opportunity Act, which applies to all public schools and all children attending those schools.

1980s

Following the 1983 publication of *A Nation at Risk,* a number of "hot" issues came to the forefront. As was the case in the post-Sputnik movement of the early 1960s, mathematics and science (as well as English) were spotlighted subjects. There was said to be a critical shortage of teachers for these subject areas, and states granted emergency teaching certificates. Alternate certification programs were initiated to help address critical teacher shortages in these subjects; many new math and science teachers came from other fields (e.g., industry). However, this raised a debate on the merits of applying a bachelor's degree in a specific subject area toward teacher certification. On one hand, in terms of content competence, the degree was seen as a good thing. On the other hand, a subject-area degree alone was considered inadequate for the responsibilities and challenges of classroom teaching. Therefore, teacher certification, even for those following alternative tracks, still required a prescribed number of education courses (e.g., psychological foundations to education, historical foundations to education, methods of subject area instruction). By the end of the decade, not only was course work required, but so was some form of new-teacher internship under the supervision of a mentor.

Ongoing professional development was encouraged, including in-service training and continuing education. Graduate degrees became required in many states. Accreditation became more critical for school districts as well as for teacher education programs. Accountability testing for teacher competence became more commonplace. Developing a comprehensive and nationally consistent teacher certification process also began.

A number of new themes emerged (or even reemerged) during this decade. First, in the 1980s, many colleges and universities initiated reforms in their undergraduate curricula. Second, there was a concerted effort by those writing science and mathematics curricula to present teaching materials about the contributions of women and racial/ethnic minorities to specific content principles. Further continuing a trend from the late 1960s, colleges and universities capitalized on social-consciousness and cultural diversity/inclusiveness movements to offer courses in women's studies, African studies, and other courses delving into the histories and sociologies of various ethnic minorities. Such issues found their way into teacher education as multicultural-education courses. Third, there was genuine outrage over specialization curricula (that is, more courses in one's major and fewer distribution course requirements or electives) at the expense of the classics and humanities; a strong call for a return to a liberal arts curriculum ensued.

By 1988, there was even a recommendation to abolish the Carnegie unit, a system of accounting for the courses students take toward graduation (e.g., bookkeeping of credits taken/earned). The primary arguments against the Carnegie unit were its contribution to uniform standards and the consequent limits placed on alternative pedagogical approaches. Of course, this recommendation was in direct conflict with considerations of time-consciousness and pedagogical efficiency. For example, team teaching was becoming a popular trend in education, for it encouraged greater consensus within schools about educational goals and served as a labor saving device. Another popular trend involved maximizing "time on task." Proponents of this theory believed that efficient learning resulted from efficient teaching, which essentially required a maximization of instructional time within a given class period.

Further contributing to the efficiency theme was a stronger commitment to ability tracking and increased concern over class sizes. Proponents of efficiency believed small, homogeneous classrooms would enable teachers to focus more on instruction and reduce time lost on disruptive or academically misplaced children.

However, efficiency proponents failed to demonstrate any appreciable relationship between "improved" classroom factors and teacher practices. In fact, many questions arose about reform movements, especially in terms of teachers' roles in reform, the hierarchical extent of school reforms, teachers' knowledge base and skills, and the daily noninstructional duties teachers performed. Ironically, during this decade ESL certification came to be required for teachers working with children of limited English proficiency, and special-education awareness began for subject-area teachers. Additionally, the 1980s saw considerable examination of teaching styles and their compatibility with individual learning styles.

Teacher education was finally undergoing a long-overdue evolution. The training of teachers was finally moving away from behaviorism and toward the concept of reflective practice, quite cognitive in orientation. Education professors, many of them specifically professors of curriculum and instruction, routinely attacked curriculum packages. These materials were criticized for constraining and controlling knowledge as well as teacher creativity and innovation. However, these efforts to do away with curriculum packages and to encourage teachers to develop their own teaching materials were in considerable conflict with reliance on the Hunter model of teaching and with the tremendous focus on teachers' knowledge base on subject matter as it related to standardized assessment and educational objectives.

Two more issues in teacher education emerged before the end of the decade: *critical thinking* and *critical pedagogy*. Although critical thinking was viewed heavily in terms of problem-solving efficiency in the sciences, a more widely accepted conception reflected the holistic and integrated thinking and learning once advocated by Dewey's humanistic curriculum movement. Perhaps the most important application of critical thinking to teacher education involved contextual thinking; this was perhaps the key salvo against the Hunter model, for pedagogical practice needed a context and could not be generic.

Whereas critical thinking reflected a humanist origin, critical pedagogy reflected a social reconstructionist origin. Advocates of critical pedagogy (e.g., Henry Giroux and Peter McLaren) noted that teaching practice should be political and ideological. Pedagogical practice was said to influence intellectual change, one's knowledge base, and how one relates to others; this meant much more than mere transmission of information. Again, here is a philosophical movement that flew in the face of current practices, for it challenged the notion that assessable educational objectives were of ultimate importance. In fact, as the decade drew to a close, one could sense the growing debate over education as a total process versus education in terms of some "bottom line." Intellectualism versus technicism was fast becoming a dominant debate theme.

1990s AND BEYOND

As this decade evolved and passed, we have seen a number of curriculum changes take place. First, we have seen a stronger commitment (albeit tenuous and halfhearted at times) to cultural diversity and sensitivity. We offer courses in multicultural education for prospective teachers, but we still do not know what they ultimately learn. There have been attempts to offer diversity education in schools, but not without backlash, especially with regards to homosexuality and alternative lifestyles (e.g., New York City's short-lived Rainbow Curriculum). We have also witnessed more accountability measures—audits, funding with strings attached, litigation, and the like—aimed at inclusiveness and equitable education, especially for children with limited English proficiency. However, there has been backlash here, too (e.g., California's Proposition 187), and bilingual education continues to struggle for its proper conceptualization and recognition in school curricula.

Second, we have seen an increased effort to provide more comprehensive and consistent curricula for our subject areas, especially in mathematics and science. Both subject areas have striven for integrated learning and standards offering considerable depth and breadth. English as a subject area offered a compromise with a curriculum balanced between grammar skills and appreciation for literature. Not only did social studies reestablish history as its dominant theme, but the globalization of America necessitated more attention to geography in the curriculum. However, foreign-language instruction has greatly suffered during this decade. Very few school systems offer foreign-language instruction to their students, and most who do only offer Spanish and French. Consequently, colleges and universities are not requiring foreign languages for admission as much as they have in decades past, and they rarely maintain a foreign-language requirement for graduation. The prospects for foreign languages are not very good in a climate where presidential candidates (e.g., Senator Bob Dole in 1996) recommend English be our national language. Although it is our de facto official language, such statements only exacerbate tensions as we strive toward a more culturally pluralistic and sensitive society.

Many issues, some contradictory, were raised during the 1990s. Teachers were said to be lacking in appropriate certification or competence, yet teacher shortages continued. Teacher education programs were finally emphasizing prospective teachers' knowledge about learners in addition to their own knowledge. As was the case during previous decades, better and more-uniform certification standards were called for. However, there was still no universal agreement as to what is the best academic preparation for a teaching career (e.g., a bachelor's degree in education or a bachelor's degree in a subject area?). In fact, undergraduate degree programs for teachers were neither consistent nor clarified. Although some programs emphasized the theoretical foundations of teaching, others emphasized pragmatic methods courses.

Further exacerbating the debate is the number of credit hours required for teacher certification versus a bachelor's degree. With normal schools and state teachers colleges long gone, teacher education essentially belongs to two primary types of institutions of higher education: large state universities and small private colleges; there no longer appears to be a happy medium. In the case of large state universities, because tuition is subsidized by federal and state funds, students are under time and credit limits for completing their degrees and any certification requirements. Consequently, the two academic programs most affected are engineering, which is now under pressure to streamline its traditional five-year bachelor's degree program, and teacher education, which is under pressure to prioritize its course requirements.

Regardless, accountability testing was rarely far from concern among teacher education programs, school systems, and state departments of education. Even presidential campaigns were run with a platform that included improving the quality of schools in terms of test scores. How schoolchildren perform on standardized tests determines how schools and states are ranked, and there may be a monetary bounty attached. This places teachers in a great dilemma, for they are expected to improve student test scores, teach more-rigorous curricula, be pedagogically inclusive, and ensure America that they will help graduate the best possible workforce for a competitive global economy. Unfortunately, we are left to wonder how much of this is ultimately possible and to what extent such expectations are mutually compatible. For example, while President George W. Bush ran his 2000 election campaign, he championed education, repeatedly proclaiming, "We will leave no child behind." However, based on the complex expectations of schools, teachers, and children in this hyper-accountability era, one cannot but wonder if children ever get ahead. Whether the ultimate goal is increased test scores or increased success rates, a proverbial lowering of the bar may be needed to ensure that accountability goals are met. As has been asked about educational standards/objectives for some time, are we dealing with standards for excellence or standards for mediocrity (i.e., minimal competency)? Is the ultimate goal for education to be the best it can be, or to be "substantially approvable," to use governmental bureaucratic language?

Furthermore, the merits of alternative certification programs continued to be debated. There was additional debate as to whether teachers should hold at least a master's degree, as a sign of increased professionalism. More and more states demand at least a master's degree for permanent certification, yet teachers are said to lack enough content knowledge to pass state certification exams, further feeding the political frenzy. At the very least, teacher education was no longer seen as peripheral to the American educational policy agenda. For better or worse, whether guided or misguided, the focus of educational reform fully enveloped teachers, as opposed to either children or curricula.

However, the most intriguing contradiction lies in the philosophy of teacher education. On one hand, teachers were and are encouraged to be reflective practitioners, constructivists, critical thinkers, and nurturing facilitators and to use alternative assessments. On the other hand, teachers were and are held accountable for students' scores on standardized exams reflecting minimal thinking skills. Considerable dichotomy and conflict continues.

This has led to a rather punitive approach to educational reform.

Rather than promoting reform as a means to improve, politicians promote reform as a threat. There have been calls for states to either take over or close down teacher education programs when their graduates cannot pass certification exams. Many university leaders have called for the abolition of colleges of education, arguing that teacher education belongs in the hands of subject-area departments, where the "real experts" are. All this took place during the same decade that John Goodlad established his Center for Educational Renewal at the University of Washington and New Jersey's Montclair State University established the nation's first Center of Pedagogy and Institutes for Critical Thinking and Philosophy of Children.

With charter schools and private schools gaining popularity, politicians have advocated school vouchers to let families choose their children's schools. State and federal grants have been awarded to school districts that collaborate with private organizations to offer programs to enhance student achievement (e.g., Project Outreach). Although such ventures may seem to be children friendly, they subtly undermine the American public school system and perhaps blatantly undermine the principle of the separation of church and state defined by the U.S. Constitution. In fact, one dominant theme during the 2000 presidential campaign was the shutting down of schools that routinely fail to succeed on standardized assessments. Such threats, in combination with calls for more accountability, standardization, and school choice, leave public education a potentially endangered species and only serve to polarize this country's citizens, with education as a powder keg.

So many of the themes described during prior decades seemed to return in the 1990s, reinforcing the cliché that education reform resembles a pendulum in motion. Although some argue that education has evolved since the mid-1800s, others can argue that it has merely oscillated between competing curricular, political, theoretical, philosophical, and intellectual agendas. In fact, one cannot help but wonder if teacher education is an application of the metaphorical question, "Which came first, the chicken or the egg?" Does teacher education drive curriculum reform, or vice versa? From a historical perspective, one might argue the former prior to 1900 yet argue the latter since. And yet we are left to wonder to what extent either provides the true impetus. As we begin a new millennium, we are left with a historical legacy of inherent contradictions, incomplete agendas, questionable continuity between school curricula and teacher education, and superficial changes, with the ultimate meaning of education still missing and in dire need of searching.

Chapter Three

⊷ The Academic Preparation of Teachers

Two decades ago, few distinctions could be made among teaching positions. Teachers were certified either as multisubject elementary school teachers, or as single-subject secondary school teachers. The lack of differentiation among teaching roles has frequently been cited as limiting teachers' opportunities to take on different school responsibilities.
—Sharon Feiman-Nemser and Robert E. Floden, 1986

The purpose of this chapter is not to describe in intricate detail all academic and certification requirements for classroom teachers. I advise the reader to contact specific state departments of education (provided in Chapter 12) for such information. Neither is it the purpose of this chapter to give a detailed historical account of what certification programs have been like since the beginning of public education. As noted in Chapter 2, teacher education has evolved in a somewhat strange manner since the latter part of the 1800s, guided directly and indirectly by various curricular, social, and political agendas.

My primary objective in this chapter is to offer some perspective on how teacher education curricula have evolved and continue to evolve in light of increasing demands that teachers be more knowledgeable about the content they teach. Furthermore, I wish to share current teacher education curricula from five different states in order to offer some global sense of what the academic requirements generally are and allow the reader to make some comparisons between various states' criteria for elementary- and secondary-level teaching.

According to Feiman-Nemser and Floden (1986), teachers are considered to be very different from academics (e.g., university professors), in the sense that teachers lack the knowledge academics possess. This view only reinforces the stereotype of schoolteachers as weakly educated semiprofessionals rather than the transformative intellectuals Freire envisioned. Although there is little consensus regarding the "ideal" teacher education program (e.g., Cochran and Jones 1998), teacher education is still considered important at the undergraduate, postbaccalaureate, and graduate levels.

To reemphasize the quotation from Feiman-Nemser and Floden above: Teacher education is typically viewed in terms of elementary and secondary school teaching. Many of us grew up with self-contained elementary school classrooms, where one teacher taught all subjects. Perhaps there were a few exceptions to the rule: a music teacher, an arts teacher, and a physical education coach. However, we viewed that self-contained classroom teacher as one who taught a specific grade level rather than a subject; he or she was a "specialist" of that grade level.

This changed significantly for many of us upon entrance to middle school or junior high school. Perhaps as early as grades 5 and 6, or typically by grade 7, we suddenly learned to have multiple teachers and to learn in different classrooms. We had science teachers, social studies teachers, mathematics teachers, English teachers, and foreign-language teachers in addition to arts teachers, music teachers, and physical education coaches. Our teachers were no longer "specialists" of grade levels; they were "specialists" of subjects.

By high school, the specialization was even more pronounced. We did not just have science teachers; we had biology, chemistry, and physics teachers. We did not just have mathematics teachers; we had algebra, geometry, trigonometry, and calculus teachers. We did not just have social studies teachers; we had civics, history (world and American), and political science teachers. We did not just have English teachers; we had literature teachers specializing either in world, British, or American literature. The teachers were now "superspecialized"; their area of knowledge was perhaps very narrow. In many respects, this seemed excellent preparation for college, where professors were considered experts in very specific and focused areas, such as early-eighteenth-century American history, urban poets during the Great Depression, or energetic processes of intestinal bacteria in donkeys indigenous only to southwestern New Mexico.

And yet an interesting question eventually arose: How did these teachers become the "specialists" they were? Was there a specific course of training for first-grade teachers versus fourth-grade teachers? Was there a specific course of training for civics teachers versus history teachers? Was there a specific course of training for algebra teachers versus geometry teachers? Was there a specific course of training for biology teachers versus chemistry teachers?

With the exception of the last question regarding science teaching, the answer to all the other questions is no. First-grade and fourth-grade teachers are similarly trained. Civics teachers and history teachers are similarly trained. Algebra teachers and geometry teachers are similarly trained. Much of teacher education has not been overly differentiated.

Because of the context of the term "specialist," academic discourse has somehow created its own differentiation. University academics became known as "experts." Secondary school teachers became known as "specialists." Elementary school teachers became known as "generalists." What one was identified as reflected a view of how one was educated. Not only do these identifiers distinguish teachers from academics, they also reinforce the stereotypical conception that secondary school teachers are inadequately educated and elementary school teachers are perhaps woefully educated.

PREPARATION OF ELEMENTARY TEACHERS

A bachelor's degree in elementary education is a long-standing program that still exists in this country. However, we should take the term "long-standing" with a grain of salt, considering that bachelor's degree programs in education were first legislated in the 1920s and were not universally required until the early 1970s. College students desiring a career teaching grades K–6 often find a curriculum with distinct requirements, typically falling into the following categories: general education, education major, and electives. Students take a number of prescribed courses in each category toward their degree (and certification). More often than not, courses in education more than dominate the curriculum.

General education courses, on the other hand, are not only limited in their proportion in the curriculum, they are limited by depth as well. What I mean by this is that the elementary teacher is expected to teach multiple subjects to children and needs academic experience with each of the various subjects. How much of general education can be dominated by mathematics or science or social studies or language arts? Since these teachers will teach a little of everything, they are required to take a little of everything in college: a little mathematics, a little science, a little social studies, and a little language arts. Consequently, they often only experience the introductory-level courses of many of these subject areas, thus giving them a hodgepodge of content knowledge, perhaps to the point of being too broad and too superficial.

This has caused concern among many, particularly within the mathematics and science education communities. Should elementary school teachers have stronger mathematics and science backgrounds? If we consider what the national mathematics and science content standards propose, there is a genuine possibility that teachers may have virtually no experience with the content they need to teach. There have been strong efforts to increase the amount of mathematics and science content elementary school teachers take during their undergraduate programs. Numbers of courses have been increased, and more effort has been made regarding the types of courses prospective teachers take, so that teachers take more credits in multiple areas of science.

However, a new challenge has arisen. There are states actually eliminating bachelor's degree programs in elementary education from colleges and universities. In these states, no longer can someone become an elementary school teacher through the traditional curriculum. They have to have an academic major; education is not viewed as an academic major (e.g., Lanier and Little 1986).

Let us assume that the elimination of bachelor's degree programs in elementary education chronologically coincides with a growing trend toward eliminating the self-contained classroom. With elementary school curricula becoming more sophisticated and with special education and team teaching becoming more relevant, the self-contained classroom is slowly giving way to multiple teachers teaching multiple subjects in multiple classrooms to multiple grade levels. Perhaps an elementary school teacher only teaches mathematics and science, or science and social studies, or mathematics and reading.

However, this creates potential problems in addition to potential solutions. Many prospective elementary school teachers do not have great confidence in or command of their content knowledge, particularly in mathematics or science (e.g., Bryan and Abell 1999; deJong, Korthagen, and Wubbels 1998; Ginns and Watters 1999; Hogan and Berkowitz 2000; Keys and Kennedy 1999; McDevitt et al. 1999; McLoughlin and Dana 1999; Raphael, Tobias, and Greenberg 1999; Smith 2000). Merely speculating, how many prospective elementary school teachers would major in mathematics or science? If they were to major in mathematics or science, why would they prepare to teach at the elementary level versus the secondary level? Neither discipline, especially science, seems an appropriate specialty at the elementary level. As noted in Chapter 1, subject specialization is seen as more relevant to secondary-level teaching, as teachers see themselves in terms of their content areas.

As a result, one would imagine few prospective elementary school teachers majoring in mathematics or science. Perhaps they major in psychology, sociology, or history. Perhaps they major in literature or a foreign language. Unfortunately, such majors lack a significant requirement for mathematics or science. Eventually, someone will be required to teach mathematics or science to many children across many grades. Who will have this ultimate responsibility, and will they be adequately prepared? Not every teacher can be so "fortunate" as to be required to teach only social studies and English.

As elementary schools perhaps evolve further and further away from self-contained classrooms and toward subject specialization, teacher education programs and certification policies are not necessarily ready, and perhaps neither are prospective teachers. Do these prospective elementary school teachers really know what they want to teach, and at what grade level, when they begin undergraduate study? What if they change their minds at some point, either during their studies or during their careers? How can teacher education programs and certification policies accommodate this? Logistically, they cannot.

Elementary school teacher education is unfortunately too generic because it serves a relatively generic yet flexibly evolving school structure. It would seem very difficult to foresee how many mathematics and science teachers elementary schools will ultimately need or how many first- or fourth-grade teachers they will ultimately need. Consequently, these prospective teachers are educated rather generically, either within a bachelor's degree program in elementary education or in education course work while pursuing a bachelor's degree in an academic major. They are all educated alike, certified alike, and hired alike. Not until they enter the classroom do they have an opportunity, albeit limited, to distinguish themselves.

Epistemological Issues

But what do prospective elementary teachers conceptualize about themselves, the profession they seek to enter, and their own curricular experiences? During a brief personal experience in New Jersey, teaching an elementary-level science methods course with approximately 80 students enrolled, I observed some troubling things. Before I delve into these troubling observations, I wish to offer more context about the curriculum prospective elementary teachers follow toward certification.

During the 1990s, bachelor's degree programs were phased out in New Jersey, so to obtain elementary-level teacher certification in New Jersey requires a bachelor's degree in a subject area (albeit loosely defined); teacher education courses are taken in addition to the degree. For comparison, consider two midsized state university teacher education programs within 20 miles of each other. At one university, all prospective elementary school teachers major in a specially constructed degree program known as Natural History and Philosophy. This degree program offers a content curriculum relatively balanced in terms of mathematics, science, and social studies. Students take introductory courses in college-level algebra/trigonometry, biology, chemistry, physics, earth science, anthropology, history, and psychology, to name a few. In addition to their content courses, students take the following education courses: (1) Educational Psychology; (2) Teacher, School, and Society; (3) Philosophical Orientation to Education; (4) Teaching for Critical Thinking; (5) Teaching Reading; and (6) Effective Teaching/Productive Learning. Furthermore, they also take a methods course, participate in a professional seminar, and have two field experiences prior to a full semester of supervised student teaching. Education courses are spread over the last three years of undergraduate study.

On the other hand, consider the university I was teaching my methods course at. First, the curriculum for prospective elementary school teachers was different from that at the first university. There was no specific major to follow; hence, there was no cohesion between education courses and arts and sciences courses. Consequently, the number of credits and courses required for teacher certification differed. This program did not offer courses analogous to the Educational Psychology, Philosophical Orientation to Education, Teaching for Critical Thinking, and Effective Teaching/Productive Learning required at the first university. It did, however, offer a Computer for the Classroom Teacher course.

Second, rather than focusing on the intellectual and theoretical aspects of teacher education, this teacher education program focused on the pragmatics of teacher education. Whereas the first program offered one unified methods course for prospective elementary school teachers, this one offered five separate subject-area methods courses: one for mathematics, one for science, one for social studies, one for language arts (e.g., English writing and reading), and one for arts/creativity. All five methods courses are taken concurrently during the semester prior to student teaching, thus back-loading the majority of teacher education courses to the final year of undergraduate study. This was the focus of the teacher education program, despite the fact that many local school districts had moved away from self-contained classrooms and toward subject specialization. Whereas the first program developed some appreciation for this new trend in schools (including thematic learning units), this one still approached elementary-teacher education as a hodgepodge of school subject matter.

Third, and more critically, nearly all of my students were majoring in psychology or sociology, which required only two introductory courses in mathematics and two introductory courses in science to satisfy graduation requirements. It should be noted that students at this particular university could major in any of the following:

- •• African, African American/Caribbean Studies
- •• Anthropology
- •• Art History
- •• Art Studio
- •• Communication
- •• English Literature
- •• English Writing
- •• Environmental Science
- •• Geography
- •• History
- •• Mathematics
- •• Philosophy
- •• Political Science
- •• Psychology
- •• Sociology
- •• Spanish

But these students chose only two possible majors, universally viewed among themselves as the least demanding majors available to them. New Jersey, which requires all secondary school teachers to hold a bachelor's degree in their primary area of certification, does not have such a specific requirement for elementary school teachers. In fact, there was no state requirement as to how many courses in specific subject areas were needed for certification, thus creating a minimalist situation for prospective elementary school teachers, and these students took advantage of it. On the other hand, this state adopted a curriculum reflective of the national mathematics and science content standards, which effectively required elementary school teachers to have better backgrounds in mathematics and science content. Even the state certification tests for content knowledge reflected this requirement.

Ontological Issues

That nearly all of these students chose one of only two majors—psychology or sociology—led to my first troubling observation: Essentially all of my students were aware of the new content standards, state curriculum, and teacher certification tests. They were also keenly aware of the statewide student assessments taking place during grades 3, 8, and 11 and of the high demands placed on accountability in mathematics and science. However, my students all sought to major in subject areas that minimized their mathematics and science requirements. Although the national mathematics standards call for the learning of geometry and basic trigonometry principles between grades 3 and 8, my students, who would become the teachers of children expected to learn such concepts, would never themselves formally learn these concepts. The same could be said for science. Many of these students took two introductory-level courses in biology but no chemistry, physics, or earth science. And yet the national science education standards expected them eventually to teach concepts related to these subject areas.

This led to my second troubling observation: Interestingly enough, a good number of my students aspired to teach only in grade levels K–2 simply because they did not want to be held accountable for teaching content relevant to the third-grade assessment. Apparently they thought teachers only began to worry about such content demands when the assessment took place; in other words, they only began to worry about the content during third grade. Of course, the two subject areas they deemed most critical were mathematics and science; they wanted no part of either, especially in terms of accountability.

Since I was their science methods professor, it concerned me greatly to think that potentially 80 elementary school teachers in one local region would consider themselves absolved from teaching mathematics or science content during grades K–2. I was not alone. The methods professors for mathematics and social studies raised similar concerns.

Consequently, these students also considered themselves absolved from understanding such content (i.e., mathematics and science), aside from what minimal concepts K–2 students were exposed to, even though the certification tests expected at least an eleventh-grade comprehension of content by teachers. Apparently the state curriculum did not seem relevant to them, which left me to wonder what they intended to do each day in their classrooms.

It was disheartening to teach lessons related to basic physical science concepts, such as inclines (or "ramps"), and be told by my students that the concept was irrelevant for their occupational goals. At best, they only wanted superficial knowledge (e.g., things go faster down a steep ramp); they did not even wish to understand *why* principles were what they were. Such a perspective contradicted what they verbally advocated about science teaching and learning in their reflection assignments (e.g., Tabachnich and Zeichner 1991). On paper, my students advocated teaching science in terms of hands-on activities, developing understanding, and not being bound to a textbook loaded with vocabulary and sterile facts. However, in practice, regardless of their interest in hands-on activities, they were not advocates of understanding, and they viewed science concepts as superficially as the textbooks might.

Also disheartening was my students' complaints about their methods courses. In my case, my students were outraged that I expected them to develop an understanding of science content they had never learned before, regardless of the national mathematics and science standards or New Jersey certification examinations. *Why*, they asked me, *do I need to understand sine, cosine, and tangent?! Why do I need to know about inclines?! Why do I need to know about force, work, and energy?! Why do I need to understand the periodic table?! I'll never teach that. . . . You don't teach that stuff to little kids!*

On a personal level, I do not think it is asking too much of an elementary school teacher to have the knowledge level expected of an eleventh grader in the State of New Jersey. Historically speaking, this is akin to what we would have expected of the graduates of a normal school of a century ago. Yes, high school curricula have changed dramatically since the late 1950s, but high school literacy is still high school literacy, regardless of era or decade. This is how we approached our methods courses, especially in mathematics and science. Our students needed to appreciate not only what was expected of elementary school children in terms of content understanding but also what knowledge base they needed as teachers. And this is where much conflict arose.

One of the activities I created for my students involved discussion in small groups and by the whole class on the national science-education standards (which New Jersey essentially adopted in its entirety). I did not want my students to feel the frustrations of science teachers of the 1960s and 1970s; I wanted them to genuinely understand and appreciate the curriculum, so it could be taught and learned successfully. For this activity, I posed the following questions for discussion:

- What are these standards telling us?
- What is expected of us prior to/after grade 4?
- What kinds of lessons can I do that "properly" reflect the standards?
- What am I supposed to know about science in order to accomplish this?
- Do you think the New Jersey Core Curriculum Content Standards for Science are a good idea? Why or why not?

Surprisingly, while my students were generally in tune with the first two questions, they progressively struggled with the next two. They acknowledged that yes, certain science concepts need to be learned prior to grade 4; however, they expressed displeasure that there were no specific guidelines as to what is appropriate content for each individual grade (the guidelines only use grades 4, 8, and 12 as benchmarks) (e.g., Pushkin 2001a, 2001d). This led to discussion, grudgingly on their part, on the developmental appropriateness of content or lessons, where decision making would be their responsibility, not that of the authors of the standards.

This eventually led to an unpleasant discussion regarding their knowledge base, unpleasant because it confronted their sense of accountability. One student was particularly vocal throughout the course, even during this early activity. She aspired to teach second grade, and only second grade, for reasons unclear to me. However, what most intrigued me was her frustration with class discussions she deemed counterproductive. Her contention was that if she wanted to teach second grade, she should be experiencing methods classes that specifically showed her how to teach second graders. In other words, since she wanted to teach seven-year-olds, it was her expectation that professors would teach her like a seven-year-old, so she knew exactly what to emulate (see Chapter 4 for similar discussion).

Never mind that this was an adult, with children of her own and in the process of completing a bachelor's degree at a state university and obtaining teacher certification. Never mind that the national science education standards do not address science content on a specific grade-by-grade basis. Never mind that I was a professor working with aspiring professionals. This was a prospective teacher wanting to know precisely what it is like to be seven years old and specifically how one must teach seven-year-olds. Of course, one must wonder what would happen to her if she were hired for a teaching position for any other grade.

While pressing this student a little further in discussion, I asked her what would happen if she had to teach a lesson on something (e.g., electricity) that she had little background for. Her response was that she would consult a *third-grade* textbook for the "facts" and design the lesson slightly below the level of that book. When I asked her to elaborate, she essentially told me that as long as she understood more than her students did, she would be fine. Never mind that textbooks are known to have glaring misconceptions, which get passed along in teaching (e.g., Slisko and Dykstra 1997). Never mind that perhaps she may have a student who already understands electricity beyond a third-grade level. Her contention was that to teach a second-grade concept, one only needs a slightly higher level of comprehension (i.e., third-grade). When I asked her about perhaps consulting a high school physics book or physical science book, her response was indignant: *Why should I get into that complex level?! I don't have to get into that kind of detail! This is just basic stuff to cover with little kids. . . . I don't need to understand the full scope of electricity!*

This was not the last frustrating encounter with this student, or with anyone else in the course. In fact, their overall judgment of the New Jersey Core Curriculum Content Standards for Science was very unfavorable because it expected too much of them and was not concrete enough to tell them what, exactly, they would be held accountable for. Sadly, although one might find comfort in the cliché "Misery loves company," my class experiences were not unique in this teacher education program. To provide further insight as to how my students conceptualized the teacher education curriculum, I wish to share a story regarding the Arts and Creativity Methods course.

I was required to observe one of our adjunct instructors for reappointment; she happened to teach the Arts and Creativity Methods course. Granted, much of the course content focused on art making, but she sought to show the students ways to integrate art with reading, art with writing, art with social studies, and art with science. Essentially, she was enlightening the students about a method of teaching art as an interdisciplinary academic subject. I found the lesson wonderful and fascinating; the students thought otherwise.

During some free time in my methods class, I asked a few of the students what they thought of that art lesson and tried to engage them in discussion on how we could possibly do similar things in a science lesson. My students were very reluctant to have a dialogue and expressed the desire to not dwell on the other methods course. When I asked why, one student replied, "Frankly this course is very disappointing. . . . I thought we would be learning how to construct bulletin boards for each month and holiday season."

Please keep in mind that each methods course ran for 13 weeks at two hours per weekly session. This accounted for 26 total hours of instruction, relatively inadequate for genuine learning and preparation for student teaching. And yet I found it humorous to think that my students honestly expected to spend 26 hours, as prospective professionals, learning how to make bulletin boards for their classrooms.

Forgive my sarcasm, but how much "instruction" is needed to learn how to cut out colored paper and pictures and to staple or tack them aesthetically to cork? Once again, we see evidence that the focus for elementary school teacher education is on concrete skill mastery rather than on the substantive curricular, pedagogical, philosophical, and cognitive issues. Although the first teacher education program I referred to delved into the intellectual aspects of teaching, this program was the complete antithesis. Two programs, same type of university, same clientele of students, yet very different approaches to elementary school teacher education. In fact, the regular professor for the Arts and Creativity Methods course once lamented, *We have 1990 state guidelines, a 1950 teacher education program, and we're producing teachers for 1920 school buildings.*

Why? What are we looking at? Are we preaching one thing yet practicing another? I cannot help but wonder if this teacher education program simply saw schools the same way Horace Mann did in the 1830s, when children were expected to be obedient. I cannot help but wonder if this teacher education program still believed in Ralph Tyler's Technical Rationalism Model of the 1940s (see Chapter 2). And yet I cannot help but wonder about the intellectual hypocrisy of this program, which advocated hands-on activities as the alternative to book-oriented lessons but took a very superficial stance toward the content children and teachers would be held accountable for.

Perhaps Steve Allen (see Chapter 1) was right after all. Perhaps we teach not how to think but what to think. Perhaps this teacher education program did not advocate comprehension of mathematics and science content. Perhaps it ultimately advocated content coverage aimed at success on statewide assessments. But what about the teacher-certification exams? If students of teacher education do not want to be held accountable for content knowledge, how can they possibly expect to pass the exams? I shudder to think about possible answers, but will later in this chapter, as well as Chapter 5.

I remember several conversations with the chairperson of that teacher education department. Her top priority was for faculty to teach students how to teach a few science lessons, hoping they would somehow learn a few concepts along the way. She did not want her students getting into theory or "deep thinking issues"; she wanted her students to be able to demonstrate they could "do the job." I was left with the impression that teaching, and teacher education, in her mind merely meant performing tasks and maintaining classroom control.

Why was she such an advocate of hands-on activities, as were the students? Why was their view of "hands-on" essentially busywork? Why was the state curriculum viewed superficially? Perhaps they had few expectations for these future teachers or the children they may someday teach. Perhaps the state curriculum lacked credibility. Perhaps hands-on lessons were generic enough to enable anybody to effectively observe and evaluate teaching practice. As discussed in both Chapters 1 and 2, teaching practice and evaluation appear to be tied to some level of conformity as an indicator of competence. Perhaps, as was the case with the seven-step lesson plans described in Chapter 2, this teacher education program misconceptualized the state curriculum from its original intention. Perhaps it was conceptualized correctly, as a means of allowing evaluators to look for physical actions independent of subject matter. Perhaps the evaluators themselves do not know the content of the state curriculum and thus de-emphasize its value for prospective teachers.

Perhaps there was something more to it. Reflecting back on Steve Allen's contention, I wonder if teaching was intended to be more of a physical act rather than a mental process. *Do the job. Don't get into theory or deep thinking issues.* Could this be a function of the program's paradigm, or perhaps a reflection of the leadership? (I will examine this in Chapter 9.) At a time when many advocate critical thinking, a holistic view of knowledge, and the process of learning (e.g., Kincheloe 2000), as discussed in Chapter 1, we sense how teachers can be viewed as being a "dime a dozen"; such instances further de-intellectualize the teaching profession. Perhaps this teacher education program perceived intellectual limitations to its faculty and students. Perhaps Shulman's (1986) notion of PCK is irrelevant, as if successful teachers can only be competent and knowledgeable to a finite extent. Perhaps the way a teacher education program functions still comes down to philosophical perspective, and this teacher education program has yet to enlighten itself.

Interstate Comparisons

And yet how could I expect my students to think any differently? Teacher education is notorious for such conservatism and concreteness. But what happens to these young adults when they finally graduate, somehow manage to pass their certification tests, and get hired by a school? Will they be able to adapt? Will they be up to the challenge? Reflecting back again to Chapter 1, I wonder if they will be able not only to teach the required content effectively but to empower children to learn it meaningfully and successfully, in terms of both state assessment and long-term understanding. Elementary school teachers work from a great disadvantage created by universities, schools of education, and state departments of education, and yet it is the teachers who are continuously held accountable, whether they know better or not.

Further exacerbating things, in New Jersey, is a limit as to how many total credits a student may have and remain at undergraduate status, regardless of whether they graduated with their degree or not. This is especially true in state universities, where tuition is subsidized. When New Jersey phased out the bachelor's degree for elementary education and required a bachelor's degree in an academic major, the number of credits in education course work were consequently reduced. In essence, education went from a major to a minor for prospective elementary school teachers (see Chapter 4 for more discussion).

The consequences reinforce my earlier points. Given a limited number of credits and courses available for teacher education, especially when teacher education becomes a nonacademic program of sorts, teacher education programs are forced to make choices and prioritize goals. In an ideal world, perhaps teacher education programs could place equal emphasis on theory and methods. To some extent, the first program I described has accomplished this. However, in the case of the second program, methods were deemed more important than theory.

Exacerbating the situation even more are inadequate academic preparation of prospective teachers, demands for teaching a state-prescribed curriculum and for accountability testing, limited budgets and resources, and the role of university faculty in preparing students for teacher certification. As will be discussed in Chapter 4, when prospective teachers begin student teaching (i.e., teaching internships), there are limited opportunities for teacher education faculty to observe and effectively evaluate classroom practice. Given those limited opportunities, many faculty do not have the luxury of genuine summative assessment and rely on short-term approaches. The difference between the two is much akin to the difference between the intentions of Madeline Hunter's theory on classroom lessons and its actual application. Crudely put, teacher education professors want to enter a classroom, see something that fits their expectation of competent teaching, complete evaluation forms as painlessly as possible, and move onto the next task of their day. So how does this relate to teaching prospective teachers? Methods courses often become very programmed in terms of *This is the way we do it. . . . Trust our expertise. . . . Learn to do it right.* Very often, the goal of this second teacher education program seemed to be to produce teachers who follow a recipe, who mimic what they are shown, so the short-term responsibilities of the faculty could be met effectively and efficiently.

In light of all these competing demands, something has to give. In a traditional bachelor's degree program in elementary education, prospective classroom teachers take courses, prior to student teaching experiences, in general psychology, educational psychology, educational theory and practice, some foundations courses (e.g., historical and sociological), and various methods courses related to subject areas. Without that degree program, teacher education faculty needed to prioritize course and requirements.

Student teaching experiences are often sacred cows in such degree and certification programs; the credits allotted to them are considered untouchable. Taking this into account, faculty need either to be creative with courses and credits or to choose some courses over others. In this growing era of accountability and pragmatic bureaucracy, educational theory and practice and educational foundations courses are sadly sacrificed from the curriculum for the sake of methods courses.

Gone are discussions about John Dewey and Paulo Freire. Gone are in-depth discussions about pedagogical content knowledge. Gone are discussions about the meaning and purpose of schools and public education. In its place are courses focusing on curriculum standards, statewide assessment, and concrete skill mastery; the priority becomes an outcomes-based focus on behavioral objective management and compliance. It did not have to be this way, but for at least one teacher education program, this was the result.

Why? We cannot help but return to this question. As the expectations for teacher credentials have increased since the 1960s, the roles of teacher education programs have dramatically shifted. At one point, the demand was for a bachelor's degree in elementary education. Then the demand was for pedagogical competency. Then the demand finally shifted toward content. Back to basics, know the facts, teach to tests . . . whatever phrase we wish to use. Rather than reconceptualize the bachelor's degree in elementary education, New Jersey eliminated it. Although one teacher education program found a way to maintain a specific degree program and retain all that it stood for in teacher education, another was unable to do so. Perhaps the latter program did not sense it had the economic and institutional support necessary to maintain its original structure. Perhaps it considered itself no longer capable of being everything it once was. Perhaps it considered prioritizing and cutting parts of its curriculum wiser than alternatives. However, I cannot help but wonder which of these two programs is better prepared to handle new demands from the New Jersey Department of Education. Even more critically, one is left to wonder which of these teacher education programs works with the Department of Education and which one works for it.

Is this unique to New Jersey or to any particular college or university? Not necessarily. In New York, Pennsylvania, and Delaware, for example, the bachelor's degree programs in elementary education still exist. Although only Pennsylvania makes a concerted effort to increase the amount of mathematics and science content taken by prospective teachers, all three states require prospective teachers to take courses in multiculturalism, writing across the curriculum, special education, and nutrition/health, in addition to educational theory and foundations courses and methods courses (general or subject-specific).

On the other hand, Michigan's degree program for elementary education has a slight twist: Although teachers earn a degree in elementary education, they graduate with both a subject major and minor, a hybrid between generalist training and specialist training. Prospective elementary school teachers choose from the following subject area majors: English, language arts, foreign language, mathematics, natural science, and social studies. Choices of minor are bilingualism/biculturalism, dance, early childhood, English, foreign language, middle schools, language arts, mathematics, natural science, physical education, and social studies. A major constitutes at least 30 credits in a given subject area, while a minor constitutes at least 20 credits.

Students take the following education courses:

- Teaching: Research, Theory, and Practice
- Teaching Language Arts
- Reading in Subject Matter Areas
- Educational Psychology
- Teaching Mathematics
- Teaching Reading
- Teaching Science
- Teaching Social Studies
- Parent Intervention Programs
- The Exceptional Child in the Regular Classroom
- Multicultural Education
- Computer Applications in Teaching

These are in addition to practice teaching courses and supervised student teaching. Although there seems to be some balance between theory and methods, the Michigan education curriculum for elementary school teachers places heavy emphasis on subject-area content knowledge. It is uncertain whether Michigan elementary schools have more self-contained classrooms or more subject specialist classrooms; however, this curriculum does indicate a possible balance between both.

Discussion

Returning to my earlier lament about the disappearance of John Dewey and Paulo Freire from teacher education classes, I wish to share this observation in some historical context (see Chapter 2). If I could describe an evolutionary trend in elementary education over the last century or so, it might reflect the following themes:

- ➥ teaching children to be obedient
- ➥ teaching children to be good and caring adults
- ➥ teaching children to be productive workers and citizens
- ➥ teaching teachers how to mold children
- ➥ teaching teachers what teaching is about
- ➥ teaching teachers how to teach
- ➥ teaching teachers what to teach
- ➥ teaching teachers to be competent and employable

As each new theme arises, teacher education programs respond in knee-jerk fashion. If schooling undergoes an evolution from curriculum movements, to social agendas, to behavioral norms, to thinking skills, to fundamental knowledge recall, and to accountability testing for content mastery, how could we expect anything different for teacher education? As will be discussed in Chapter 9, one consequence of teacher education's evolution is that teaching is viewed as a collection of occupational skills to be mastered rather than as an intellectual career/vocation.

However, perhaps the most important theme we could reflect upon from this section of the chapter is one depicting elementary school teachers as unsuspecting victims within a clash of conflicting agendas. On one hand, they are expected to be competent in pedagogical skills according to some criteria for observation and evaluation. On the other hand, they are supposed to be creative agents of change within their classrooms. On yet another hand, they are expected to have strong content knowledge, while on another hand, they are expected to teach multiple subjects. Just like Tevye in *Fiddler on the Roof,* one soon runs out of hands on which to ponder. Some teacher education programs seek to address all dimensions of what a teacher needs to be. Others only focus on the intellectual/philosophical dimension. Others focus only on pedagogical pragmatism. Others try to focus on pedagogy with content knowledge. In many respects, a teacher education program's focus depends on how it responds to its state certification tests and on what those tests primarily emphasize. One would expect such tests to emphasize all dimensions of what a teacher needs to be, but tests differ from state to state, as do certification requirements. Perhaps some tests place heavy emphasis on educational theory. Perhaps some place heavy emphasis on subject-matter knowledge. Perhaps some place heavy emphasis on teaching skills.

However, it remains to be seen how successful elementary school teachers are on these tests. Perhaps this is a function of how compatible the tests are with teacher education curricula. Perhaps prospective teachers are ultimately taught to these tests, as is said to happen in many American schools as accountability testing approaches. Nonetheless, some elementary school teachers are placed at great disadvantage by the colleges and universities that train them. There is no easy solution to propose; in many cases, to prepare elementary school teachers for a utopian view of what schools should be and what teachers should be could conceivably lengthen university training by two years.

PREPARATION OF SECONDARY TEACHERS

Just like elementary school teacher education, secondary school teacher education has undergone somewhat of a degree program shift during recent years. Many secondary school science teachers went through a bachelor's degree program in secondary science education, with an emphasis in biology, chemistry, physics, or earth science; in many cases teachers also earned certification specifically for general science instruction or environmental science instruction. Depending on state and university requirements, these bachelor's degree programs were interdisciplinary, and teachers experienced considerable content in subject areas other than their primary emphasis.

However, concern arose as to whether secondary teachers knew enough of their subject matter or whether they were taught enough subject matter in college to be qualified as science teachers. Much has been written about high school science and mathematics teachers lacking an appropriate major or minor for their teaching certification area (e.g., Allen 1998; Cochran and Jones 1998; Gabel 1994; Lanier and Little 1986). However, the question arises as to whether this is because the bachelor's degree program in secondary science education lacks sufficient science content or whether it is because of the structural nature of the degree program. In other words, is there genuinely a lack of content, or is there simply no mechanism to declare a major or minor beyond secondary science education?

Case in point: Consider a semi-outdated bachelor's degree program in secondary science education with emphasis in biology. There may very well be some credit and course discrepancies relative to the upper-level courses of the biology major curriculum, courses perhaps sacrificed for other science (i.e., chemistry or earth science) or education courses. However, the curriculum more than represents a minor in biology and may indeed represent the minimum requirements for a major in biology. The same could be said for certification emphasis in chemistry or physics. In fact, the missing credits or courses appear to represent advanced theoretical or laboratory courses in each major, perhaps prerequisites for graduate study in those disciplines.

But does such a bachelor's degree program in secondary science education provide prospective teachers a mechanism for declaring a major or minor? Are biology, chemistry, or physics departments flexible enough with their advanced course requirements to allow substitutions and still grant a major? In fact, the potential lack of flexibility by academic departments may contradict certification requirements by national professional teaching societies (e.g., National Science Teachers Association [NSTA]) and teacher education accreditation agencies (e.g., NCATE). Furthermore, this contradicts the mission of many national curriculum standards efforts, especially in science, where interdisciplinary curricula are recommended not only for elementary schools but for secondary schools as well (e.g., Pushkin 2001a, 2001d).

This may be an issue related more to university structure and policy than to the quality of a degree program's curriculum. To include bachelor-of-education type programs, in which the student may not be able to declare a major and/or a minor, into national statistics regarding the academic qualifications of high school science teachers may not be fair or appropriate. Is a minor in the view of an academic department sufficient for a teaching certification? Perhaps the debate should not focus exclusively on the issue of academic major. The reality is that many secondary school teachers are certified in multiple subject areas (especially in the sciences, where a teacher might have, for example, a chemistry/physics or biology/chemistry certification); perhaps we need to take a closer look at the second certification area versus the first.

As was the case for elementary education, many states (e.g., New York and New Jersey) have phased out the bachelor's degree program in secondary education and required a bachelor's degree in an academic discipline instead. On the other hand, some states (e.g., Delaware, Michigan, and Pennsylvania) still maintain the bachelor's degree program in secondary education but require students to take essentially as many courses in their subject area as they would for a subject degree major.

In essence, social studies teachers need a degree in a social science, mathematics teachers need a degree in mathematics, biology teachers need a degree in biology, and all high school teachers were considered to be better qualified as a result of this. Again, this reflects the historical shift toward expecting teachers to know more content and the earlier-mentioned theme of teaching teachers what to teach.

However, a question arises. If a bachelor's degree in an academic discipline is supposed to improve a teacher's qualifications and competency with subject matter, why do we still consider nonteacher college graduates incompetent in their subject matter (e.g., Pushkin 1994, 1998a, 1998b, 1998d, 2001b, 2001c)? Is the amount of content coverage necessarily a prerequisite for competence? It is debatable what we are guaranteeing with requirements of academic majors and minors defined by academic departments rather than by schools of education. The terms "qualified," "certified," and "competent" may or may not be equivalent in teacher education.

Another question arises. Just as with elementary school teacher education, what education courses are sacrificed for secondary school teachers when certification requirements compete with credit requirements? As discussed earlier, states such as New York, New Jersey, Delaware, Michigan, and Pennsylvania offer various theory and foundations courses and methods courses. One might expect these states to offer more theory and foundations courses to prospective secondary school teachers than to prospective elementary school teachers, simply because the curriculum for prospective secondary school teachers is less dispersed among subject area courses. However, this is not necessarily the case.

For example, in both New York and New Jersey, a prospective high school chemistry teacher not only needs to earn a bachelor's degree in chemistry, he or she must earn a degree accredited by the American Chemical Society. Although this offers a very extensive content background, it does not provide much flexibility in terms of taking education courses within the possible credit limits (described earlier) on those attending state universities. And yet the first New Jersey teacher education program I described earlier offers the same core education courses to both prospective elementary and secondary school teachers (the second college essentially has no undergraduate secondary education program). In New York, however, because of the way teaching internships work in large urban regions (e.g., New York City), education course work takes a different twist for prospective science teachers (see Chapters 4 and 5).

In Pennsylvania, prospective high school teachers all take courses on multiculturalism, writing across the curriculum, educational theory, and educational psychology in addition to general methods and subject-specific methods courses, field experience courses, and supervised student teaching. In Delaware, prospective high school teachers take two educational psychology courses (one focused on social aspects, the other on cognition), a cultural diversity course, a reading-in-content-area course, a classroom management course, a subject-specific methods course, and supervised student teaching. In Michigan, students take courses on teaching theory, multiculturalism, computer applications, educational philosophy, exceptional children in regular classrooms, reading in a subject area, and adolescent psychology in addition to field experiences and supervised student teaching.

It should be noted that prospective high school teachers face scheduling issues for education courses similar to those described earlier for elementary-teacher education. For example, in New Jersey (at least in the first teacher education program), prospective teachers take education courses spread over the last three years of undergraduate study. This is also generally true for prospective high school teachers in Michigan and Pennsylvania. However, in Delaware, the course work is more back-loaded to the last two years, and in New York, it could be condensed within a final year of study.

One approach to dealing with the challenge of balancing education course work with subject-area course work is what Judith E. Lanier and Judith W. Little (1986) refer to as the "4 + 1" program, in which prospective teachers pursue their academic discipline degrees during a four-year period and then spend a fifth year taking education courses toward certification. In some cases, the course requirements only meet minimum certification; in other cases, the courses meet the requirements for a master's degree. Ohio, during the 1980s, was one of the first states to adopt this program. This five-year approach has addressed issues such as critical teacher shortages, alternative certification routes, career changes, and increased professionalization. Interestingly, such a program was developed with only secondary teachers in mind, rather than elementary, perhaps reflecting how distinctly different we consider elementary education and secondary education.

Yet other questions arise. Although the five-year approach has been somewhat successful, there have been drawbacks. For instance, I wonder to what extent one single year of education courses ultimately influences a prospective classroom teacher, when non-education faculties provide four years of unbalanced influence. Teaching itself is viewed rather negatively by non-education faculty (e.g., Feiman-Nemser and Floden 1986; Lanier and Little 1986; Pushkin 1994, 1998d, 2001b). This is a very sensitive issue in science education, where science faculties have excessively high opinions of themselves (e.g., Thomas 1990) and lack genuine sensitivity for the prospective high school science teachers in their courses (e.g., Coppola and Pearson 1998; Pushkin 1998d, 2001b, 2001c). The dominant influence of insensitive pedagogical practice may be too much to overcome with merely one year of education experiences.

There is also concern about how college graduates may perceive this one additional year of education course work relative to the four-year degrees they have already earned. For example, consider a student who has recently earned a bachelor's degree in chemistry and is weighing the choice between getting a job with a chemical company or remaining in college one more year for teaching certification. From personal experience, I can say that most university chemistry faculty would encourage the student to choose the former and not the latter. Why? To begin with, the starting salary for a chemist with a bachelor's degree is significantly higher than that for a high school chemistry teacher. Even Randi Weingarten, president of the United Federation of Teachers in New York City, noted in a recent editorial that teacher salaries are too low to attract qualified professionals graduating from college (*USA TODAY,* August 16, 2000). Add to the mix the image of unruly students, crumbling facilities, and professors' views of teaching as subprofessional, is it any wonder a young adult takes his or her degree to the corporate world?

Certainly, the requirement that a student earn a bachelor's degree in an academic discipline poses a double-edged sword. One edge cuts at the image of teachers' allegedly inadequate content knowledge; the other cuts at the image of underpaid chumps who allegedly missed a real professional calling. Even fifth-year master's degree programs pose a double-edged sword. Although states and universities attempt to improve the professional image of certified teachers, local school systems play a low-ball game of trying to hire lesser-educated and cheaper college graduates from elsewhere.

I used to be a proponent of the "4 + 1" approach to teacher education until I observed how university science faculty taught and speculated on the quality of student that graduated from their programs (e.g., Pushkin 1998a, 1998b, 1998c, 1998d, 1999, 2000, 2001b). Somehow, there needs to be more cohesion and better coordination between education faculty and arts and sciences faculty. Quite frankly, regardless of whether teachers are prepared through a four-year or five-year program, they should continuously experience classes from both "sides" of the college or university campus during all years of study. Although there are pragmatic considerations in favor of "4 + 1" (or even "3 + 2") programs—in terms of resources and scheduling of classes, as well as ensuring adequate preparation for the profession within a reasonable number of years—we have to appreciate that teaching is a profession of intellectual growth. In other words, teachers should probably not be prepared by cramming a number of education courses into a short period of time and then being certified immediately into teaching positions. Just as there is debate over the merits of teacher effectiveness for teachers certified by alternative routes versus teachers trained only in subject areas, there is debate on these merits for teachers certified by alternative routes versus teachers certified by traditional routes. Not only is there debate regarding teacher effectiveness (usually in terms of children's performance on outcomes-based assessments), teacher retention is also an issue. Many new teachers in American schools fail to stay in the profession more than 3–5 years, and questions have arisen regarding the potential impact of the duration of education course work (e.g., Darling-Hammond 1996, 1998).

Furthermore, there need to be courses taken with arts and sciences faculty who demonstrate and reinforce the progressive and constructivist pedagogical approaches advocated by education faculty (e.g., Pushkin 2001b). As long as prospective teachers continue to experience diametrically opposed teaching practices and philosophies at the university level, they will continue to struggle with their own epistemological and ontological foundations, thus stunting their intellectual development toward future classroom teaching and the teaching profession.

I agree teachers should possess a master's degree, but not at the risk of being underpaid or unemployable. Also, there needs to be equitable consideration for professionalization among elementary school teachers as well. Such academic innovations and expectations should not apply exclusively to high school teachers.

Yes, teachers do need to have better understanding of their content matter, but content matter is probably not the only component to be concerned about. Everything still comes back to epistemologies and ontologies; until teachers are educated about critically exploring and embracing their philosophical and intellectual views, each course, credential program, and degree program merely remedies an artificial symptom of teacher incompetence. Just as is the case with elementary teacher education, high school teachers are potentially caught between the battle lines of competing agendas. However, by comparison, high school teachers are less victimized than their elementary school counterparts, simply due to the structural nature of high schools versus elementary schools. Additionally, high school teachers have the advantage of history. High school curricula and teacher credentials were more firmly established early in the twentieth century compared to those of elementary education. However, the counterargument is that perhaps high school education is more inertial and less evolved compared to elementary education. In some respects, it is a matter of historical reference and perception. However, it is not too far-fetched to think the launching of Sputnik in 1957 was the seminal moment for high school education, and the publishing of *A Nation at Risk* in 1983 was that seminal moment for elementary school education.

FINAL DISCUSSION

As we continue to debate the merits of teacher education degree programs and certification requirements, we must remember that teaching is a multifaceted profession requiring multiple competencies, regardless of whether one teaches at the elementary, middle, or high school level. In fact, I should note that many of our teacher education and certification programs fail to develop distinct middle school teacher education. More often than not, prospective middle school teachers are caught between state certification requirements for elementary school or high school teaching (i.e., K–6 and 7–12 versus K–8 and 7–12).

Certainly content knowledge is important. Elementary school teachers need more experience with subject matter on a deeper and broader level. Whether this means requiring more courses within schools of arts and sciences or developing specialized subject matter courses within schools of education, prospective elementary school teachers need to be more appreciative of subject content for *all* elementary grades, not just a grade of their choice. They need to be more appreciative of the interdisciplinary nature of knowledge, whether they teach in self-contained classrooms or not. And they need to be better prepared for the demands of accountability assessment, specialized teaching, and team teaching.

However, as noted throughout this chapter, not all teacher education programs see schools and teacher education in terms of a big, inclusive picture; neither do state departments of education. Some programs do attempt to address teacher education from all dimensions, yet some are constrained by either academic regulations, budgetary factors, statewide assessments, accountability measures, or certification exams. Teacher education programs are forced to satisfy the demands of so many masters (e.g., departments of education, state legislatures, and accreditation agencies) that their curricula look like the ultimate compromise, in which no one is really satisfied. What to stand for, what to prioritize, and what to ultimately focus on are complex issues, even though we may think the thought process was myopic and hasty. As mentioned earlier in this chapter, perhaps Shulman's (1986) theory of PCK is too much to ask of teacher education programs. Perhaps there are too many competing demands to do justice to genuinely comprehensive teacher education.

Similar things can be said for secondary school teachers. They need to be more competent with content matter. Whether this translates to degree requirements for a subject area, more flexible majors, and more adequate minors is subject to debate. It is also debatable whether more responsibility should fall on schools of arts and sciences, considering the negative view many arts and science faculties have toward teacher education (e.g., Feiman-Nemser and Floden 1986; Lanier and Little 1986).

But schools of education should be viewed in terms of more than mere pedagogy (e.g., Lanier and Little, 1986). In fact, as conflicts continue to arise due to the demands of certification requirements, we cannot simply reduce teacher education to content and pedagogy aspects. I hate to sound pessimistic, but as we begin to see just from a glimpse at five different states, teacher education is shaping up into the site of a heated turf war. As will be discussed further in Chapter 9, schools of education have historical roles, as well as historical persecution from other branches of higher education. However, the slings and arrows are not one-directional. Education faculty are quick to criticize arts and science faculty for their pedagogical skills, and in many respects an adversarial relationship is the consequence.

But there is hope. Of interesting note, in Michigan, elementary education majors take a prescribed number of mathematics and science courses, regardless of major or minor. These courses reflect the state's theme of teaching teachers what to teach. However, what is really interesting is who teaches these courses (i.e., education faculty or math/science faculty?). I have had the opportunity to visit three universities in Michigan during the past few years, and each one presents a different approach. For example, one university gives the sole responsibility of teaching these courses to the math/science faculty, because they are the "content experts." The second university gives the sole responsibility to education faculty, because they are the "content-teaching experts." The third university advocates team teaching these courses by both education and math/science faculty, so students get the best of both perspectives and education and math/science faculty work collaboratively. In Pennsylvania, prospective teachers experience all three approaches, depending on the subject area.

We still have a long way to go. Foundations courses related to the theory and practice, as well as the sociohistorical aspects, of education need to remain in the curriculum. It is genuinely disconcerting that we move further away from the principles of John Dewey and minimize the importance of pedagogical content knowledge. What we are losing in this evolution of teacher education is the holistic perspective of teaching and learning. Just as we continue to lose the notion of liberal arts education and Renaissance thinking throughout higher education, we continually lose that intellectualism within teacher education (e.g., Richardson and Pushkin 2000). Yes, there are constraints and competing demands, but teacher education cannot be a perpetual Ping-Pong ball between "either-or" philosophical extremes. Somehow, we need to have better balance.

Sadly, teacher education is becoming more localized, concrete, prescriptive, mechanical, and bureaucratic. There are those who think this is all well and good. But look where it leads. Think about those two teacher education programs in New Jersey. Think about those three universities in Michigan. Perhaps this is hyper-localization; at the very least, there is considerable inconsistency among teacher education programs, not only from state to state but within states. Is anybody on the same page? I would not dare to ask if everyone is, for the answer is self-explanatory. Although the pendulum currently swings in the direction of social conservatism and bottom-line, ends-justifying-means policies, we are left to wonder if the late Steve Allen was a sage as well as comedian.

Critics rage against teacher education in terms of noncompliance, illiteracy, and incompetence, but when exactly did these attributes become so apparent? Teacher education has somehow lost touch with its process and focused too much on products, and this trend needs to be reversed for teacher education programs to improve and thrive. In other words, teacher education has lost touch with its epistemological and ontological roots, roots in need of reacquaintance if teacher education is to be reconceptualized. Just as we cannot build houses from the roof down, teacher education programs need to be built from a firm philosophical base, one that can remain intact during the swings of the agenda pendulum. Then again, maybe if the philosophical base was genuinely firm to begin with, the pendulum would not need to swing so often.

REFERENCES

Allen, S. 1998. *"DUMBTH": The Lost Art of Thinking.* Amherst, NY: Prometheus Books.

Bryan, L. A., and S. K. Abell. 1999. "Development of Professional Knowledge in Learning To Teach Elementary Science." *Journal of Research in Science Teaching* 36, no. 2: 121–139.

Cochran, K. F., and L. L. Jones. 1998. "The Subject Matter Knowledge of Preservice Science Teachers." Pp. 707–718 in *International Handbook of Science Education*. Edited by B. J. Fraser and K. G. Tobin. London: Kluwer Academic Publishers.

Coppola, B. P., and W. H. Pearson. 1998. "Heretical Thoughts II: On Lessons We Learned from Our Graduate Advisor That Have Impacted Our Undergraduate Teaching." *Journal of College Science Teaching* 27, no. 6: 416–421.

Darling-Hammond, L. 1998. "Teachers and Teaching: Testing Policy Hypotheses from a National Commission Report." *Educational Researcher* 27, no. 1: 5–15.

———. 1996. "The Right To Learn and the Advancement of Teaching: Research, Policy, and Practice for Democratic Education." *Educational Researcher* 25, no. 6: 5–17.

deJong, O., F. Korthagen, and T. Wubbels. 1998. "Research on Science Teacher Education in Europe: Teacher Thinking and Conceptual Change." Pp. 745–758 in *International Handbook of Science Education*. Edited by B. J. Fraser and K. G. Tobin. London: Kluwer Academic Publishers.

Feiman-Nemser, S., and R. E. Floden. 1986. "The Cultures of Teaching." Pp. 505–526 in *Handbook of Research on Teaching*, 3rd ed. Edited by M. C. Wittrock. New York: Macmillan.

Gabel, D. L., ed. 1994. *Handbook of Research on Science Teaching and Learning*. New York: Macmillan.

Ginns, I. S., and J. J. Watters. 1999. "Beginning Elementary School Teachers and the Effective Teaching of Science." *Journal of Science Teacher Education* 10, no. 4: 287–313.

Hogan, K., and A. R. Berkowitz. 2000. "Teachers as Inquiry Learners." *Journal of Science Teacher Education* 11, no. 1: 1–25.

Keys, C. W., and V. Kennedy. 1999. "Understanding Inquiry Science Teaching in Context: A Case Study of an Elementary Teacher." *Journal of Science Teacher Education* 10, no. 4: 315–333.

Kincheloe, J. L. 2000. "Making Critical Thinking Critical." Pp. 23–40 in *Perspectives in Critical Thinking: Essays by Teachers in Theory and Practice*. Edited by D. Weil and H. K. Anderson. New York: Peter Lang.

Lanier, J. E., and J. W. Little. 1986. "Research on Teacher Education." Pp. 527–569 in *Handbook of Research on Teaching*, 3rd ed. Edited by M. C. Wittrock. New York: Macmillan.

McDevitt, T. M., A. L. Gardner, J. M. Shaklee, M. M. Bertholf, and R. Troyer. 1999. "Science and Mathematics Instruction of Beginning Elementary Teachers." *Journal of Science Teacher Education* 10, no. 3: 217–233.

McLoughlin, A. S., and T. M. Dana. 1999. "Making Science Relevant: The Experiences of Prospective Elementary School Teachers in an Innovative Science Content Course." *Journal of Science Teacher Education* 10, no. 2: 69–91.

Pushkin, D. B. 2001a. "The Atheoretical Nature of the National Science Education Standards? There's More Theory Than We Think. A Response to
  Thomas Shiland." *Science Education,* in press.

——. 2001b. "Cookbook Classrooms; Cognitive Capitulation." In *(Post) Modern
  Science (Education).* Edited by J. Weaver, P. Appelbaum, and M. Morris.
  New York: Peter Lang. In press.

——. 2001c. "Science Learning: Is It Genuine or Cognitive Capitulation?" Man-
  uscript.

——. 2001d. "To Standardize, or Too Standardized: What Becomes of Our Curriculum? In *The Encyclopedia of Educational Standards.* Edited by J.
  Kincheloe and D. Weil. Santa Barbara, CA: ABC-CLIO Publishers. In
  press.

——. 2000. "Critical Thinking in Science: How Do We Recognize It? Do We Foster It?" Pp. 211–220 in *Perspectives in Critical Thinking: Essays by Teachers in Theory and Practice.* Edited by D. Weil and H. K. Anderson. New
  York: Peter Lang.

——. 1999. "Post-Formal Thinking and Science Education: How and Why Do
  We Understand Concepts and Solve Problems?" Pp. 449–467 in *The Post-
  Formal Reader: Cognition and Education.* Edited by J. Kincheloe, S.
  Steinberg, and P. H. Hinchey. New York: Falmer Press.

——. 1998a. "Introductory Students, Conceptual Understanding, and Algorithmic Success." *Journal of Chemical Education* 75, no. 7: 809–810.

——. 1998b. "Is Learning Just a Matter of Tricks? So Why Are We Educating?"
  Journal of College Science Teaching 28, no. 2: 92–93.

——. 1998c. "Teacher Says; Simon Says: Dualism in Science Learning." Pp.
  185–198 in *Unauthorized Methods: Strategies for Critical Teaching.* Edited
  by J. Kincheloe and S. Steinberg. New York: Routledge.

——. 1998d. "Undergraduate Science Education: Improvement, Initiative, and
  Willingness to Change." *Journal of College Science Teaching* 28, no. 2: 8.

——. 1994. "Should the APS Get Involved with Education? Yes, but Look Before
  You Leap!" *American Journal of Physics* 62: 696.

Raphael, J., S. Tobias, and R. Greenberg. 1999. "Research Experience as a Component of Science and Mathematics Teacher Preparation." *Journal of
  Science Teacher Education* 10, no. 2: 147–158.

Richardson, A., and D. Pushkin. 2000. "An Educator To Compare to Erasmus?"
  Presentation at the Biennial Meeting of the International Cultural Research Network in Beijing, China, July.

Shulman, L. S. 1986. "Those Who Understand: Knowledge Growth in Teaching."
  Educational Researcher 15, no. 2: 4–14.

Slisko, J., and D. Dykstra. 1997. "The Role of Scientific Terminology in Research
  and Teaching: Is Something Important Missing?" *Journal of Research in
  Science Teaching* 34, no. 6: 655–660.

Smith, D. C. 2000. "Content and Pedagogical Content Knowledge for Elementary Science Teacher Educators: Knowing Our Students." *Journal of Science Teacher Education* 11, no. 1: 27–46.

Tabachnich, B. R., and K. Zeichner, eds. 1991. *Issues and Practices in Inquiry-Oriented Teacher Education.* London: Falmer Press.

Thomas, K. 1990. *Gender and Subject in Higher Education.* Buckingham, UK: Open University Press.

Chapter Four

◀◆ The Student Teaching Experience

Tovia Rosenfeld

BEGINNING A NEW CAREER PATH

In May 1996, my father showed me an article in the *New York Times* about an upcoming shortage of science teachers. I saw this as an opportunity to enter the New York City public school system and immediately updated my resumé and mailed one to all the schools in proximity to my neighborhood in Brooklyn. I was in the process of completing my applications to medical schools and deliberating over what to do during a year of potential waiting to matriculate. Although I had the academic credentials to pursue a medical degree, I was somewhat ambivalent toward the years of study, long hours, lack of sleep, considerable debt, and delay of a family life. Teaching, in my view, could be something worthwhile and economically wise to do in the interim before medical school.

A couple of days later I telephoned the different public schools to find out if they had received my resumé. Most said yes and acknowledged that positions were available. However, they would be willing to give me an interview only if I met the Board of Education's requirements. Among those requirements were a bachelor's degree in one's subject area, college credits in a foreign language, and courses in education and special education. Ironically, I did not meet any of the requirements in a literal sense, though I did technically. My bachelor's degree from Brooklyn College was in psychology, but because I had followed a pre-med route in college, I was required to take all the biology, chemistry, physics, and mathematics courses required for a biology degree. Furthering my serendipity, a few of my undergraduate psychology courses were counted as education courses. So although at first glance I failed to meet any of the Board of Education's criteria for employment, "upon further review" my transcripts told a different story. I am quite certain that my opportunity came about because of the shortage of science teachers; I doubt that anyone would have looked at my transcript so closely and broadly had there been a teacher surplus.

Around the same time, I accidentally discovered that Brooklyn's Edward R. Murrow High School was having a day of interviews and sign-in for prospective new teachers. Being opportunistic, I went. When I arrived, I found many long lines. No one knew what they were waiting for, yet they stood patiently. I decided to ask someone at the front desk what the lines were for, but they turned me away and said I had to wait in line to ask a question. My Board of Education experience had just begun.

To make a long story short, I waited for three hours (one of those hours was spent waiting in the wrong line). While I was waiting, an assistant principal approached me, recognized my resumé, and asked if I wanted a position. I eagerly said yes and was then sent to 65 Court Street, the Board of Education Processing Center. The line there extended out into the hallway. After I had waited eight hours, we were all sent home because the line was impossibly long. Those of us who were turned away were given special tickets that would allow us to cut the line when we returned the next day. When we returned the next day, the line of people with tickets was so long that it still took another full day to be processed. But by the end of the day, we had been fingerprinted, our transcripts had been evaluated, and we had been given "provisional probationary teaching licenses."

The day I started teaching was the same day I received a copy of the curriculum I was to teach. I was also barraged with attendance forms, book receipts, referrals, student program cards, planning/grade books, seating-chart forms, grading procedures, and tons of paperwork. All of my 170 students (five classes, 34 students per class) wanted me to pronounce their names correctly (not too much to ask, albeit challenging for a first-day novice), hand out books, and assign them seats.

On the second day, I found that 30 of my students were mine no longer. They had been switched out of my classes due to program changes and conflicts in their schedules. I was further shocked when I picked up my pile of mail (a.k.a. paperwork). It was then that I discovered my classrooms had been changed! I also had to deal with teaching two different subject areas: biology and psychology. These subjects were familiar to me, but to prepare for both simultaneously, with all the aforementioned happening, was an absolute nightmare.

After the first two weeks things began to settle down. My students remained my own, as did my classrooms. But lesson planning still remained problematic. There was not enough time in the day to mark homework, design quizzes, answer student questions, and discuss lesson plans with other teachers. Furthermore, there were some teachers whom I never met because our free periods never coincided. I was dropped into a sea of children without a life jacket and with no land in sight (Darling-Hammond and Sclan 1996).

SEASONING THE SHOCKED ROOKIE

In order to prepare new teachers to handle these problems, a form of teaching internship is required. This internship program, called "student teaching" in my case (a somewhat confusing terminology I will clarify later), is supposed to provide new teachers with classroom experience and ease their way into the teaching field (Driscoll, Peterson, and Kauchak 1985). Furthermore, student teaching, or any teacher-internship program, is generally required if teachers intend to upgrade their teaching certificate from provisional to permanent/professional status. The implementation of teacher internship became a necessity in response to critical teacher shortages and to teachers entering the profession through alternative certification routes. This internship program typically takes place sometime during the first two years of classroom teaching for those pursuing alternative certification routes. Ideally, the internship takes place during the senior year of college for prospective teachers taking a traditional route into the profession.

HOW THE INTERNSHIP WORKS

My internship experience was divided in two parts: a *learning* part and an *experience* part. The original conception, according to Jean D. Clandinin and Michael Connelly (1995), came from John Dewey (1938), who saw "laboratory" and "apprenticeship" components to teacher education. When I refer to the *learning* part, I am essentially referring to the concept of "apprenticeship," or what a teacher education program would call a methods/seminar course. When I refer to the *experience* part, I am essentially referring to the concept of "laboratory," or what a teacher education program would call student teaching. However, in my own situation, the entire internship was called "student teaching," with its presumed two parts. For reasons not completely clear to me (although I presume due to some institutional pragmatism), the university overseeing my academic training for certification did not have distinctly separate courses indicating "laboratory" or "apprenticeship."

For college students pursuing a teaching career through the traditional route, an internship program typically involves a methods course related to one's subject area, taught by a professor, and actual off-campus student teaching experience at a local public school. Sometimes multiple student teaching experiences are part of a university's teacher education program, in which a student takes a methods course in conjunction with an abbreviated "student teaching practicum." This is followed by a full semester of off-campus student teaching at a public school, which may or may not be local to the university. However, for those entering the profession via alternative routes, an internship program could span the entire first two years of public school teaching, during which a new teacher is supervised by multiple veteran teachers and school administrators. Depending on the new teacher's academic credentials, he or she may or may not be required to take further education courses at a local university during this time. According to Sharon Feiman-Nemser (2001), 28 states currently require district-supported internship programs, and 8 more are expected to have such requirements during the next few years.

The learning part of an internship program is designed to accomplish many goals. The first goal is to enrich new teachers with as much "teaching" knowledge as possible, thereby equipping them for any classroom situation. It also empowers new teachers to express their ideas and questions to an audience of their peers while a professor leads the topic of discussion. On the whole, the program is designed to help guide new teachers by showing them how to put into action all they have learned over the years. This program is trying to prepare teachers for the classroom. In my case, I was already teaching in the classroom while being "prepared."

In fact, my personal experience is a perfect illustration of the cliché "There's 'in theory,' and then there's 'in practice.'" When I was hired by the New York City Board of Education, I was issued a provisional teaching license to teach full-time at Edward R. Murrow High School. I had never taught before, nor had I ever taken an education course; I was deemed qualified by technicality. I was effectively thrown into the classroom with no systematic guidance. By the time I finally registered for my internship at Brooklyn College, I had already been employed as a full-time classroom teacher for nearly two years. I was about to take a class to "prepare" me for what I had already experienced.

But the class was a requirement for my certification, even though it seemed rather late for me (when certification rules change, similar situations can occur for veteran teachers who entered the profession via alternative certification routes). In light of my teaching experience, it was deemed I should only require the learning part of student teaching and not the experience part. My formal student teaching experience effectively was one of attending a class for required academic credits. I never worked under anyone's supervision; I was, essentially, my own intern. Ironically, six student teachers have interned under my guidance since my internship three years ago. Therefore, as I describe the learning part of the internship, it will reflect my own experience as an "apprenticeship" student. However, as I describe the experience part, it will reflect my "laboratory" perspective as a metaphoric captain who was never a private.

The Learning Part

The learning part takes place at a local university, usually once a week for three hours, during a single semester. Fortunately for me, Brooklyn College's School of Education building is a mere two blocks from my high school. An experienced professor teaches this learning part. The professor discusses curriculum writing, teaching skills, classroom technique and management, and a multitude of teacher-related topics. In many respects, this could serve as an additional workshop for new teachers who do not enter the profession in a more traditional way.

However, the learning part was not all it was cracked up to be. Much of what was taught was either outdated or not taught well. In fact, the learning part offered its share of dichotomies.

For example, students left the university knowing about the different modalities of learning; this was good. On the other hand, professors could stun students with a plethora of polysyllabic words, such as "multiculturalism" and "mainstreaming." They could put students in a trance while speaking about motivational techniques and classroom logistics. I soon wondered if teaching was more than subject matter and interacting with students; I was interminably sitting and listening to a collection of new jargon.

And that is what I took from student teaching. Student teachers do not know how to incorporate any of the ideas presented in these classes into their lessons, and no wonder. Student teachers are really more "students" than "teachers." Students learn how to teach not only according to what they read but also according to their professors' actions. New teachers try to model themselves after their own teachers. This is not much different from novices trying to emulate experts when learning to cook, play an instrument, or solve mathematical problems.

Lo and behold, new teachers like me had a professor to emulate who talked the talk but didn't walk the walk. My professor sat behind a table and *talked at us,* as if teaching was telling and learning was listening. Whatever happened to show and tell? Students cannot simply discuss the ideas; they need to do something with them, either physically or mentally.

It is somewhat of an oxymoron for professors to teach good teaching techniques by sitting down and *talking* for three straight hours. If we were lucky, we might get a five-minute break at some point in the lecture. Professors must not only talk the talk; they need to present the different learning methods and show how they can be used in a classroom setting. This means they need to illustrate good teaching practices (e.g., Clandinin and Connelly 1995; Dewey 1938; Feiman-Nemser 2001); they need to demonstrate (or at least stimulate discussion on) the same lesson using the many different teaching styles. This way, a new teacher can see how one method differs from the next. Seeing content in various contexts is invaluable; it is essentially an opportunity to think critically.

But this is not always possible, for many reasons. Many professors have been out of the school classroom environment for many years. Perhaps they are full-time professors at the university. Perhaps they are part-time professors working full-time as school-district administrators. Regardless, they are considerably removed from the trenches, and what they remember may significantly differ from what new teachers experience on a daily basis.

These professors have read about the new standards and teaching methods. It is highly probable they have even discussed new teaching strategies around a water cooler. But it is very difficult to teach material without firsthand knowledge about it. These professors have not had the opportunity to see or experience what they are teaching. This is not to say all education professors do a disservice to new teachers, but from the new teachers' perspective, there is a degree of credibility lost.

Another problem with the learning part is the makeup of a student teaching class. Many student teachers are under the false impression they are entering an internship program geared toward their needs. They presume the class will be full of new teachers teaching the same content area. However, when they arrive at the first class, they notice it is composed of people entering the teaching profession from *all* backgrounds. The class does not have new history teachers alone, or new biology teachers alone, or new mathematics teachers alone; it contains new teachers from *all* subject areas. Just for some spice, there are even people from the special education program.

Why is this the way it works? In my particular case, it was considered cost-effective. It is too costly to reserve a class for new teachers of one subject area; there may not be enough new teachers enrolled in a given semester to justify the class. Of course, given the variety of new teachers in a given semester and their need for student teaching, there was a "logical" solution: Each new teacher had a course number, specific to their subject area, they could register for, but everyone met at a common time in a common place with a common instructor. Theoretically, this served everyone's needs. The new teachers get their required student teaching course, the university can offer student teaching cost-effectively, and only a minimum of professors are burdened with the responsibility to teach the course.

In reality, no one's needs are being served particularly well. It is not the professors' fault; they do not determine enrollment policies. Consequently, as well-meaning instructors, they try to accommodate all these different student teachers by spending a few days catering to each individual's field. In other words, they attempt to divide the course into equal portions, so no one will be neglected. Unfortunately, as noble as this is, the more subject areas one seeks to accommodate the greater the potential for a logistical nightmare. In my particular experience, we had new teachers representing approximately a dozen different subject areas.

Given the length of a semester, this essentially meant only one week of the semester focused on my specific curricular needs, while the remaining three months of the semester focused on everyone else's. Objecting to this may seem a tad egocentric on my part, but I was obliged to attend all class meetings, whether they related to me or not, and as a new, anxious teacher, this did not sit well with me. I definitely did not think I was getting my tuition's worth. One could argue that a variety of diverse subject areas enrich the learning part, but this is not how a novice teacher sees things when he or she perceives the need to learn *everything* about teaching their subject area in one semester.

The Experience Part

The Logistics

The experience part (akin to Dewey's concept of laboratory) takes up the rest of the student teaching curriculum and is accomplished with a mentor. Mentors are supposed to be established classroom teachers who volunteer to share their day with a teacher-to-be over the course of a semester. Most importantly, mentors can offer new teachers various means of support (e.g., Little 1990) and opportunities to further educate themselves through their classroom practices (e.g., Feiman-Nemser 2001).

It should be noted that mentors are not necessarily uncompensated for their volunteerism. In some school districts, mentors may be paid a stipend (for some teachers, mentoring becomes an automatic routine undertaken for the extra pay). In other school districts, such as in New York City, mentors who volunteer to take a student teacher from the CUNY system are allowed to attend a free three-credit class, a definite bonus to those trying to pursue additional credits toward certifications or advancements (e.g., administration or supervision).

It is extremely important that a mentor and a student teacher have comparable interests in such areas as (1) age group (e.g., high school versus elementary school), (2) subject area (e.g., science versus history), and (3) type of student (e.g., honors level versus general level). One positive aspect of pairing up with a mentor of a similar interest is that the material being studied will be identical to what the student teacher will be required to teach. Furthermore, lesson plans and handouts, homework assignments, and study guides used during the semester will be made available by the mentor to the student teacher to look at and photocopy. Again, the only way to accomplish this is by appropriately matching mentors and student teachers.

It should also be noted that in addition to the mentoring classroom teacher, at least one faculty member from the university may serve as an institutional supervisor/mentor for the student teacher. Sometimes classroom teachers mentor multiple student teachers; sometimes university professors supervise multiple student teachers as well. In some states (e.g., New York), students must be supervised by one university professor, typically coming from a school of education. Other states (e.g., New Jersey) require two university professors, one from a school of education and the other from a school housing the department of the subject area (e.g., biology within a school of science and mathematics). Although the classroom teacher works with a student teacher on a daily basis, university professors may only visit the student teacher a few times during the entire semester.

In fact, these visits typically coincide with observations, in which the student teacher is observed and evaluated (formatively, that is, in a formal/official process) with written notes. At the minimum, each professor formatively observes a student teacher twice, as does the mentor. At the end of the semester, both the mentor and the professor(s) write summative evaluations of the student teacher, which ultimately determine if the internship was successful and could count toward certification requirements.

The idea behind this experience part is to give the student teacher a taste of what the job will require while having someone for continuous classroom support. Most teacher education programs want a student teacher to "clock in" with their mentor between 15 and 20 hours per week. This averages to about 3.5 hours per day (essentially the duration of five class periods), assuming a Monday through Friday schedule.

The "Illogistics"

However, class periods and actual hours sometimes create interesting situations (and epiphanies) for a student teacher. The aforementioned hours do not include time spent on any other education courses, at a part-time job, or creating and preparing lesson plans; these hours are strictly intended to be "classroom contact hours." Student teachers thus have a grueling schedule with very little leeway. This program, which is designed to help student teachers, has built-in time constraints that make it a very difficult program to benefit from.

For example, suppose a student teacher has the opportunity to internship in my high school while completing a degree at Brooklyn College. The first thing this student teacher needs to realize is that teachers rarely teach five consecutive periods, primarily due to our large student enrollment and staggered class schedules. My high school cannot logistically have all four grades, 9 through 12, in the building at the same time for any extended period. First, the building is too small; second, ninth, and twelfth graders are not a particularly healthy combination. Consequently, our schedules are staggered. Grades 11 and 12 come to school earlier in the morning and leave earlier in the afternoon, and grades 9 and 10 arrive later in the morning and leave later in the afternoon. Only during a few periods in the middle of the day are all four grades in the building together, which is less than ideal but manageable.

That being said, let us return to student teachers and their mind-set. Student teachers try to organize their schedules in time blocks at this stage of their academic careers just as they have from youth: *Okay, I'm here doing this for three hours, then there doing that for two . . . then we go there for another hour, then back to there for two more.* Unfortunately, such scheduling does not work so cleanly for student teaching, simply because too many schedules are nonsynchronous and in competition with each other.

Let us suppose, hypothetically, that the student teacher needs to take classes at Brooklyn College, which are offered in the midafternoon, and works a part-time job in the evenings. In the mind-set of the student teacher, 3.5 hours of daily student teaching should be an easy requirement to meet: *Student teach from 8:00 to 11:30 A.M., have a leisurely lunch, attend classes from 2:00 to 5:00 P.M., get a quick dinner, then head off to work.* But not so fast . . . what makes the student teacher so sure that 8:00 to 11:30 A.M. covers 3.5 hours of actual classroom teaching? Sometimes student teachers fail to realize that although children are in classrooms essentially all day long, that does not mean individual teachers are. It is quite possible a teacher may only teach two or three of their five classes during the morning and the rest during the afternoon.

What do teachers do with all that "free" time? That is when student teachers learn about planning periods, duty periods (e.g., patrolling the halls or rest rooms), and incredibly brief lunch breaks.

For all intents and purposes, student teaching becomes an all-day obligation. In fact, in the traditional route of teacher education programs, that is exactly what student teaching is and should be for a full semester. Student teachers should experience the classroom and building aspects of the school day; after all, they will inevitably experience all aspects upon employment. However, this is not always feasible or practical with alternative-route programs.

Believe it or not, alternative-route certification programs are becoming more common than not. Why? In states (e.g., New York) where a bachelor's degree in a subject area is required for teacher certification, teacher education programs are no longer degree-granting programs; they are auxiliary programs. For example, within the CUNY system, all secondary-level teacher-certification programs are de facto alternate route in nature. It is very rare to find a college student with an entire semester solely reserved for student teaching, especially in large, urban, public institutions like CUNY. Education courses are often crammed into a packed schedule of advanced-level subject-area courses. Student teaching is essentially just another course, competing with other courses, while college students race to complete their degrees and certification requirements in a timely fashion.

Somehow, student teaching needs to be more student oriented, or at least student sensitive. It should allow students to gain full benefits through flexibility. Although I will expand upon this further, I do wish to address the issue of the nonsynchrony of university and high school daily class schedules. As we should be well aware, the typical university class does not meet five days per week during a semester as a high school class does. University classes sometimes meet twice per week or three times per week; students can often construct their schedule to minimize the number of days they spend on campus.

Sometimes this can work to the advantage of a student teacher. For example, suppose a student teacher takes classes at the university only two days during the week (e.g., Tuesday and Thursday). This leaves the remaining three days exclusively for student teaching. Is this ideal? No, it is not. However, it does offer a creative compromise between competing necessities. A student teacher who only "clocks in" for three days a week with a mentor (essentially only 11 hours of "classroom contact hours") is still potentially able to spend three entire school days at the school. This allows the student teacher to perhaps follow the mentor around during duty periods, to work with him or her during planning periods, and to have opportunities to work with other teachers in the department and develop socializing skills and collegiality. Perhaps in the long-term development of a new teacher, three full days may be more beneficial than five partial days. Perhaps the number of hours a student teacher is required to serve needs to be looked at more flexibly as certification requirements and pursuing a college education become more complex.

Exacerbating Conditions

In my experience with Brooklyn College, student teachers are responsible for finding their own mentors. This requires a lot of footwork, a lot of traveling from school to school hoping to find someone who will take a new teacher under his or her wing. Ideally, it should be the responsibility of all teacher education programs (most do) to find mentors and match them with their student teachers. These volunteers should be preselected, experienced teachers who have a successful track record with their teaching skills and who are reformers in their schools (Cochran-Smith 1991).

With Brooklyn College's approach, a student teacher is faced with many questions when looking for a mentor:

- •◦ Which school is best for me to student teach?
- •◦ How do I contact a teacher to be my mentor?
- •◦ Which teacher should I ask to be my mentor?
- •◦ How do I know if the mentor is any good?
- •◦ What are my mentor's responsibilities?
- •◦ What are my responsibilities to the mentor?
- •◦ What if I don't like my mentor?

Additionally, student teachers are probably unfamiliar with the teachers of a school district. These questions and unfamiliar circumstances create a student teacher ill-equipped to find an appropriate mentor. Nevertheless, many teacher education programs give this responsibility to the student teacher (Tharp and Gallimore 1988). This is one of several limitations I perceive of the student teaching process.

As noted before, mentors are not necessarily uncompensated, and there is the inevitable risk of a mentor perpetually volunteering in order to get the compensation, with no genuine interest in helping the student teacher succeed. As much as teacher education programs seek to ensure that their mentors are of top quality, there is a limit to how much scrutiny they can use when school districts, as quite often happens, preselect their mentors for the teacher education programs. Potentially caught in the middle of this political and public relations dance is the student teacher, who may end up being an indentured servant for a well-connected but ill-intentioned mentor.

Furthermore, *all* mentors should have some recent training from the teacher education program. Teaching biology is one thing, but teaching someone how to teach biology is really something very different. How can a teacher who is constantly behind a closed door know how to deal with a student teacher (Little 1990)? I am a perfect example: I became a teacher without any education courses and became a mentor immediately after my internship. I had barely two years of teaching experience, had taken virtually no education courses, and yet I was a mentor. Now I finally have five years of teaching under my belt, along with a master's degree in secondary science education. However, the call to mentor probably came well before I was ready for it.

In some school districts, finding a mentor makes a student teacher feel like Goldilocks sampling bowls of porridge: *This one's too young and inexperienced, and this one's too old and outdated, . . .* Mentors are often very senior members of a school's faculty, possibly several years removed from *any* teacher education courses. This could be very detrimental for student teachers trying alternative pedagogical approaches; a very senior, inertial mentor could feel threatened by alien methods and potentially quash efforts to use them. On the other hand, very new teachers serving as mentors could also be detrimental, especially if they are still struggling to understand what they are doing.

Communication is another exacerbating issue in student teaching. Believe it or not, experienced teachers (even genuinely progressive ones) somewhat take their skills for granted. To them, the class just flows by itself, moving in the fashion they desire. Not only must mentors teach and provide guidance, they must also explain how and why things are accomplished (e.g., Feiman-Nemser 2001). They may need to make this explicit for any aspects of classroom experience: teaching of content, writing assignments, or maintaining classroom decorum.

There is also an accountability issue to consider; in this case, I interpret accountability in terms of *credibility/verification*. As of 2001, I am unaware of any definitive requirements for becoming a mentor. Although Cochran-Smith (1991) makes recommendations for what mentors *should* be, my experience within the New York City public school system is that mentors are conveniently available warm bodies (this may be true for many school systems). In fact, there are school districts where experienced teachers avoid mentoring student teachers, perceiving the opportunity as too much of an imposition with too many responsibilities. This is often how relatively new teachers become mentors.

I am also unaware of mentors extensively checking student teachers' references or academic records. Essentially, all any teacher needs to do to become a mentor is accept a student teacher's request. Granted, mentors could contact the teacher education program, or vice versa, for verification of students' backgrounds. However, given how many teacher education programs possibly place the responsibility of finding mentors on the student teachers, one wonders whether potential mentors have the time or means to verify backgrounds. And whether backgrounds are checked or not is a mystery to the student teachers, for they really do not understand the process beyond its mere requirement.

Another inherent limitation of mentoring lies with scheduling. Returning to the issue of nonsynchrony, public schools do not typically run on the same timetable as universities do. This creates a tremendous challenge for student teachers, as well as a humbling learning experience.

For example, at Brooklyn College, student teachers first register for the "student teaching" course (learning part) knowing that mentoring (the experience part) is required. Sometimes, this registration only takes place at the start of the semester (versus preregistration the semester before). Compounding matters, student teachers, primarily due to lack of foresight, often only begin to look for mentors at least two weeks into the semester.

Student teachers do not think in advance of what they need to do; they simply assume they only need to worry when they are physically on campus, disregarding or neglecting the responsibility of preplanning. In other words, semester or summer break is viewed as a vacation, reinforcing the notion that student teachers, in many cases, are still college students. If anything, student teachers learn very quickly that education is a year-round profession, not one of merely 180 days a year. We keep working even if school is not in session.

Hopefully, mentors are found within the first month of looking. Ideally, student teachers would like to get started with their mentors immediately, but they are sometimes lulled into a false sense of security regarding the total number of "classroom hours" expected of them. Student teachers who are expected to maintain 15 to 20 hours of "classroom hours" may assume that lost hours can be made up before the semester ends. In theory, this seems reasonable, until one considers the extraneous demands on student teachers. If anything, lost hours are rarely made up; they unfortunately *catch up* to a very stressed student teacher at inopportune times.

Furthermore, by the time the college semester or term begins, public schools have often already begun their academic terms, not waiting for student teachers, and valuable days of teaching experience are long past and effectively lost. Why? Student teachers have lost out on an opportunity to follow their mentors' classroom from the beginning of a term (academic year, semester, or quarter). Granted, in some cases, even for student teachers who do plan ahead and begin at the start of the university's semester, there is no guarantee of synchrony with a public school's calendar. However, the chances for it are somewhat improved.

Most critically, however, the student teachers have missed some of the most important aspects to a classroom: setting it up, gaining the children's respect, establishing and developing rapport and a sense of community, seating arrangements, assigning monitors, and dealing with the paperwork. By the time student teachers enter the classroom, it is awkward, if not impossible, for them to establish themselves. When a student teacher enters an established classroom, it is a totally new experience. However, it is not necessarily new for the children in the classroom; they may have already been there for some time. The student teacher is a sudden stranger to the community, a potential intruder. There is no guarantee children will want to redevelop their community for the sake of one person who will only be there for a short period of time. When the experience part begins has not only pedagogical and cognitive implications but psychosocial implications as well. The longer student teachers' entry into the classroom is delayed, the longer their development as teachers is delayed.

RECOMMENDATIONS FOR STUDENT TEACHING

For the first few weeks of student teaching, the number one job of student teachers is to observe the mentors. They must actively watch and figure out what happens inside the school walls. During this period, student teachers gain insight and firsthand experience into activities, homework assignments, and motivational techniques that have been tried and found true. Additionally, student teachers should be

- watching how students interact with teachers and friends
- observing classroom management
- reading and grading student homework
- watching class participation
- listening to students' ideas and questions
- viewing hallway behavior
- memorizing students' names

Student teachers should also be learning many basic skills. Some of these are how-to skills:

- ➡ preparing a lesson plan
- ➡ writing on the blackboard
- ➡ communicating with students
- ➡ speaking publicly
- ➡ answering student questions
- ➡ keeping classroom order

None of these skills should seem new to student teachers. As stated before, the overall goal is to give student teachers an opportunity to demonstrate those skills learned at the university. This "getting their feet wet" will allow student teachers to see how these skills are used and applied in the classroom. Student teachers should observe not only their own mentors but other teachers as well in order to see as diverse a view of teaching and classrooms as possible. They must understand that their own mentors are their guides, but not their only guides; an entire department (or school) of teachers is there to help them in any way possible.

Sometimes other teachers are not inclined to let student teachers observe them because it interferes with student participation or simply makes teachers feel uncomfortable. Yet even these teachers are happy to share their lesson plans and prior quizzes or tests. This gives student teachers access to a wide variety of teaching aids and a wealth of ideas in their subject area. These materials can later be used as a springboard for the student teachers' own future lesson plans.

After observing different classrooms, student teachers should become comfortable with the environment and begin to present lessons to their classes. A first lesson does not have to take up a complete period. It has to be long enough, though, for student teachers to teach one topic, concept, or idea. This first lesson should have a lot of mentor input, providing guidance on

- ➡ what topic should be taught
- ➡ how to teach the topic
- ➡ which handouts to use
- ➡ how long to spend on the subject
- ➡ how to motivate the students
- ➡ what to write on the blackboard

While providing guidance, mentors must remember that there is no guaranteed right way to teach a topic, concept, or idea. The teaching method depends entirely on class culture, teacher experience, and student capabilities. All teachers must be flexible, as each class has a different population requiring unique teaching techniques, which should match (or at least acknowledge) the student (e.g., Shulman 1986).

Because each person is comfortable teaching in his or her own way, it might appear to student teachers that one's own method is the only method. It is, therefore, imperative that student teachers and mentors understand and appreciate different perceptions and perspectives. For student teachers, this means they should not feel required to teach just as their mentors do. For mentors, this means that in order to promote learning and reform, they must allow their student teachers to grow and fulfill their own potential (Feiman-Nemser, Parker, and Zeichner 1993).

Student teachers' first post-teaching observation is important to both student teachers and mentors. Too much criticism will turn student teachers away from teaching. Too little criticism will only allow the same mistakes to be repeated the next time. One idea is to let student teachers critique themselves. Student teachers should generally know what went wrong in their lessons (Bell 1997). It is always best to ask student teachers what they think took place during the lesson. And then the dam bursts. Usually, student teachers know exactly what went wrong. They can see it in the children's behaviors and reactions. This is where the mentors' job continues, showing student teachers what went wrong and letting them learn from their experiences (Haney 1997). This is essentially what reflective practice is all about.

It is to student teachers' benefit to keep running self-journals of their teaching experiences. Student teachers should keep track of their successes as well as their failures. Lessons that worked should be examined and explored for future use. Ideas that failed should be studied in depth to understand the reasons for failure and how not to repeat them again. Most student teachers find their first lesson to be the most difficult one. They are frightened of the unknown and afraid to get up in front of a class of children. But once they actually do it, they are relieved to know that it is not so terrible.

There is a tremendous benefit to serving as a mentor. Because student teachers are fresh out of school, their ideas are new and sometimes interesting. They are also looking at their mentors' classrooms from a new perspective, eager to learn and teach. Student teachers should shadow their mentors throughout the entire day. It is an opportunity to view a teacher's world in ways few have. Sometimes, sitting in the back of the room, one can see things that typically go unnoticed (a proverbial "third eye"). Discussions with student teachers can be very eye-opening, as they reveal what occurs in the classroom when the mentors are not looking.

Another benefit to mentoring is that student teachers typically have access to a huge number of new resources (e.g., articles, books, and Web sites). Mentors can use these resources to supplement their lesson plans with new homework ideas, interesting hands-on activities, and intriguing motivational concepts. Consequently, student teachers will get good practice when it comes time to develop their own lesson plans.

For student teaching programs to be successful, many changes must be implemented. As previously discussed, it is of utmost importance that mentors are trained. This training should be offered and controlled by the university. Mentors must be taught how to convey their teaching skills to student teachers. This training is also beneficial in that it allows mentors from different schools and backgrounds to meet and compare methods. They can use their time together to discuss problems and solutions. By surrounding mentors with their peers, a learning and instructional environment is being created that will be of value to all parties. Furthermore, the university can instruct the mentors on how to rate their students. This will eliminate the need for a third-party evaluator (e.g., professors) who only comes to see the student a few times during the semester.

Another way to help student teachers is by requiring a full year (according to the public school calendar, not the university's) of training (in some schools of education, this is already the requirement). By having a full year of experience, student teachers will experience an entire school year, from start to finish, and not enter at midyear. This allows them to become genuine members of the classroom community and minimizes the risk of floundering as a temporary addition to an established classroom.

A full year of experience consequently extends the number of student teaching hours, thus also extending the student teacher's responsibilities. The first semester should be set aside for learning and discovery. The second semester should be used as real-time training. Each student teacher should be given one class that is completely and exclusively his or her own, a class he or she has already developed several months of rapport with. Every aspect of that class belongs to the student teacher (e.g., lesson plans, teaching, and assessment). As a reward for accepting more accountability, student teachers should be offered an incentive, which could range anywhere from free additional courses or credits at the university to job placement when they finish the teaching program.

Some other ideas for student teaching programs are these:

•➤ Student teachers should spend one day with their mentors even before the school year has begun.
•➤ Mentors should have an extra free period to instruct their student teachers.
•➤ Student teachers should have time to become familiar with all the audiovisual, technological, and curricular resources in their department.
•➤ Student teachers should be given a complete copy of the curriculum they are assigned to teach.

All in all, student teaching programs have a lot of positive attributes and potential. Such programs can be very useful and beneficial. However, as teacher education programs evolve with state certification requirements, so too should student teaching. Until all programmatic capabilities are maximized, the most important goals will not be accomplished.

REFERENCES

Bell, C. R. 1997. "The Bluebird's Secret: Mentoring with Bravery and Balance." *Training and Development* 51, no. 2: 30–33.

Clandinin, J. D., and M. Connelly. 1995. "Narrative, Experience, and the Study of the Curriculum." Pp. 48–57 in *Revisioning Curriculum in Higher Education.* Edited by C. F. Conrad and J. Grant-Haworth. Needham Heights, MA: Simon and Schuster.

Cochran-Smith, M. 1991. "Learning To Teach against the Grain." *Harvard Educational Review* 61, no. 3: 279–310.

Darling-Hammond, L., and E. M. Sclan. 1996. "Who Teaches and Why: Dilemmas of Building a Profession for Twenty-First Century Schools." Pp. 67–101 in *Handbook of Research on Teacher Education,* 2nd ed. Edited by J. Sikula, T. J. Buttery, and E. Guyton. New York: Macmillan.

Dewey, J. 1938. *Experience and Education.* New York: Macmillan.

Driscoll, A., K. Peterson, and D. Kauchak. 1985. "Designing a Mentor System for Beginning Teachers." *Journal of Staff Development* 6, no. 2: 108–117.

Feiman-Nemser, S. 2001. "Helping Novices Learn To Teach: Lessons from an Exemplary Support Teacher." *Journal of Teacher Education* 52, no. 1: 17–30.

Feiman-Nemser, S., M. B. Parker, and K. Zeichner. 1993. "Mentoring in Context: A Comparison of Two U.S. Programs for Beginning Teachers." *International Journal of Educational Research* 19, no. 8: 699–718.

Haney, A. 1997. "The Role of Mentorship in the Workplace." Pp. 211–228 in *Workplace Education*. Edited by M. C. Taylor. Toronto: Culture Concepts.

Little, J. W. 1990. "The Mentor Phenomenon and the Social Organization of Teaching." Pp. 297–351 in *Review of Research in Education,* vol. 16. Edited by C. Cazden. Washington, DC: American Educational Research Association.

Shulman, L. S. 1986. "Those Who Understand: Knowledge Growth in Teaching." *Educational Researcher* 15, no. 2: 4–14.

Tharp, R., and R. Gallimore. 1988. *Rousing Minds to Life.* Cambridge: Cambridge University Press.

Chapter Five

⊷ The Certification Process

As already noted in Chapters 3 and 4, the minimum requirements for a teaching certificate are generally a bachelor's degree in either education or a specific subject area, a prescribed number of education courses, and some form of supervised-teaching internship. However, that is not all there is to it. As noted in Chapter 1, permanent certification requires passing state licensure exams, and a teacher has only so many opportunities to take these exams before a state or school district is required or compelled to remove him or her from the classroom. Furthermore, as noted in Chapters 3, 4, and 7, a master's degree is required by many states (e.g., New York) for permanent certification. Finally, as will be noted in Chapter 7, certification does not necessarily ensure employment.

Nonetheless, certification is an important part of the teaching profession, especially for public schools (private or parochial schools tend to be more lenient in terms of teacher certification). State funding is tied to the number of certified teachers in a school district. Certification is an accountability issue, and for many school districts, a credibility issue. As I discuss later, certification also creates accountability and credibility issues for teacher education programs.

Historically speaking, teacher certification really did not become an issue until the early 1900s, when criticisms were aimed at teachers' qualifications and knowledge levels (Nichols and Good 2000). Although the concept of employment contracts for teachers had been around since the 1850s (Blount 2000), the accountability issue had more to do with social behaviors than with subject competence. In fact, it was not until the early 1960s that teacher certification requirements and teacher education programs came under close scrutiny (Lanier and Little 1986). There was very little consistency between states—or, for that matter, institutions of higher education—in certification requirements. Interestingly, even two decades later, when a bachelor's degree was no longer a novel requirement for teachers, the vast inconsistencies remained (see Chapter 3) (Lanier and Little 1986).

PROGRAM MATRICULATION REQUIREMENTS

How does one get into a teacher education program? When one follows a traditional route (i.e., undergraduate study), there are minimum entrance requirements to be met. For example, in Pennsylvania, students need to meet the following requirements prior to acceptance to a teacher education program:

- a minimum cumulative grade point average (GPA) of 2.50
- an assessment of reading, writing, and computation skills
- completion of an education core (i.e., educational psychology and educational theory and practice, or their equivalents)
- an "early field experience," preferably in a diverse setting (one with at least 25 percent minority students)
- documented evidence showing completion of at least 80 hours of paid or volunteer work in a setting with an age-appropriate population, in settings involving students from an underrepresented group or whose home area, whether urban or rural, is different from the candidate's own background
- approval by the professional education adviser and the head of the department in which the teacher certification major or option is located

On the other hand, in New Jersey prospective teachers have the following requirements (many similar to Pennsylvania's):

- three letters of recommendation: two from faculty members and one from an off-campus educator
- cumulative overall GPA of at least 2.50, as well as a cumulative GPA of 2.50 with no failing grades in their major or in prerequisite courses in the professional sequence (some departments require a higher GPA for their majors)
- speech proficiency prerequisite
- successful completion of prerequisite courses (i.e., General Psychology, Growth and Development, Initial Field Experience, and Educational Psychology)
- successful completion of course requirements for their major
- evidence of active interest in community affairs and teaching

➦ approval of a screening committee with representation from the college of education and the student's major field
➦ passage of Basic Skills Requirement at their university
➦ a self-rating scale
➦ any special criteria (e.g., portfolio review, writing samples)

Prospective teachers in Michigan also need to have a minimum GPA of 2.50, must pass proficiency tests in English and mathematics, and must be sophomores before they can enter teacher education programs (unlike in New Jersey, where one essentially needs to be a junior). Interestingly, matriculation to a teacher education program has no specific education course prerequisites. In Delaware, there are specific course prerequisites, but GPA requirements appear to be waived. In New York, it appears that prospective elementary school teachers can matriculate immediately upon entering college; for prospective secondary school teachers, matriculation can occur at any time, presuming satisfactory progress in their subject major.

Each state has its own requirements. Some states' requirements exactly match, but this is rare. There is usually enough variation that prospective teachers must meet additional requirements when they move from one state to another. There are, however, several states with reciprocity agreements, which allow a certificate from one state to be exchanged for an equal certificate in another state. Readers should contact the appropriate state department of education for more comprehensive information (see Chapter 12).

It should be noted that some teacher education programs do make probationary admissions. However, such admissions could depend on the area of certification, the needs of that area, and any extenuating circumstances for the student. One extenuating circumstance is the case of a prospective teacher having a documented physical or learning disability. As dictated by the Equal Educational Opportunity Act of 1974 and the Americans with Disabilities Act of 1990, one cannot deny a student acceptance into a teacher education program on the basis of a physical or learning disability. If special arrangements need to be made for course work or diagnostic testing, the teacher education program is obligated to do so.

This raises interesting questions. In New Jersey, if a student has a speech impediment such that he or she cannot successfully meet the speech proficiency prerequisite, does excluding him or her from the teacher education program constitute discrimination? What if the aspiring teacher is deaf or blind? What if he or she is a paraplegic or a quadriplegic? Where does a teacher education program draw the line between honoring the civil rights of the college student and considering the best interests of school districts? The issue is not as black-and-white as one might think; there are many shades of gray involved.

This is what makes the issue of minimum requirements potentially volatile. On one hand, requirements may be too lenient. On the other hand, perhaps some requirements are blatantly discriminatory. This is a delicate balance teacher education programs are forced to deal with in the face of teacher shortages and demands for more teachers and for highly qualified teachers. As has been the case throughout the last century, what deems a teacher "certified," "qualified," or "competent" is subject to intense debate. Caught in the middle of this debate are teacher education programs, whose primary function is to produce certified teachers for school districts.

As discussed in Chapter 1, if we raise the entrance requirements for teacher education programs, as advocated by Arthur Levine of Columbia University's Teachers College, we potentially shrink the number of teachers for the job market. Perhaps the teachers who are left are better qualified, but will this solve the problem of teacher shortages? Not necessarily. Fewer teachers for school districts already plagued by overcrowded classrooms is not a pleasant prospect.

So do teacher education programs cater to the law of supply and demand? The consequence of that would be increasing the number of qualified candidates to meet the stricter entrance requirements. If the entrance requirements involve better grades in college course work, and more candidates are needed, artificial grade inflation seems to be the likely result. By grading college students more liberally, teacher education programs can admit an artificially high number of qualified candidates to meet the needs of the job market. Unfortunately, this puts teacher education programs right back where they started. Whether the GPA requirement is 2.50, 2.75, 3.00, or even 3.50, there will be students entering teacher education programs who are qualified by academic technicality, but unqualified in terms of ultimate competence. Pennsylvania, in fact, is soon to find out the implications of this, as recent state legislation has raised the GPA requirement to 3.00.

PRAXIS AND STUDENT TEACHING

There are safeguards to minimize the number of unqualified or incompetent teachers a teacher education program produces. Perhaps this is a harsh way to look at it, but teacher education programs need some mechanism of quality control just as many other professions do.

Suppose a student, Mary Bookworm, wants to become a physician and is really good at taking tests in science. On paper, she's a whiz in biology, chemistry, and physics. She has straight As in all her college courses and scores among the very best on the entrance exam for medical school (i.e., the Medical College Admissions Test [MCAT]). The medical school interviews her, accepts her, and she begins her studies.

She takes a year or two of course work and does very well on her exams. Then, it finally happens. She has to start working with patients in a hospital clinic. On her very first day she sees a man with a severed hand, a woman badly beaten in a domestic attack, gunshot wounds, car accident victims, and blood, Blood, BLOOD everywhere. Finally, before she gets her lunch break, a sick child spews projectile vomit on her new white doctor coat. Well, how does a medical career strike Dr. Bookworm now?

Believe it or not, the "disgusting," "yuck," "gross me out" part of medicine turns many good students away. It happens. The gore is a little more than some people bargain for. Somehow the luster, the glamour is lost.

What is not to say this does not happen in teaching too? As described in Chapter 4, student teaching is somewhat of a baptism by fire for many. Student teaching is supposed to be an opportunity to learn to teach by teaching, or as said in Latin, *docendo docere,* which essentially means "learn to do by doing" (Brubacher and Rudy 1997). However, in actuality, student teaching can often lead students to ask whether this is *really* what they want to do for the rest of their lives.

In 1993, while I was pursuing my doctorate, I had the opportunity to observe and supervise student teachers for the first time in my career. It was a wonderful learning experience! Most of the student teachers I worked with were wonderful and talented. However, there were exceptions.

One student teacher was assigned to teach eleventh- and twelfth-grade social studies. She wrote wonderfully detailed lesson plans, was very punctual and organized, and was definitely *not* teacher material. To begin with, she was afraid of her students, many of whom were much taller than she was. In fact, when she taught, she either sat or stood behind her desk. When she worked at the chalkboard, she wrote with one hand and clung to the chalk rack with the other. Second, she never learned anyone's name; she simply pointed at students who raised their hand and said "Yeah, you." Third, she mumbled when she spoke, and she often presented wrong information, even though her lesson plans were correct.

To make a long story short, she did not belong in a classroom, especially a high school one. She was incredibly uncomfortable in the environment and never tried to develop a rapport with the students (who were not horrible monsters, I might add). After her student teaching experience, I sat down with her and gave her my overall assessment, which was not particularly good. This was not a news flash for her; we had discussed her discomfort before. However, now the time had come for me to assign a grade for her student teaching. Hardly being an expert on assigning grades, I set up my own protocol.

I asked myself this: If I were a high school principal and needed to hire a teacher immediately, would I take a chance on a student teacher? If my answer was yes, that told me the student teacher deserved an A. If I thought the student teacher was not quite ready for the job but thought he or she would be good with a little more experience, this told me the student teacher deserved a B.

In this case, I gave the terrified social studies student teacher a C. No way would I ever hire her, unless I had no other choice. I certainly did not want her to fail, nor did I want to prevent her from graduating and gaining her certificate. But she was clearly unemployable. Naturally, she raised a ruckus over the grade; after all, she had done everything we had told her to do (e.g., Hinchey 1995). She completed all her written tasks on time and never missed a day of school. But aside from the clerical aspects, she floundered at student teaching.

The teacher education program concurred and offered her the following options: repeat her student teaching experience, take the grade and complete her certification requirements, or opt for a degree without certification. Devastated by her prospects, she took the third option. Although this was harsh, and she probably never became a teacher, it was better she found out then rather than three to five years into a potentially unfulfilling career.

Now we come to *praxis,* which is essentially the testing part of certification. As noted in Chapter 1, there are many teachers who repeatedly fail their licensure exams after graduation and after securing employment, only to lose their jobs. Licensure exams generally involve teaching theory and practice, general knowledge, and specific subject matter. There are national exams as well as individual state exams. Depending on the state or teacher education program, these exams are taken either before or after graduation. In the case of teacher education programs that are sanctioned to certify their graduates, these exams must be taken and passed prior to graduation. Teacher education programs that only offer courses and supervised student teaching may not be able to grant certification, and in that case the responsibility belongs to the state department of education. Under these circumstances, licensure exams may be taken after graduation. It is not much different than the situation of someone taking a state bar examination after completing law school. One can be a degreed lawyer, but one cannot practice law without passing the bar exam.

This, of course, creates an interesting accountability issue for teacher education programs. If teacher education programs are supposed to produce new, qualified teachers for the demands of school districts, the measure of their success is the number of certified teachers they turn out. If the teacher education program is responsible for granting certification, they can control their accountability. If the state holds that responsibility, accountability is essentially out of the hands of teacher education programs.

What are the implications? If teacher education programs grant certification, they know exactly how many "qualified" teachers they produce. They control the entire process, from admissions to graduation, and are able to regulate the number of students in their program.

On the other hand, when the state grants certification, this limits the control teacher education programs have in terms of student entrance and graduation. Students can conceivably enter a teacher education program, take classes, do their student teaching, and graduate with a degree and yet never be certified to teach. Why? They failed to pass the licensure exams.

Although this may appear to be a nonissue, we need to think about the political climate of teacher education. States are confronted with a shortage of teachers and look to teacher education programs to ease these shortages. If teacher education programs are graduating people who cannot pass the exams, the shortages are not eased. The teacher education programs failed to meet the demands of the state. Will states blame themselves? Hardly. They consider their certification requirements fair and are unlikely to attack their own licensure exams. So who gets the blame? Teacher education programs do, regardless of whether they grant certification or not.

For example, one teacher education program in Delaware has a way of dealing with this dilemma. Although the state department of education grants teaching certification, it places accountability on its teacher education programs in terms of the number of certified teachers graduated. This particular program requires all of its prospective teachers to pass licensure exams prior to student teaching. Although this is not unique (other states and teacher education programs have a similar requirement), this particular teacher education program enjoys boasting a 100-percent exam-passing rate among its graduates.

Is this an institutional miracle? Hardly. If passing the licensure exam is a prerequisite for student teaching, and if successful completion of student teaching is the final requirement for graduation, it stands to reason that 100 percent of the school's graduates would pass the exam. However, this is a little misleading.

First, this teacher education program only prepares teachers for early childhood or elementary-level teaching/certification. This particular program offers bachelor's degrees specifically in early childhood and elementary education. This particular program also has open admissions, meaning anyone can matriculate to the college (its mission statement), and anyone can matriculate into the teacher education program, regardless of GPA, skills competency, or academic course work. If anyone can matriculate into the program, there is the distinct possibility that some candidates for the teaching profession are unqualified. To combat this, this program uses student teaching as its institutional gatekeeper; without successfully completing student teaching, a student cannot graduate and become a teacher.

Consequently, anyone can enter the program, but not everyone can graduate. Because of the college's mission statement, the teacher education program cannot dismiss a student. However, it can prevent a student from graduating. Essentially, a student can remain in academic limbo until he or she passes the licensure exam. Although statistics are unavailable, one could speculate, based on the nationwide issue of teachers' inability to pass licensure exams, that a reasonable number of this college's teacher education students do not graduate in a timely fashion. However, this information is unlikely to be presented to Delaware's Department of Education. If a teacher education program is held accountable, and if the information it provides to its state department of education determines its success, then that program will essentially put its best foot forward and report the most positive statistics it can (more on this in Chapter 9).

THE ELEMENTARY CERTIFICATE

As noted in Chapter 3, elementary schools have changed in many respects: from self-contained classrooms to subject-specific ones and from K–8 to K–6 to K–4 buildings. Some teacher education programs have addressed this in their curricula, and some have not. However, one thing that has yet to fully adapt is the nature and scope of certification. In more cases than not, elementary school certification covers grades K–6 for all subject areas (note that early childhood certification covers grades N–3).

However, there are some "quirks" among certificates. For example, in New Jersey, although early childhood education can be an academic specialization or major at some universities, elementary certification generically covers grades N–8. Unfortunately, middle school, which requires subject specialization, begins at grade 5 or 6. This creates a void for prospective middle school teachers, especially if they receive their preparation from a teacher education program like the one I taught in (see Chapter 3). All methods courses for prospective teachers of grades 5–8 (or 6–8) were the same as those for prospective teachers of grades N–4 (or N–5).

This created a messy situation for student teaching assignments as well as for prospective employment. Any aspiring second-grade teacher majoring in sociology was as likely to be placed in a middle school science classroom as any aspiring seventh-grade teacher majoring in mathematics, and vice versa. As long as a certificate reads "grades N–8," teachers are at risk of placement in any classroom, whether they are properly trained for it or not.

On the other hand, Michigan has attempted to rectify this problem. As noted in Chapter 3, prospective elementary school teachers are expected to declare a subject major and minor. The purpose of this is to prepare teachers for three employment situations: (1) a self-contained classroom for grades K–5, (2) a subject-specific classroom for grades 6–8, or (3) a self-contained K–8 classroom (note that Michigan has a separate early childhood option). What this essentially means is that grades K–5 require generalists and grades 6–8 require specialists. Although all prospective teachers declare a major and minor, teachers of grades 6–8 essentially need to declare a Middle Schools minor (see Chapter 3). Although this is far from perfect, it at least minimizes the chances for misplacing student teachers or hiring inadequately prepared teachers for subject-specific classrooms.

THE SECONDARY CERTIFICATE

At face value, one would expect secondary school certificates to be relatively straightforward by comparison to elementary school certificates. This is not necessarily the case. When "secondary school" exclusively meant "high school," life was simpler. High school involved grades 9–12. This has not necessarily been the case in approximately half a century because of the introduction of junior high schools in the 1950s (see Chapter 2).

In most states, secondary certification covers grades 7–12. The original logic behind this was to address middle schools and junior high schools, especially the latter. Junior high schools were (and still are) sub-

ject-specific environments. Teachers needed some level of content specialization, as in an academic major (or in some cases, a bachelor's degree in a subject area).

In light of the previous section, dealing with elementary certification, one sees potential problems. For example, how do prospective middle school teachers get their methods training? In New Jersey and Michigan, such training falls under the domain of the elementary-education
program. However, in New York, Delaware, and Pennsylvania, it falls
under the domain of secondary education.

Please note that in the case of New Jersey, only one teacher education program includes middle school methods training within an elementary education program, and for undergraduate study only. At another teacher education program (the first of my two examples in
Chapter 3), elementary methods training only covers grades K–5; secondary methods training covers grades 6–12. At the graduate level, for
both teacher education programs (e.g., postbaccalaureate), secondary
methods training covers grades 6–12.

MIDDLE SCHOOL CERTIFICATION

Middle school certification is relatively rare, as are middle school
teacher education programs. Some teacher education programs do
offer specific middle school teaching methods courses (e.g., in Michigan
and Delaware). However, as noted in the previous sections, certification
either covers grades K–8 or 7–12, and methods courses are typically the
domain of elementary or secondary teacher education programs.

Middle school seems to be a no-man's-land, an academic structure with ill-defined boundaries. Some states (Florida, in the 1980s and
1990s) offered specific subject certification for grades 6–9 to accommodate middle school and junior high school employment, but depending
on the state, a prospective middle school teacher could have the right or
wrong certification for employment.

Then again, middle schools can potentially hire ill-qualified
teachers based on confusing certificates. For example, suppose a middle school principal needs to hire a teacher. How does he or she know
whether a teacher with K–8 certification is equally, more, or less qualified than a teacher with 6–12 (or 7–12) certification? In many cases, the
principal does not know or perhaps does not want to know. As is the
case with pragmatic functionalism, the principal may only think about
needs on a myopic level. After all, perhaps the middle school serves
grades 5–8. If a teacher with K–8 certification is hired, he or she could be

shifted among all grades if necessary. A teacher with 6–12 (or 7–12) certification may not be as interchangeable and may therefore be less attractive for employment. Some states are prepared for this challenge; others may not be.

K–12 CERTIFICATION

We typically see K–12 certification for subjects that cover the entire spectrum of schooling (e.g., art, music, and physical education). Although some states (e.g., Michigan) may offer specific training in these subjects for elementary school teachers, such training is rare in others. This creates challenges for prospective teachers and for teacher education programs.

For example, I have had graduate students in New York and New Jersey who took teaching-methods courses specifically to train and certify them as high school art, music, or physical education teachers. However, because of the blanket K–12 certification applied to their subject areas, they could easily be placed in elementary schools for student teaching or hired to teach in an elementary or middle school. Just like middle school certification, K–12 subject certification represents trouble for teacher education programs. Under which domain should methods training courses fall: elementary, secondary, or both? Should prospective art, music, and physical education teachers take methods courses for both elementary and secondary schools? What about middle schools? Perhaps there could be a methods course sequence addressing each type of school setting covered by K–12 certification.

ALTERNATIVE-ROUTE CERTIFICATION

As discussed in Chapters 3 and 4, alternative-route certification has been the "answer" to the critical teacher shortages of the past two decades. In some cases, the alternative route has become the *only* route (see Chapter 4). The general premise behind the alternative certification route is to use alternative criteria in order to quickly provide qualified teachers for classrooms. Many of these teachers come from other professions (e.g., engineers teaching science, journalists teaching English, or attorneys teaching history). These teachers have the academic credentials for a subject area but do not have the pedagogical training required for certification. Advocates and critics of alternative-route certification continue to debate the merits of hiring these teachers, particularly as it influences student achievement (e.g., Greenwald, Hedges, and Laine 1996; Ingersoll 2001).

Alternative-route certification programs serve professionals from other fields who are hired by school districts in critical need of teachers, especially in mathematics and science. These new teachers have been issued a provisional teaching certificate but need to meet certain requirements toward permanent certification, typically within a two- to three-year period. These new teachers come to teacher education programs to take prescribed education courses (as well as any additional subject-specific courses) while they teach full-time in classrooms (under some level of administrative supervision). These new teachers are also expected to pass all licensure exams.

When all requirements are met, these new teachers are granted permanent certification and are viewed in the profession as equal to teachers who traveled a more traditional route. They may be equal in theory, but in practice there are concerns. For example, do alternative-route teachers have sufficient experience and insight to deal with the classroom environment effectively? There are opinions on both sides of this issue. Those who think these teachers do have enough experience and insight point to maturity and subject-matter knowledge as positive factors. Opponents of alternative-route certification argue that alternative-route teachers may not have sufficient pedagogical experience (e.g., Ashton 1996). In some respects, it seems as if adherence to Shulman's (1986) theory of PCK is a demarcation between advocates and opponents of alternative-route certification.

DISCUSSION

The issue of certification is fairly sticky, and yet certification is a litmus test of sorts for ensuring that school districts have qualified and competent classroom teachers. However, what is required for certification is far from universal. States cannot agree on certification requirements. Inconsistencies and overlaps between certification coverages may work for or against a teacher, depending on his or her school district. Even what teacher education programs offer in terms of subject-area methods courses contributes to confusion.

As noted in Chapters 3, 4, and 7, the relationship between academic preparation and certification is somewhat confusing. In some cases, a bachelor's degree in a subject area, without any education course work, warrants certification. In some cases, a bachelor's degree in education does. In some cases, the bachelor's degree area may be irrelevant if sufficient academic credits in education and a subject area are demonstrated. In some cases, a master's degree is the ultimate criterion. And yet certification is never guaranteed; nor is employment.

Although academic course work continues to be a point of contention, there is little argument over the impact of licensure testing. All states have some level of testing. However, according to a recent Associated Press article, thirty-four states require teachers to pass a series of national competency tests in order to gain certification (*Philadelphia Inquirer*, March 4, 2001). Such a requirement involves high stakes. For example, in 1998, fifty-two teachers from Mississippi, Georgia, Louisiana, Tennessee, and Arkansas were alleged to have taken part in a cheating scheme, paying hundreds of dollars to exam supervisors at one specific site to help them pass the tests. The consequences were severe; as of 2001, twelve teachers from Mississippi had been stripped of their certificates.

On what grounds can a teacher be certified? What makes him or her qualified? This chapter has not answered these questions particularly well, primarily due to inconsistent information. This inconsistency, to say the least, exacerbates the conflicting views of what qualities makes a successful classroom teacher. Shulman's (1986) theory of successful teaching has four dimensions. Unfortunately, various state departments of education and teacher education programs seem unable to consider all four dimensions concurrently. Consequently, certified teachers are potentially incomplete and therefore not fully prepared to teach successfully.

REFERENCES

Ashton, P. T. 1996. "Improving the Preparation of Teachers." *Educational Researcher* 25, no. 9: 21–22, 35.

Blount, J. M. 2000. "Spinsters, Bachelors, and Other Gender Transgressors in School Employment, 1850–1990." *Review of Educational Research* 70, no. 1: 83–101.

Brubacher, J. S., and W. Rudy. 1997. "Professional Education." Pp. 379–393 in *The History of Higher Education*, 2nd ed. Edited by L. F. Goodchild and H. S. Wechsler. Boston: Pearson Custom Publishing.

Greenwald, R., L. Hedges, and R. Laine. 1996. "The Effect of School Resources on Student Achievement." *Review of Educational Research* 66, no. 3: 361–396.

Hinchey, P. H. 1995. "The Human Cost of Teacher Education Reform." *Education Week* 25, no. 9: 39.

Ingersoll, R. M. 2001. "Rejoinder: Misunderstanding the Problem of Out-of-Field Teaching." *Educational Researcher* 30, no. 1: 21–22.

Lanier, J. E., and J. W. Little. 1986. "Research on Teacher Education." Pp. 527–569 in *Handbook of Research on Teaching,* 3rd ed. Edited by M. C. Wittrock. New York: Macmillan.

Nichols, S. L., and T. L. Good. 2000. "Education and Society, 1900–2000: Selected Snapshots of Then and Now." Pp. 1–52 in *American Education: Yesterday, Today, and Tomorrow.* Edited by T. L. Good. Chicago: University of Chicago Press.

Shulman, L. S. 1986. "Those Who Understand: Knowledge Growth in Teaching." *Educational Researcher* 15, no. 2: 4–14.

Chapter Six

Recruitment and Hiring

As discussed in Chapter 1, there is supposed to be a teacher shortage in the United States. The current teacher population is graying, classrooms and schools are overcrowded, and more (and younger) teachers are needed in order to reverse this trend. Compounding this problem are issues of curriculum reforms, accountability testing, licensure/certification standards, school-district demographics, and budget resources.

However, as alluded to in Chapter 4, one must wonder if school districts are genuinely prepared to handle the task of recruiting new teachers. In the classified section of any given Sunday newspaper, the "cattle calls" are posted as if written by central casting for movie extras:

> *Wanted: teachers for upcoming school year in the following areas: English, ESL, Math, Science, Social Studies. All levels. Show up at district office 10 A.M.–1 P.M. Bring resumé and copy of certificate.*
>
> *Teacher openings for the upcoming school year: English, Math, Science, Spanish. Must hold certification. Fax resumé to 123-456-7890.*
>
> *Teachers wanted. All subject areas. Must be certified. Mail resumé to P.O. Box 123, Any Town, Any State. No phone calls.*

The ads give no specifics, no contact person, and no professional expectations to guide applicants. Warm bodies are needed to fill slots. Let us see your union card, they say, and we'll find a classroom to stick you in—we're never short of those. How can a school district intelligently determine who it is most appropriate to hire? Perhaps such a determination is not part of the process. It is ironic that in a society that requires workers to have specific, albeit broad, competencies (e.g., computer literacy, interpersonal skills, a teamwork philosophy, and creative-thinking skills), teachers are viewed as certified but generic cogs for a giant and dysfunctional machine.

THE JOB MARKET

Dee Ann Spencer (2000) noted that the U.S. Department of Education predicts a potential shortage of 2.2 million teachers during this decade. Many of the issues noted in the first paragraph above reflect factors contributing to this predicted shortage. However, as Spencer also noted, according to a Schools and Staffing Survey (SASS) report, school districts did not necessarily experience severe teacher shortages during the 1990s. Granted, there were significant shortages for certain geographic regions and for certain subject areas (e.g., mathematics, science, special education, and bilingual education), but the situation was not as dire as had been predicted in the 1980s.

Perhaps the teacher shortages were less severe during the 1990s as a result of various stopgap efforts developed in response to the critical teacher shortages of the 1980s. Alternative-route certification programs, emergency certificates, out-of-field hiring, and creative recruitment efforts managed to temporarily alleviate the need for classroom teachers, and yet at the same time, these measures undermined the credibility of school systems and teacher credentials (Ingersoll 1999, 2001; Spencer 2000).

On the bright side, school districts rarely report unfilled teaching positions at the start of a school year, simply because they cannot afford to have unfilled positions. This keeps classroom sizes from growing even larger and makes running of schools more cost-effective. However, on the down side, because of alternative-route certification programs and other hiring practices initiated during the 1980s, the typical teacher, one who graduated from an undergraduate teacher education program, is a vanishing breed. Consequently, the definition of a "new teacher" has changed (e.g., Spencer 2000).

Unfortunately, this raises some concerns. First, as demands increase for stronger teacher credentials (e.g., bachelor's degree in subject area, master's degree, and advanced education course work), we must wonder whether the new breed of "new teachers" can quickly enough meet the demands to develop professionally. Second, licensure examinations are critical gatekeepers in many states; can these "new teachers" pass the exams and gain permanent certification? Considering how many "new teachers" leave the profession within three years, the demands for increased professionalism may drive them away as much as school-related and economic stress factors do.

However, a third concern, the most critical, reflects recent calls for recruiting the "best and brightest" into teaching. Advocates of this call, from Arthur Levine and Leon Botstein (see Chapter 1) to the

Carnegie Forum on Education and the Economy (Spencer 2000), seek better-educated and more-knowledgeable teachers, and yet the aforementioned stopgap measures to alleviate teacher shortages, especially in urban school districts, undermine this call. By hiring "underqualified" teachers (Ingersoll 1999, 2001), school districts send the message that they are most concerned with the number of warm bodies in classrooms and with short-term expedience. Never mind the long-term effects. Never mind the potential implications of the instability accompanying perpetual turnover. Never mind the image that "anybody can teach. . . . we'll hire anybody."

Given budgetary constraints and comparatively low salaries, many school districts still struggle to find the "best and brightest"; the economic incentive to teach is still relatively weak. Given the shrinking pool of graduates from undergraduate teacher education programs, school districts are often forced to seek quantity over quality. School districts, like the American health care system, operate reactively rather than preventively. Although educational organizations, such as the Carnegie Foundation, and governmental organizations, such as the U.S. Department of Education, look to and plan for the future, school districts plan for the much shorter term. School districts operate in crisis mode. Immediate needs take top priority; making sure a school year opens smoothly with a teacher in every classroom casts a big shadow.

The "teacher shortage" is in a vicious cycle. On one hand, state legislatures and departments of education dictate stronger academic credentials for teachers, striving to make teaching a more professional field and schools more accountable. On the other hand, by raising the bar, fewer "new teachers" come from traditional academic routes, creating projections of a teacher shortage. In knee-jerk fashion, state politicians and educational leaders seek to solve the shortage crisis by encouraging the alternate route. Teachers of marginal qualifications are hired to solve one crisis, but hiring them exacerbates another.

Further compounding this vicious cycle is a new trend toward eliminating middle schools in Philadelphia, Cleveland, Cincinnati, Milwaukee, and Brookline, Massachusetts, among other metropolitan-area school districts (Harrington-Lueker 2001). Given the quirky certification coverages in many states (see Chapter 5), many prospective teachers may find themselves unemployable in districts that only have K–8 and 9–12 schools. It should be noted that middle schools are rare in private and parochial school systems; even charter schools tend toward the K–8 approach (Harrington-Lueker 2001). However, according to Danny Weil (2000), charter schools have been initiated at the elementary, middle, and secondary levels; charter schools are not necessarily unique to a specific grade level.

Another factor to consider is that private, parochial, and charter schools do not typically require teachers to hold certification (Weil 2000). Consequently, advocates for public school systems fear the qualified teacher pool will be drained, in light of the fact that certification is the ultimate indicator of school accountability. In fact, certification may be a misleading indicator, given the number of creative ways school districts hire teachers without proper certification.

As public schools are continuously branded as failures, the job market, as teachers typically know it, may change dramatically (e.g., McLaren and Farahmandpur 2001). Perhaps cattle calls will no longer be placed in the newspapers. Perhaps there will no longer be more calls for resumés. Perhaps these public schools (or entire school districts) will be taken over by their state governments. Politicians who want to see schools become more efficient, more cost-effective, and more accountable in terms of standardized performance measures deem schools need to be overhauled and run by, as the saying goes, "those who know what they're really doing" (e.g., Finkelstein and Grubb 2000).

Case in point: Consider President Bush's Campaign 2000 promise to shut down public schools that routinely underachieve and reopen them under "new management," especially if such schools expect to continue receiving federal funds (barely 6 percent of an overall operating budget). Funding becomes a form of ransom for such public schools, especially those in urban regions, where funding is already severely and disproportionately limited compared to more affluent, suburban schools. A war is currently brewing over five New York City public schools in Brooklyn, the Bronx, and Harlem. The *New York Daily News* reported on March 15, 2001, that three of every four New York City public schools are failing to meet state performance standards. Harold Levy, chancellor of the city public school system, advocates that five particular schools be taken over by Edison Schools, an "innovative educational reformer with a proven track record of success." In theory, parents and taxpayers have the final say on this recommendation by means of a state-mandated vote. In practice, Chancellor Levy holds the proverbial gun to their heads, as if the deal is already done.

According to an editorial written by Ramon C. Cortines, chancellor of the city public schools from 1993 to 1995, Edison Schools offers children a research-based, well-rounded, technologically advanced curriculum in the classroom and focuses on professional development for teachers (*New York Daily News*, March, 18, 2001). Cortines endorses Levy's recommendation. However, one wonders whether this endorsement reflects a genuine desire to improve the educational lives of children, considering that Cortines serves on Edison's board of directors.

U.S. Representative Charles Rangle (D.–Harlem, N.Y.), in a countereditorial, questions Levy's motives, as the chancellor has offered to finance a public relations campaign on Edison's behalf aimed at parents and taxpayers (*New York Daily News,* March 18, 2001). The crux of the debate centers on school improvement: Has there been enough improvement to justify shielding the school from corporate takeover? According to the New York State Department of Education and Chancellor Levy, the answer is no. In a typical knee-jerk reaction, a system that has chronically neglected a number of schools suddenly reaches its tolerance limit and calls out the cavalry. Never mind that some of these schools have made concerted and successful efforts to hire and retain appropriately certified teachers. Never mind the recent record of stability in these schools. Never mind the small but steady improvement in achievement. Enough is apparently enough. Failing schools need to be made an example of. Coincidence or not, Edison Schools appears to be in the right place at the right time.

But who foots the bill for this takeover? Taxpayers. According to Congressman Rangle, New York City taxpayers will end up paying $250 million to Edison Schools over a five-year period to run five schools. Who benefits from this venture? Edison Schools? The odds are good it will make a handsome profit. The New York City Board of Education? The odds are good it will derive some economic benefit too. The five schools in question? That remains to be seen.

The most obscene part in this debate is Chancellor Levy's statement to the parents of the children attending these five schools that Edison Schools is the last hope for their schools and children. Unless Edison Schools takes over immediately, he has told them, the future is hopeless, failure will be irreversible, and their communities will serve as the standard for all of New York City's ills. Such scare tactics motivate some parents to scream that the sky is indeed falling and to demand a quick turnaround in their schools' prospects. On the other hand, such tactics alienate parents, sending the message that ethnic minorities really do not know what is good for their schools and communities, so politicians and corporate honchos need to save these people from themselves. Whichever way the vote eventually goes, the patience and faith of parents are severely tested.

What does this mean to the job market? If Edison Schools takes over these five schools, it will mark a great win not only for Chancellor Levy, a former Wall Street executive, but also for Mayor Rudy Giuliani and Governor George Pataki, as well. Mayor Giuliani has never hidden his feelings about the New York City public school system (see Chapter 1); neither has Governor Pataki. They view public schools from a functionalist, pro-capitalist perspective, and they see many schools (most serving ethnic minority children, lower-income children, and children of limited English ability) as the equivalent of failed corporations. In their minds, sweeping foreclosures and hostile takeovers are long overdue. As noted in Chapter 1, the teachers are to blame in the Giuliani-Pataki paradigm. In their view, teachers are typically the products of failing schools, and they return to perpetuate the failure. Consequently, the first ones to go in the school takeovers will be the teachers. Since they cannot do the job right, the thinking goes, they should be replaced by those who can, and in due time, well-qualified, certified teachers may be replaced by corporate trainers, "results guys," and troubleshooters. Schools facing a free-market paradigm suddenly need teachers who fit that paradigm. Teacher education programs do not prepare teachers, whether by traditional or alternative route, for such a paradigm (see the section "Postscript" at the end of this chapter).

SCHOOL DISTRICTS' AGENDAS

Personnel Needs

There always seems to be a need for teachers. Look at the number of advertisements in the Sunday classifieds. Look at the number of emergency certifications issued by school districts. Look at the growth of substitute-teacher pools in any school district. As discussed earlier in this chapter, school districts' top priority is to ensure every classroom has a teacher (or a semblance of one) by the first day of a school year.

In order to attract and retain better teachers, some states (e.g., Massachusetts) offer signing bonuses; other states (e.g., Utah and Florida) are considering this practice as well. The premise behind these bonuses is not much different from the premise behind bonuses for professional athletes. A school district offers a certain amount of money up front to a new teacher. This money counts as salary; however, it is not part of the teacher's annual salary; it is above and beyond it. This financial incentive is believed to help schools fill positions typically difficult to fill, and to help new teachers with possible relocation expenses associated with their new job. However, as noted by the American Federation of Teachers (AFT), such bonuses may still fail to make up for the low annual salaries earned during a career (AFT 2001). For example, in Massachusetts, new teachers receive a $20,000 signing bonus; however, it is paid out over a four-year period. In Florida, the proposed signing bonus would only be $1,000. Furthermore, such bonuses are only offered to new teachers (either from traditional or alternative-route certification programs), which potentially offends veteran teachers (AFT 2001).

Yet another practice used to fill positions is to recruit foreign teachers, particularly in mathematics, science, and foreign languages. This is becoming very common for urban school districts in Chicago, New York City, Dallas, and Los Angeles (AFT 2001). These teachers are recruited through Global Educators Outreach Programs and come from twenty countries (e.g., Nigeria, Germany, Austria, and Russia) where there are teacher surpluses. In some urban districts, this initiative is very popular; in others there is considerable opposition.

Proponents of this initiative point to the benefits of cross-cultural education, filling vacancies with well-educated candidates, and cost-effectiveness. Opponents point to compromises in already questionable alternative-route certification programs, salary and working condition issues, and a potential for culture shock as these new teachers cope with American schools and inherent attitudes and behaviors very different from what they encounter in their native countries (AFT 2001).

The chief opponents of both signing bonuses and the recruitment of foreign teachers are teachers' unions (AFT 2001). These unions, for better or worse, are primarily concerned about the implications of these initiatives, especially for veteran teachers who have worked for many years at much lower salaries than their newer colleagues are now earning but who may not be close enough to retirement to opt for a big payoff like a severance package. Just as middle-aged employees fear downsizing in the corporate world, so too do middle-aged teachers in school systems. The concern that one segment of the professional population will benefit at the expense of another goes beyond signing bonuses and foreign recruitment. Similar concerns were raised in the 1980s at the height of the merit-pay movement (i.e., salary increases according to classroom performance) and during the recent charter school movement (e.g., Weil 2000). How generations of teachers affect each other will be discussed more later in this chapter.

Teacher shortages are most critical in some of America's poorer, urban school districts (e.g., Ashton 1996), where salaries are often noncompetitive and applicants may have marginal qualifications. The subject areas most affected are English, mathematics, and science, where the pool of traditional graduates from teacher education programs is shrinking (e.g., Darling-Hammond 1996, 1998; Ingersoll 1999, 2001). Consequently, poorer school districts are forced to take any warm bodies they can get. When confronted with the choice of hiring an uncertified teacher or no teacher at all because an appropriately certified teacher is not available, *no teacher* is no option. School districts essentially need to choose the lesser of two evils: no teacher, or an unqualified but physically present teacher.

Rarely do affluent suburban districts have this problem (the same could be said of some affluent or well-off rural districts). Why? As discussed in Chapter 5, I had the opportunity to supervise student teachers, and although most of them were wonderful to work with, there were exceptions. One of those exceptions was discussed in Chapter 5; now I will discuss the other exception.

This particular student teacher was teaching high school mathematics (in fact, she was co-placed with another student teacher who was the best mathematics teacher I ever saw). She was terrible. Well, not terrible—but certainly uninspiring. She certainly knew her subject matter, and she understood her responsibilities in the classroom. But she spoke in a monotone and did not make eye contact with her students. Needless to say, she cured my insomnia every time I observed her teach a lesson.

Her heart really was not in it. She did not particularly enjoy teaching and planned to pursue a master's degree in mathematics after graduation anyway (she opted for a noncertified degree). However, it was her social attitude that troubled me most of all.

At the end of the student teaching experience, I set up appointments to meet with each advisee individually to see how they enjoyed student teaching, to find out to what degree I had been a helpful supervisor, and to find out what their concerns were, as they would soon enter the professional ranks. I also asked them standard interview questions, as if I were a school principal, just to help them think about some issues as they embarked on future job interviews.

Among my questions, I asked them all what kind of school setting they would prefer to teach in: rural, suburban, or urban. Considering they came from a variety of communities, I was curious how they would answer. Many of them took a kind view of the community surrounding the university they attended in central Pennsylvania. Happy Valley, the locals called it ("Winnie the Pooh Land," according to my Brooklyn perspective). It *was* a nice place. Granted, it was not perfect, but it was closer to perfect than many other places. It did not surprise me to hear my student teachers state a preference for a suburban or a nice rural environment.

However, it was encouraging to also hear them say, "If the only opportunity is in the inner city areas of Philadelphia or Pittsburgh, hey, I'll take the job." Let's face it, not everyone can find a job in Shangri La, and most of my student teachers were realistic. I am not knocking the urban experience. One person's Happy Valley is another's Haight-Ashbury. One person's Flatbush is another's Fargo. But many teacher education students understand and appreciate the realities of the profession and the job market. The greater number of job openings, especially in English, mathematics, and science, are in urban school districts.

Do all teacher education students want to teach in the inner city? No, and who can blame them? Would we fault an attorney who graduates law school and prefers to practice in the suburbs rather than as a public defender for a major city? Would we fault a young physician who would rather be a "country doctor" than work in an inner-city trauma center? So why should we blame teachers for desiring a career in a nice, well-funded, suburban school district? The working conditions and image of teaching are not particularly good to begin with (e.g., Glenn Group 2000).

Does this mean every attorney, physician, and teacher gets what he or she wants in life? No, of course not. Law firms, hospitals, and school districts simply do not have enough jobs to accommodate every applicant, especially in nice, well-to-do environments. This is how job markets work. Candidates who want jobs badly enough will go where the jobs are, even if the jobs are not in an environment to their liking— maybe for the rest of their lives, maybe only for a short time. But candidates who understand the nature of their professions and who care about their professions need to make difficult choices.

Getting back to the monotone mathematics student teacher: She was perhaps the only student teacher who absolutely refused to teach in an urban environment. She grew up in a semirural part of Pennsylvania, and either she was going to get a teaching job in a similar environment or she would not teach at all. Keep in mind, she was a really bad teacher—even the worst schools in Philadelphia would have hired her only out of desperation. But she wanted no part of it. In her own words, "I'd rather flip hamburgers at Wendy's than teach in Philly."

Now that is a serious declaration. Here is a math teacher, bad as she was yet potentially employable in a poor, urban school, and she would rather work in a fast-food setting. For all I know, she may be a shift manager by now. If this was her level of commitment to teaching, maybe she and schools are better off without her in the classroom. Sadly, when I pressed her for some justification on her stance, she blurted out, "I don't want to deal with black people!" My response was, "Well, chances are they're not too thrilled to deal with you, either!"

But this is what urban school districts face as they try to fill vacancies. The supposed "best and brightest" that educational leaders talk about do not want to teach there without sufficient reward or incentive. They want to teach in "good" school districts. So who is available to the "bad" school districts? The "good" districts' rejects? The "not exactly the best or brightest"? Even the worst student from a good teacher education program did not want to teach there. Is the only choice for these districts whoever is available from urban teacher education programs or alternative-route certification programs? Urban districts have personnel needs. They do not have time to worry about who does not want to teach there; they can only worry about who wants to teach there.

This could be said for all "poor" school districts, be it in the urban jungles of New York, Philadelphia, or Chicago or the rural boonies of the American heartland and Bible Belt. Some teachers want to go there; others do not. School districts are often forced to hire whomever they can, simply because applicants are not breaking down the door. This is part of the vicious cycle for many school districts. Their reputations are poor, and new, high-quality teachers prefer not to come. Classrooms need teachers, so the districts hire teachers who will come. Some of these teachers are qualified, and some are not. If student achievement is considered substandard, politicians and educational leaders point their accusatory fingers and demand changes and improvements. But how does a school system change and improve if it cannot break the cycle?

Minority Issues

That being said, this raises the issue about schools serving ethnic-minority children. According to Anna María Villegas (1998) and Beatriz Clewell and Anna María Villegas (1998), ethnic-minority children fare much better when taught by a teacher of similar ethnicity. At a time when the U.S. Census Bureau is publishing its population figures for the year 2000, educators and school systems are encouraged to take a close look at their ethnic demographics.

For example, the total population of New York City has topped 8 million people. Furthermore, its ethnic demographics have changed considerably since 1980. According to 1980 census data, the white, non-Hispanic population of New York City was approximately 50 percent; now it is approximately 35 percent. The shift in population, primarily the result of immigration, now presents a citywide African American/black population of approximately 27 percent, a Hispanic (white and black) population of approximately 27 percent, and an Asian population of approximately 10 percent.

If we were to apply Clewell and Villegas's (1998) assertion to the New York City school system (assuming the school population demographically mirrors the city), the public school teaching workforce should be 35 percent white, non-Hispanic; 27 percent African American; 27 percent Hispanic; and 10 percent Asian. Do New York City public school teachers reflect these demographics? Probably not; however, given the political and media attacks on the city's school system (see Chapter 1), it is possible the demographics may be closer than we think. As discussed in Chapter 1 and earlier in this chapter, New York City public schools are considered academically substandard. A large part of the student population are members of an ethnic minority. These students graduate high school and then attend their local CUNY campus. Perhaps they graduate and become teachers, returning to their former public schools. The politicians and media brand this a perpetuation of failure. Clewell and Villegas might consider this appropriate demographic diversity. If both are true, if "perpetuation of failure" somehow occurs despite "appropriate demographic diversity," then perhaps there is a flaw in Clewell and Villegas's theory.

But there is some merit to what Clewell and Villegas recommend. An African American teacher can present a good image and role model for African American students. A Hispanic teacher can present a good image and role model for Hispanic students. An Asian teacher can present a good image and role model for Asian students. Then again, why can't African American, Hispanic, and Asian teachers present a good image and role model for all students, including white students? If we truly want our educational systems to be rich in ethnic, cultural, and philosophical diversity, we should have students and teachers learning from everyone, not just from their own kind (e.g., McAllister and Irvine 2000; Sleeter 2001).

This is the flaw in Clewell and Villegas's (1998) theory; schooling is a matter of learning not only from one's own group but from and among everyone. Trying to match the demographics of school populations and their teaching workforces is a contrivance. It is diversity for diversity's sake, which may or may not benefit schools and children. Could African American, Hispanic, and Asian children achieve (not to be confused with "learn") better having teachers like themselves? Perhaps they can; then again, perhaps they might achieve well regardless of their teachers' ethnicities. Unfortunately, there is also evidence that African American, Hispanic, Asian, and white children underachieve regardless of teacher ethnicity. It is a complex issue lacking a simple answer. On one hand, it involves cultural (in)sensitivity issues, where children's self-efficacy or alienation is at play. On the other hand, it involves issues of academic achievement, accountability, and competency.

During recent doctoral dissertation defenses (e.g., Hallock 2000; Reinard Stock 2000; Shiels 2001; Williams 2000), this dilemma has been discussed. Particularly discussed was the issue of school desegregation, still a touchy issue in Delaware and along the lower eastern shore of Maryland. During discussions, a "loaded" question was raised: Was desegregation, in retrospect, such a good idea? No one was interested in turning back the clock to the days of Jim Crow laws or overturning *Brown vs. Board of Education,* but we did wish to examine the issue of caring, in terms of pedagogical and curricular practice. Prior to desegregation, black children were taught in black schools, primarily by black teachers. Many black children succeeded, and although they were often restricted to attending black colleges and universities (e.g., Howard, Spelman, and Grambling), they became educators, scientists, physicians, engineers, and attorneys. They were taught by teachers like themselves.

However, since desegregation, many black children still succeed, attend colleges or universities of their choice, and become professionals. Some of them had black teachers; some had white teachers. Is their success rate the same, better, or worse compared to the days of segregation? I honestly do not know, and we may not have such data available to answer this question.

For argument's sake, let us assume their success rate is worse. Why? Are minority children suddenly more intellectually defective than they were before the 1950s? Are minority teachers suddenly more incompetent than they were before the 1950s? Some argue that the quality of teachers and students has drastically declined since the 1950s; however, even if true, is desegregation the sole catalyst? This seems highly unlikely.

There could be many factors at play; however, the issue of caring looms large. Prior to desegregation, children were taught by their own kind, went to school with their own kind, and cared about each other. Schools were a community. They still are supposed to be, but the nature of the community has changed. Schools are no longer as homogeneous as they once were (at least by constitutional design). At least in public schools, students no longer go to school with and are no longer taught by just people from their own group. However, members of the school community, whether student, parent, or teacher, now need to care for more than only their own kind. This is the essence of multicultural education. Our schools as learning communities have diversified; all members need to have mutual empathy if society is to succeed as a whole.

Have we lost that empathy? Perhaps that sense of empathy never genuinely existed. Perhaps teacher education programs failed to prepare for this. Perhaps politicians and education leaders underestimated the value of empathy. Perhaps desegregation forced teachers to pretend to care about children they do not genuinely care about. Can caring be legislatively enforced? Perhaps this is why Clewell and Villegas (1998) advocate what they do. Perhaps underachievement, achievement gaps, and failing schools are the manifestation of fifty years' worth of white teacher backlash. Perhaps there is some merit to this view, but it unfortunately does not explain everything.

But school systems are concerned about the issue of demographic balance and about achieving a teaching population reflective of its student population. This is not a concern just for ethnicity or race; similar issues have been raised regarding gender, especially in mathematics and science (e.g., Fennema and Carpenter 1998). However, most educational scholars discuss how we, as educators, can be more conscious, more empathetic, and more nurturing to a diversity of learners. Ultrasegregation is rarely advocated, even though many school systems and educational leaders translate demographic balance between teachers and learners this way.

However, the application often tends toward contrivance. For example, Delaware's population breaks down to approximately 75 percent white, non-Hispanic; 19 percent African American; 5 percent Hispanic; and 2 percent Asian. Many school districts and educational leaders are attempting to create a teacher population that exactly matches the state demographics. In fact, in many schools, especially in the southern part of the state, there are virtually no minority teachers, even though there is a visible minority student population.

Southern Delaware, along with the lower eastern shore of Maryland, has great difficulty recruiting and hiring minority teachers, specifically African Americans. This is hardly surprising. Historically, Delaware fought for both sides during our nation's Civil War; the Mason-Dixon line essentially divides the state through its capital, Dover. Even today, traveling through southern Delaware and the lower eastern shore of Maryland, one can sense those old Confederate leanings. It is not difficult to imagine the discomfort an African American might feel living in such a region, or any region that prided itself on racism. Who could blame an educated African American for not wanting to teach there?

Nevertheless, schools are making very concerted efforts to entice African American teachers, albeit with marginal success. Educational leaders want to change the image of their schools and region, and yet they struggle to overcome their historical reputation. In many respects, African American teachers want to make a difference, but they are hesitant to become "symbols for the marquee."

It is unfair to African American teachers; are they recruited and hired for their talent and credentials or for their skin color? We might wonder if Delaware and similar states are making such concerted efforts to hire Hispanics, Asians, women, gays, lesbians, Catholics, Jews, Muslims, or Hindus. Consequently, we still need to know the ultimate impact on achievement, since this is what drives school reforms.

Again, the issue of diversity is incredibly complex, and yet educational leaders and school systems try to oversimplify it. Like an open can of worms or a Pandora's box, such practices challenge our sensitivities and sensibilities to governmental safeguards like Affirmative Action and the Equal Opportunity Employment Act, as well as simple human decency. As Jennifer M. Gore (2001) points out, diversity (and equity) mean more than simply a balance in numbers. School systems and educational leaders still need to come to terms with this.

THE APPLICATION PROCESS

There are typically two routes by which to submit an application for a teaching position: the unsolicited route, and in response to an advertisement. In either case, the applicant is required to fill out a school-district employment application and provide a resumé, reference letters, and proof of certification. An applicant may be required to provide academic transcripts as well as the results of his or her licensure exams. Perhaps the school district will require some form of teacher portfolio, where administrators can take a close look at how an applicant writes lesson plans, assesses learning, and reflects upon his or her practice.

In school districts under minimal pressure to fill many teaching vacancies, an application may get a thorough examination. This may be common practice in "better" school districts. Schools and administrators can afford to be choosy. The resources are probably strong, parental involvement and influence may be considerable, and there may be many applicants applying for one position. Under these circumstances, administrators truly want to ensure they hire the "best and brightest" for their students.

On the other hand, in "poorer" school districts, maybe the number of teaching vacancies outnumber the applicants. Maybe the personnel office is understaffed and overwhelmed with pressure to fill positions urgently. Maybe applications receive only a superficial examination. Maybe the personnel office will review enough of a file to consider an applicant employable, but maybe they will review it carelessly and mistakenly deem the applicant unqualified. How an application is put together is critical when those reviewing it lack time and patience. It is important to be as thorough and concise as possible in providing pertinent information. Would-be teachers are challenged to put together an application that tells a school district everything it needs to know without turning the application into the Great American Novel.

Applicants taking the unsolicited approach have three options. They can mail a resumé to every school in any district they seek to teach in. They can contact a school-district personnel office for an application package and return it there. They can do both. Some people find success one way versus another; some people like to cover all bases.

When I sought a public high school teaching job many years ago (after teaching five years in either private high schools or community colleges), I contacted the personnel office for every school district where I was interested in teaching. In addition to requesting a district application package, I requested a listing of every high school (and its principal) in that district. I then spread my resumé over a large radius in Florida, sending completed application packages to fifteen different district personnel offices and individual applications to at least fifty high school principals (I informed them that a completed district application was concurrently on file). All told, I was contacted for more than a dozen interviews and was offered three jobs. I accepted one and stayed at that school for four years before leaving to pursue my doctoral studies in Pennsylvania. Sometimes unsolicited applications are successful; sometimes they are not.

Some people prefer to wait for advertisements of a vacancy. Sometimes this is successful; other times it is not. From personal experience, I found the unsolicited route much more successful. Depending on the geographic region and the type of school systems, vacancies are routinely and openly advertised; sometimes vacancies are advertised on a limited basis within the school district. The application process is still the same. Duplicate applications may need to be submitted to the district personnel office and specific school principal. Sometimes an advertisement does not give the name of administrators; sometimes letters need to be addressed to "Personnel Director," "Human Resources," or "Sir/Madam." Just as with an unsolicited application, there is a wait for a response. However, one disadvantage to replying to an advertisement is that the applicant does not know whom he or she really applied to, so it is not clear whom to contact to find out the status of an application.

THE INTERVIEW PROCESS

In the event an application has passed a certain level of initial screening, a candidate will be contacted by either the district personnel office or a school principal for an interview. For lack of a delicate way to put it: Interviews are interviews; there is no rhyme or reason behind them, and there is no standard protocol. However, there are certain things to be prepared for.

First, applicants should be prepared to bring any pertinent documents with them (e.g., certificate, academic transcripts, or portfolio), just in case people wish to see original documentation or take a closer look at documents they may not have access to.

Second, they should arrive on time and be dressed professionally.

Third, they should be prepared to meet a variety of people (e.g., teachers, administrators, and department heads).

Fourth, they should be prepared to demonstrate their skills. For example, would-be teachers may be required to teach a brief lesson to students between interview meetings. How they teach the lesson could be critical to employability. I have been guilty of teaching "too hard" in the eyes of administrators. Perhaps I overestimate the abilities of students; perhaps they underestimate their students. There is no easy way to prepare for this task; applicants run a 50–50 chance of teaching too hard or "too easy," which in turn raises speculation about the appropriateness of their teaching methods (more on this in Chapter 8).

Fifth, applicants should be prepared for a number of questions, some appropriate, some inappropriate. There are certain questions potential employers can legally ask, and others they cannot. For example, to ask about prior employment history or academic record is legal and reasonable. To ask about religious affiliation, marital status, or sexual orientation is neither legal nor reasonable. Principals may ask certain questions to see how candidates respond to certain situations. Sometimes they are interested in the applicants' thoughts; sometimes, they are interested in how well applicants guess *their* thoughts. Although teachers are supposed to be individuals, many administrators only view teachers in terms of conformity and compliance (again, more on this in Chapter 8). Applicants need to appreciate that school principals juggle competing political and social agendas, which may or may not be their own (e.g., Riehl 2000); however, they intend to carry out those agendas, since their jobs depend on it.

SECURING EMPLOYMENT

This is the final step of a potentially long sequence of hurdles. So many factors determine success at obtaining a job offer as a teacher. One factor is geographic region. Another factor is subject area or area of certification. A third factor is the type of school and the type of school district. A fourth factor is the needs, priorities, and agenda of the school district, and even of the school administration. In many cases, an applicant may do all the "right" things and yet be unable to obtain a full-time classroom job. Rebecca Fabiano will discuss such a situation in Chapter 7.

As much as our school systems advertise teacher shortages, and the odds seem encouraging, gaining full-time employment may be a matter of being in the right place at the right time. It is not easy for an applicant to prove he or she is exactly what a school principal is looking for. So many complex issues, many beyond applicants' control, determine this. Somehow, obtaining a job is the first step in yet another series of hurdles one endures during a career. These hurdles often present themselves in the form of "tests." These tests typically force teachers to find a balance between what they believe about education, how they were trained as teachers, and what their new employers expect them to believe and do. This will be explored in Chapter 8.

POSTSCRIPT

A follow-up to the Edison Schools story: Parents in the five school districts overwhelmingly voted against letting Edison take over their schools (*New York Daily News*, April 3, 2001). Less than 50 percent of the eligible voters showed up at the community polls, yet approximately 80 percent of those who did voted a resounding no. Although this may have been a victory of sorts for parents, children, and their schools, the criticism was swift and pointed from Mayor Giuliani, Chancellor Levy, and editorialists in the *Daily News*. Rather than accepting the blame for the "ills" of a selected number of schools, the critics pointed to democracy, teachers' unions, and the unwise vote exercised by parents as the ultimate culprits.

REFERENCES

American Federation of Teachers (AFT). 2001. "New Spins on Recruiting Teachers." *AFT on Campus* 20, no. 6: 12.

Ashton, P. 1996. "Improving the Preparation of Teachers." *Educational Researcher* 25, no. 9: 21–22, 35.

Clewell, B., and A. Villegas. 1998. "Introduction." *Education and Urban Society* 31, no. 1: 3–17.

Darling-Hammond, L. 1998. "Teachers and Teaching: Testing Policy Hypotheses from a National Commission Report." *Educational Researcher* 27, no. 1: 5–15.

———. 1996. "The Right To Learn and the Advancement of Teaching: Research,

Policy, and Practice for Democratic Education." *Educational Researcher* 25, no. 6: 5–17.

Fennema, E., and T. P. Carpenter. 1998. "New Perspectives on Gender Differences in Mathematics: An Introduction." *Educational Researcher* 27, no. 5: 4–5.

Finkelstein, N. D., and W. N. Grubb. 2000. "Making Sense of Education and Training Markets: Lessons from England." *American Educational Research Journal* 37, no. 3: 601–631.

Glenn Group. 2000. "Act Fast To Lure, Keep Good Teachers." *Education USA* 42, no. 20: 1, 4.

Gore, J. M. 2001. "Beyond Our Differences: A Reassembling of What Matters in Teacher Education." *Journal of Teacher Education* 52, no. 2: 124–135.

Hallock, S. 2000. "A Transition Intervention Program for At-Risk Students in a Rural Public High School." Ed.D. diss., Wilmington College of Delaware.

Harrington-Lueker, D. 2001. "Middle Schools Fail To Make the Grade." *USA TODAY*, March 15, 15A.

Ingersoll, R. M. 2001. "Rejoinder: Misunderstanding the Problem of Out-of-Field Teaching." *Educational Researcher* 30, no. 1: 21–22.

———. 1999. "The Problem of Underqualified Teachers in American Secondary Schools." *Educational Researcher* 28, no. 2: 26–37.

McAllister, G., and J. J. Irvine. 2000. "Cultural Competency and Multicultural Teacher Education." *Review of Educational Research* 70, no. 1: 3–24.

McLaren, P., and R. Farahmandpur. 2001. "Teaching against Globalization and the New Imperialism: Toward a Revolutionary Pedagogy." *Journal of Teacher Education* 52, no. 2: 136–150.

Reinard Stock, D. 2000. "A Qualitative Examination of the Processes of Racial and Gender Identity Development in Female Multicultural Facilitators." Ed.D. diss., Wilmington College of Delaware.

Riehl, C. J. 2000. "The Principal's Role in Creating Inclusive Schools for Diverse Students: A Review of Normative, Empirical, and Critical Literature on the Practice of Educational Administration." *Review of Educational Research* 70, no. 1: 55–81.

Shiels, K. 2001. "A Qualitative Analysis of the Factors Influencing Stress and Second Language Acquisition in Immigrant Students." Ed.D. diss., Wilmington College of Delaware.

Sleeter, C. E. 2001. "Preparing Teachers for Culturally Diverse Schools: Research and the Overwhelming Presence of Whiteness." *Journal of Teacher Education* 52, no. 2: 94–106.

Spencer, D. A. 2000. "Teachers' Work: Yesterday, Today, and Tomorrow." Pp. 53–83 in *American Education: Yesterday, Today, and Tomorrow.* Edited by T. L. Good. Chicago: National Society for the Study of Education.

Villegas, A. 1998. "Increasing the Number of Teachers of Color for Urban

Schools: Lessons from the Pathways National Evaluation." *Education and Urban Society* 31, no. 1: 42–60.

Weil, D. 2000. *Charter Schools: A Reference Handbook.* Santa Barbara, CA: ABC-CLIO Publishers.

Williams, H. E. 2000. "A Descriptive Study: African-American Adolescent Males, Absenteeism, Mentoring, and Alienation in Rural Public Schools." Ed.D. diss., Wilmington College of Delaware.

Chapter Seven

‱ Teaching out of One's Field

Rebecca Fabiano

A PERSONAL AND PROFESSIONAL JOURNEY

I recently had the opportunity to attend a breakfast given by the Upper West Side Chamber of Commerce. The relatively new chancellor of the New York City schools, Harold Levy, a former Wall Street executive, was the guest speaker. He talked about his first ten months as chancellor and his goals for his tenure.

He also shared many statistics with us, including the number of teachers employed by the New York City Board of Education. Levy also noted that 12,000 of these teachers were actually unlicensed to teach in their fields. Although that number might be somewhat surprising to some, it was not to me. It just so happens that I was once hired to teach outside of my licensed field while briefly employed by the Board of Education.

It is important to be clear and recognize the fine distinction between not having a license to teach in one's field and being hired to teach outside one's field of license. Levy did not necessarily make such a distinction regarding those 12,000 teachers. Some may not have met all licensure requirements to teach in their subject areas (e.g., science, mathematics, or English); some may very well have been hired to teach outside their licensed subject area (e.g., a math person teaching science, or a chemistry person teaching biology or physics). In my situation, I was specifically licensed to teach in one field but hired to teach in another.

In 1996, I started the long and arduous journey toward becoming a licensed high school health education teacher. At that time, I had been involved in health education for over five years. I was "teaching" health education in various venues, including as a guest lecturer in many New York City high schools, for PTA groups, and for not-for-profit organizations. I had been an HIV-prevention educator for six years and coordinated a well-known HIV-prevention education program for teens. I held certificates of completion from many well-known health-education-training organizations, including the New York City Department of Health.

However, I was told this was not enough to be hired as an employee of the Board of Education; I must follow the proper procedures and get licensed in order to teach health education. Because I was eager to get a foot in the door and begin teaching, I paid for my substitute-teachers' license and began subbing immediately. In addition to subbing, I entered a graduate program (working toward my master's degree) in secondary education with a concentration in health education.

Ironically, although I have years of experience writing health-based curricula and teaching health-related topics, my undergraduate degree was in English, not health education. I was not particularly interested in becoming an English teacher, although literature fascinated me; my interests were really more relevant to health education. Changing my major did not occur to me; I thought a degree in English gave me many postgraduate options (e.g., employment or graduate school).

I wanted to be up-to-date on my pedagogy and happenings in the field of health education, and I obviously wanted formal academic training. I also did my student teaching, a requirement for this graduate program, and graduated with my master's degree in 1999. I was finally licensed to teach health education in any high school in New York State.

A LESSON LEARNED

While finishing up graduate school, I was offered the chance to teach at an alternative high school in Manhattan where I had been a regular substitute teacher. However, at the time, the then principal told me, "We can't hire you as a health teacher at this time. We need a dance teacher— you have a background in dance, don't you?" Actually, I do; it just so happens I am a paid, professional dancer. I danced with a troupe in college, and in 1999–2000 I performed with the Brooklyn Arts Exchange in New York City. However, I never considered teaching dance. After all, I also have experience cooking vegetarian dishes, but that does not make me a home economics teacher.

Because I had taken several classroom-management classes, not to mention hundreds of dance classes over the years and because this principal intimated that the job could possibly lead to a position as a health teacher, I took it. Using the Board of Education's logic, I viewed this new job as a means to an end: I would enter the system whatever way I could and eventually find my proper niche. But logic does not necessarily work in practice as it does in theory.

As the year went on, a teacher was needed to teach a reading class, and my principal said to me, "You have an undergraduate degree in English, right? Would you like to teach this class?" Again, I saw this as an opportunity to gain teaching experience, and I began teaching reading. With each thing I was willing to do, I assumed the payoff would be appropriate placement as a health education teacher. I was trying to be a good employee, patiently waiting for my reward, making use of my varied background in hopes of ultimately focusing on my primary area of interest.

All the while, my principal assured me that she would try to find the funds to hire me as the health teacher in the upcoming year. I was patient and hopeful. However, I was not hired to teach health. Actually, no one was hired to teach health, for she saw no need for a full-time health education teacher anyway. I did not get my reward, and now this school and principal can only be viewed as past history for me, for I no longer teach there. What I valued as a teacher was not valued by my administration; what purpose I served to them was not what I desired.

A PERSONAL INTEREST IN HEALTH EDUCATION

The existence of licensure seems to imply a need for health education teachers, yet I feel a need to justify why we need health education teachers, particularly me. My interest in young adults, health, and health education is long-standing. As a teenager, I was a peer educator in high school and was trained to teach fellow students about date and acquaintance rape. My interest in health grew in college, as I received further training as a peer educator and as a resident assistant, leading discussions and workshops on various health topics for campus residents.

I found that when I gave workshops on topics such as HIV prevention, the warning signs of alcoholism, and eating disorders, people always came up to me for information about other topics as well. They were thirsty for knowledge, for skills, and for suggestions about how to change or enhance certain behaviors; they wanted to be able to talk with someone they trusted with this sensitive information. I discovered that the topics about which I was learning and which I was teaching to others were relevant to my (and their) everyday life and to my interpersonal relationships in ways that required classes, like algebra and Western civilization, were not.

This piqued my curiosity further; I began reading about various health topics and taking courses and workshops over the years. My professional life has revolved around health and teens in various capacities since the early 1990s. As I found out, a degree specifically in health education and the desire to teach health education were simply not enough.

My interest in teens is very much married to my interest in health. After I successfully made it through adolescence, a harrowing experience for me as it is for so many teens, I realized how much I enjoy being around teenagers. They are curious, awkward, challenging, open, and *refreshing* to be around in ways that adults are not. And they exude energy and life in ways that adults do not.

When I worked as an Outreach Worker in an after-school peer-education program (for more than two years in the mid-1990s), I spent the morning working with adults, going to meetings, writing grants, and so on. Around 2:45 in the afternoon, my day would change. I knew young people would be arriving soon, and I could literally feel a positive change in my own energy as I anticipated their arrival. My heart would race excitedly in anticipation of their arrival. When they finally bounded through the door, no matter what I had faced that morning or what I would face that afternoon, I knew my time with these teens would be fun, challenging, and a mutual learning experience.

We often refer to our teens as our future, yet we forget how much of an impact they have on our present. To think of them as our future without preparing them to meet it as physically and emotionally healthy adults is doing them and us, as a society, a disservice. If we take the time to teach young people about health and health-promoting behaviors, we contribute to a society that is healthier overall. A society whose members treat themselves and each other better, more healthfully, is potentially less dependent on the health care system as it exists now.

By including a comprehensive health-education program in every school and as part of all curricula for grades K–12, we send a strong message to young people that we care about them as whole people, not just about the academic part of them. By whole people, I include their emotional, physical, and mental selves. This supports a concept, originated approximately a half-century ago by a well-known physician named H. L. Dunn, known as "wellness." Wellness comprises five components addressing the needs of the whole person and intended to "enhance the quality of life and maximize personal potential." These components are the spiritual, the social, the emotional, the intellectual, and the physical. A comprehensive school health program can be designed to reach and enhance all of those areas.

WHY DO WE NEED HEALTH EDUCATION?

For the first time in our history, American teenagers are less healthy, less cared for, and less prepared for life than their parents were at the same age (O'Rourke 1996). Consider for a moment a high school class in the year 1999 of 30 students: Of them, 19 will have used alcohol, 6 will have been drunk within the preceding two weeks, 13 will have had sex at least once, 3 will have a sexually transmitted disease (STD), 10 will think seriously about suicide, and 4 will attempt it (Spalt 1995).

Every hour in America, two teens between the ages of 16 and 24 are diagnosed with AIDS, and three people under the age of 25 die from AIDS (the Centers for Disease Control and Prevention classifies teens as people up to the age of 24). D. J. Anspaugh and G. Ezell (1998) present some intriguing yet disturbing statistics. For example, marijuana is used by 19 percent of tenth graders. Seventy-five percent of all sexually transmitted disease occurs among people ages 15–24. One out of 100 girls between the ages of 12 and 18 suffer from anorexia nervosa (a serious and life-threatening eating disorder), while at the same time, obesity among young people is increasing at an alarming rate. One million teens become pregnant every year.

Each day, firearms kill 16 youths. According to D. L. Kerr and J. L. Gascoigne (1996), homicide is the number one cause of death among African American youths and the second leading cause of death among all adolescents. From 1988 to 1991, the rate of death due to firearms for people 15–24 years of age increased 40 percent (Anspaugh and Ezell 1998). Anspaugh and Ezell also report that the leading causes of death among Americans—heart disease, hypertension, and cancer—are related to lifestyle factors. These factors include lack of exercise, use of tobacco products, poor diets, being overweight, and stress. All of these are *serious* health issues that our young people face. And most of them are preventable.

Because of improved sanitation, advances in vaccines and medication, better hygiene, and education, young people are not plagued with some of the diseases that might have affected them had they been alive a century or more ago. Instead, according to the Centers for Disease Control and Prevention, teens of the 1990s were mostly dealing with issues associated with "risk-taking behaviors," which have both immediate and lasting effects on the individual and our society at large. Many of these are behaviors that can be influenced and changed, for the better, with access to and participation in comprehensive school-based health-education programs.

HEALTH EDUCATION'S FOUNDATION

Health education has been offered in some form almost as long as formal education has existed in the United States. As early as 1818, Harvard

University required that all of its seniors take a course in hygiene. This was innovative for the time, but given the epidemics of the time, it was not such a far-fetched idea. By requiring students to take a course in hygiene, Harvard sent a message to its graduates and society that it considered hygiene to be an important topic as part of a complete education and important for being a successful graduate of their institution.

Nearly 200 years later have we not yet learned from Harvard's initiative? How can we continue to graduate students without comprehensive health education? What messages are we sending to students when we send them off to the workplace, to college, or to engage in interpersonal and romantic relationships, where they often are required to make decisions based on health-related issues?

Consider the decision to get drunk or not the night before an exam. Consider the decision to have unprotected sex or not. Consider the decision to use food as a coping device for depression. Consider the decision to fight with a coworker rather than using conflict-resolution skills. Do we adequately teach students how to recognize such crossroads and make wise decisions? I am rather skeptical of this.

Learning about and having the chance to practice effective interpersonal skills are as important as classical academic curricula; health education considers the whole person, not just the academic part. Just as a person should graduate from high school knowing when the Civil War was, a person should know how to communicate with others and how to make effective decisions. Effective decision making is crucial to all aspects of a successful, healthy, and educated life. One needs to be able to identify the warning signs of alcoholism and how to prevent cardiovascular disease. If people are not emotionally and physically healthy, what good is knowing how to solve a linear equation? To paraphrase a cliché, a sound mind alone is not good; neither is a sound body alone. A healthy, whole, person needs both a sound mind *and* a sound body.

It was not until the late 1800s, with epidemics continuing to plague school-aged children, that health education became a part of the American educational system. Teachers were instructed to make daily health inspections and were required to teach children about health and hygiene. This was a "reactive" or "crisis-oriented" approach to dealing with health and health education, unlike the current focus in health education, which is on prevention.

In the early 1900s, with immigration from Europe on the rise, health education became more common. In fact, support for health education initially came in the mid-1800s from the likes of Horace Mann (an early pioneer in the field of education) and the American Academy of Medicine. The original Cardinal Principles of Secondary Education of 1918 (a U.S. government commission document that promoted active citizenry at the local, state, and national level) stated that "the health of the individual is essential to the vitality of the Nation" (cited in Brophy, Alleman, and O'Mahony 2000). And so it was that health was placed first as one of its educational objectives; a secondary school should encourage good health habits, give health instruction, and provide physical activities.

Good health should be taken into account when schools and communities are planning activities for youth. The general public should be educated on the importance of good health. Teachers should be examples of good health; schools should furnish good equipment and safe buildings (Barger 1998). Reinforcing the aforementioned statement from 1918, physically fit and healthy individuals potentially lead to a vibrant and productive society as a whole. Healthy people (physically and emotionally) are contributors to society rather than people who drain society of its energy and resources.

WHO TEACHES HEALTH EDUCATION?

It has been determined that in order for health education to be effective it must be *taught by qualified health teachers*. However, trained health educators do not teach many classes, and teachers of other subjects are often asked to teach health-related topics. The topics discussed in health education can be extremely sensitive and sometimes difficult to talk about. This requires rigorous training and a comfort level talking about these topics.

The Association for the Advancement of Health Education (AAHE) recommends that all teachers teaching health education at the high school level or higher hold state certification in health education (Summerfield 1992). This comes after a long fight, going back to the 1920s, to enhance qualifications of school health teachers. One of the first graduate programs to offer health education came out of the Harvard-MIT School of Public Health in 1921. Since then, according to L. B. Bensley (1990), there has been an increase in the number of graduate schools, to approximately 140, that offer programs in health education. However, these growing programs have been considered lacking in adequate guidelines and professional standards.

In the 1970s, there was a strong movement to upgrade and redefine qualifications for school health teachers, qualifications that had not been reviewed since the 1940s. According to Anspaugh and Ezell (1998), in 1924, only four schools in the country had certification requirements for its secondary school health-education teachers. Twenty-five years later, only five states provided certification for teachers of health education.

By 1970, 31 states had certification programs for teachers of health education. New York State has been one of those states since the 1940s. However, there was not then nor is there currently a certification plan agreed upon by all of these various states; essentially, there was national discontinuity (Veenker 1971, 1985).

In other professions, such as medicine, law, social work, business administration, and even law enforcement, there are accreditation programs ensuring that graduate programs meet minimum standards in those fields (Bensley 1990). Although there are state guidelines for health-education teachers and some national standards for general teacher education and professionalism, there is only scant collective consensus on standards compared to other professions. In some respects, this is no great surprise, considering the image of teaching compared to other professions in American society.

Of 27 states surveyed between 1949 and 1970, none required health teachers to have a background in all 22 health-related topics noted in the survey; some topics were commonly required. In 1970, states required, on average, approximately 28 hours of health and physical education courses at the college or university level. Each state required that teachers have a background (i.e., course work) in different content areas. Some common content areas ("content area" was defined somewhat differently and more narrowly in 1949 than in 1970, dictating different state requirements, and it may have been viewed interchangeably with "topics") included

- ➛ health counseling
- ➛ community health resources
- ➛ personal health
- ➛ mental health
- ➛ family life and sexuality education
- ➛ accident prevention

New York State's requirements did not change from the 1940s to the 1970s. Teachers were required to have a background in

- ➛ school health programs
- ➛ health counseling
- ➛ personal health
- ➛ community health

•◦ foods and nutrition
•◦ safety education
•◦ first aid
•◦ family life and sex education
•◦ mental health
•◦ accident prevention

No explanation is offered for why certain topics were required rather than others. One can speculate that as times changed and society continued to evolve, the media's potential impact on society's access to information became more widespread and more pronounced; consequently, it became more relevant to teach some health concerns rather than others, requiring health teachers to become familiar with them.

As of 1992, according to L. Summerfield (1992), in 39 different states teachers required certification in health education in order to teach it. However, a study conducted in Texas between 1993 and 1994 (Jacobs and Wylie 1995) revealed that many teachers who teach health have a limited background in health education and not all who teach health are certified to do so. In this study, 205 health teachers were randomly selected from Texas schools to determine who were trained, certified health teachers. Only 50 percent of the respondents held a degree in health education (the vast majority reported only holding a bachelor's degree; a mere 7.8 percent held a master's degree). Of those not holding a health-education degree, teachers reported holding degrees in various disciplines, including history, biology, English, home economics, and physical education.

Of full-time teacher respondents (based on school employment status, not subject-specific teaching load), 64 percent reported having a combined certification in health and physical education. Full-time teachers were twice as interested in pursuing a master's degree as were their part-time counterparts. However, more than 47 percent of part-time respondents reported having certification in other content areas (e.g., biology, home economics). Only one respondent was a Certified Health Education Specialist (CHES, i.e., health education was this respondent's only area of certification and teaching duties). When asked about their level of confidence as health teachers, those with no background in health education expressed a significantly lower level (Jacobs and Wylie 1995).

Since 1989, the National Commission for Health Education Credentialing (NCHEC) has offered certification independent of state requirements. Any person who has a bachelor's degree with a health emphasis (either a bachelor's degree specifically in health education or a

general bachelor's degree with a major in it) can take the NCHEC certification exam and become a CHES. According to Summerfield (1992),
the exam measures competency in the following areas:

- assessing, planning, implementing, and evaluating health
  education programs
- coordinating provision of services; acting as a health resource person
- communicating health and health education needs, concerns, and resources

At this time, there is no designed coordination between CHES and state
certification programs, although this would be a way to develop some
types of national standards for health education teachers.

A study conducted by the School Health Policies Program Study
(SHPPS) found that only 4.4 percent of all lead teachers (i.e., teachers essentially in charge of a subject area, such as a subject coordinator) majored in health education; less than half (46.2 percent) were state certified in health education (Collins et al. 1995). Most disturbing of these
results was that 10 percent of participants reported having no background whatsoever in health education (Jacobs and Wylie 1995).

Although 10 percent may seem like a small percentage, what
would be our reaction if that one-in-ten teacher was the one teaching
health to our children? Would we want an art-certified teacher teaching
our children chemistry? Or a math-certified teacher teaching Spanish
class? Generally, no. For many reasons, there are many "misplaced/mis-
hired" teachers who are teaching outside of their certification fields, but
teaching in fields distantly related to what one is certified for presents a
major concern. When it comes to "important" (i.e., classical academic)
subjects, we take great exception to out-of-field classroom teachers.

However, because health education is not considered as "important" as other subjects, schools do not set standards or requirements for
who should teach this subject. Consequently, when a health-education
teacher is out of field, the alarm is not as great, for obvious reasons.
Somehow, health education is not viewed as vitally academic or as a
subject that could make or break a child's academic progress or career.
Is health education emphasized on the SAT or American College Testing
(ACT) exam? Is one's grade in health education taken into account for
college admissions? Do we typically view health education as a "real
major" for college? Health education is viewed somewhat as an ap-
pendage of compulsory education; we tend not to place high value on it.

Another disturbing result noted by the SHPPS was that 13 percent of the full-time health-education teachers surveyed reported a prefer-ence to teach something other than health education, even though all respondents felt health education was "as important as other courses." By comparison, 93.3 percent of the part-time health education teach-ers surveyed felt that health education is as important as other topics; more than 23 percent of these teachers would rather be teaching some-thing else.

Such findings are very upsetting. It is hard to believe such senti-ments are not somehow conveyed through classroom teaching. Thus, at the very least, a subtle message is sent to students that health education is unimportant or less important than other subjects taken in school; health education is potentially deemed "trivial."

Many teachers in the SHPPS reported wishing they had received more training and professional development, especially in the areas of alcohol and drug use, conflict resolution, emotional and mental health, and suicide prevention. The SHPPS reported that within the two years prior to this study, most districts (83.6 percent) offered training to health educators. The most common topics were HIV prevention, alcohol and drug use, STD prevention, tobacco use prevention, and conflict resolu-tion. This request came from people who (supposedly) had a back-ground in health education but wanted more training. Imagine what type of training a person who does not have a background in health ed-ucation might need.

According to the New York State Department of Education, stu-dents in New York City are required to graduate from high school with only one semester of health education (quite inadequate, and I will ex-plain why later). Many schools, including the one where I taught, out of my licensed field, as a dance and reading teacher, get away with not of-fering a health-education class by incorporating some topics (e.g., HIV/AIDS, reproduction/anatomy) into biology classes. In fact, in many southern rural school districts in the United States, health education is considered taboo, since it is often synonymous with sex education, often banned where religious conservatism is dominant.

Additionally, some alternative high schools, such as the one where I taught, conduct "advisory classes," which are comparable to homeroom periods in larger public schools. Teachers are instructed to offer health-related lessons during their advisory classes. Many teachers I have spoken with feel inadequately trained to offer effective lessons on today's health topics, let alone a semester's worth of lessons.

In the six years the school where I formerly taught has been op-erating, there has never been a single health-education class. When I asked my former principal why, she told me that it is more cost-effective to have health topics taught in biology classes and that many of her colleagues at other small, alternative high schools share the same view and do not have separate health teachers. It leaves one to wonder which is worse: eliminating health education because of community norms or teaching health education on the cheap.

This is problematic, given the health-related issues facing today's youths. If not in school, where they spend eight hours a day, where are children supposed to receive information about health and health-promoting behaviors? Schools are logical places to provide health information, not only to improve health during the childhood years but also to prevent illness, disability, and health care costs later in life. Health education literally empowers students to avoid health risks (Summerfield 1992).

WHAT DO I DO NOW?

I was frustrated at my situation. I grew comfortable at the school where I was teaching; I got along well with the faculty and the students and hoped the principal would find the funds to hire me as the health teacher. When that did not happen, I decided that over the summer, I would explore teaching opportunities at other public high schools. With stellar letters of recommendations and "real" teaching experience, I thought for sure I would have no problem getting hired as a high school health teacher.

Feeling very confident, I took all of my papers, letters of recommendations, completed forms, and blank money orders to 65 Court Street (home of the New York City Board of Education). I hoped that, in exchange, I would walk out with my health-education license and a list of schools looking to hire a qualified, licensed health teacher that coming fall.

I could not have been more disillusioned! When I met with a staff person from the Board of Education to discuss any possible openings, I was told there was an "excess of health teachers" and no openings at this time. Year after year, as budgets get cut, positions for health teachers get cut as well, because as already mentioned, many positions for health teachers go to physical education teachers, because they can be hired to fill what are essentially two positions. Because of the view of health education as "trivial," schools sometimes do not offer enough health-education classes to justify hiring a full-time health teacher. Teachers with multiple certification areas are as valuable as gold, especially when they can help fill multiple gaps within a school's schedule.

Perhaps I should have pursued multiple certifications and taken advantage of my other "talents" (English and dancing). Perhaps that would have made me more marketable. Perhaps I would have solid job security. Then again, perhaps I would still never get to teach health education.

Over the summer, I continued to receive invitations to attend job fairs sponsored by the Board of Education and letters indicating which districts were hiring and in which subjects. In all of those forms, letters, and job announcements, I did not see one opening for high school health teachers. So I began looking outside of the Board of Education. I really wanted to stay within the fields of secondary education and health education, if at all possible.

I was lucky enough to be hired to direct an after-school program at a Manhattan high school. As the director, I oversee all aspects of programming and have designed the program so there is a health-and-wellness component, allowing me to still "teach" within my area of expertise. Is this necessarily what I ideally planned for myself? No, not really; however, I know I am finally in the right place at the right time for me. I have some degree of professional security, and my education and interests are not going to waste.

It is sad to think I could not have my fair opportunity to affect an entire high school of kids in need of comprehensive health education. But the system had more influence on the circumstances than I could. I am not sure that I would ever be able to go back to teaching as a classroom teacher for the Board of Education. So far, the Board of Education has not needed me in the appropriate way I needed to be needed. It certainly made things extremely difficult for me to be able to make a contribution in my chosen area, and I do not hold much optimism that this will change in the near future.

My experiences present a unique challenge to the teaching profession. On one hand, we strive to become well-trained experts in our field of passion. On the other hand, educational systems essentially dictate to us which fields are worthy of passion and which ones are not. Consequently, many teachers, like myself, are caught in a certification no-man's-land, unable to teach in our appropriate subject area because we are not "needed" or deemed "vital." The choices we are then left with are very difficult and challenge our desire to stick with our beliefs and find our proper niche in education.

Although some (e.g., Friedman 2000; Ingersoll 1999) debate the issues of underqualified and miscertified teachers in American secondary schools, I think we need to go beyond the tabulation of data. Yes, there are many unqualified and uncertified teachers in our classrooms today, but the onus to improve this situation is not simply limited to teacher education programs. State departments of education need to better conceptualize their school curricula and requirements for teacher subject-area certification. These same departments need to have better-articulation agreements with colleges and universities (much like ministries of education do in Canada and several European countries). Unless there is better communication among departments of education, school systems, and colleges and universities, either curricular or staffing loopholes will continue to exist. As long as those loopholes continue to exist, teachers will continue to be misplaced or hired for the "wrong reasons," ending up as negative statistics for educational leaders, researchers, and policymakers to debate.

REFERENCES

Anspaugh, D. J., and G. Ezell. 1998. *Teaching Today's Health.* 5th ed. Boston: Allyn and Bacon.

Barger, R. N. 1998. "The Cardinal Principles of Secondary Education. History of American Education Web Project." Web site: *http://www.ux1.eiu.edu/~cfrnb.*

Bensley, L. B. 1990. "A Perspective on Lack of Continuity and Standards for Master's Degree Programs in Health Education and Health Promotion." *Health Education* 21, no. 2: 59–60.

Brophy, J., J. Alleman, and C. O'Mahony. 2000. "Elementary School Social Studies: Yesterday, Today, and Tomorrow." Pp. 256–312 in *American Education: Yesterday, Today, and Tomorrow.* Edited by T. L. Good. Chicago: National Society for the Study of Education.

Collins, J. L., M. L. Small, L. Kann, B. C. Pateman, R. S. Gold, and L. J. Kolbe. 1995. "School Health Education." *Journal of School Health* 65, no. 8: 302–311.

Friedman, S. J. 2000. "How Much of a Problem? A Reply to Ingersoll's 'The Problem of Underqualified Teachers in American Secondary Schools.'" *Educational Researcher* 29, no. 5: 18–20.

Ingersoll, R. M. 1999. "The Problem of Underqualified Teachers in American Secondary Schools." *Educational Researcher* 28, no. 2: 26–37.

Jacobs, W. J., and W. E. Wylie. 1995. "Who Teaches Health Education in Texas Secondary Schools?" *Journal of School Health* 65, no. 9: 365–369.

Kerr, D. L., and J. L. Gascoigne. 1996. "Getting To Know Generation X: Health Education for the Thirteenth Generation." *Journal of Health Education* 27, no. 5: 268–272.

O'Rourke, T. 1996. "A Comprehensive School Health Program To Improve Health and Education." *Education* 116, no. 4, 490–494.

Spalt, S. W. 1995. "A Letter to My Principal." *Journal of School Health* 65, no. 2: 69–70.

Summerfield, L. 1992. "Comprehensive School Health Education." ERIC Clearinghouse on Teacher Education.

Veenker, C. H. 1985. "Future Options: Professional Preparation Programs in Health Education." *Health Education* 15, no. 7: 36–38.

———. 1971. "Certification of Health Educators: A Priority for the Seventies." *School Health Review* 2, no. 1: 3–7.

Chapter Eight

☛ The Probationary Period

What is this "probationary period"? What is the concept of "probation"? It is common practice for an employer to hire new employees on a probationary (or "trial") basis. Perhaps the new employee struggles to perform his or her duties. Perhaps he or she conducts him- or herself unprofessionally. Employers need to protect themselves, their organizations, and their customers from unsatisfactory employees. If a new employee performs unsatisfactorily within a given period of time (typically between 30 days and six months), an employer can terminate him or her.

However, what if the organization in question is a school? What would define the probationary period? Although some advocate applying organizational (e.g., corporate) principles to educational settings (e.g., Senge 1990), the transfer is somewhat incomplete. For example, it is difficult to hire teachers the same way salespeople or office workers are hired. Granted, we are in an era of downsizing that views workers as generic, interchangeable cogs (e.g., Kincheloe 1995, 1999; McLaren and Farahmandpur 2000, 2001). However, teachers are not typical workers.

Usually, one cannot simply terminate a teacher and immediately hire a replacement (although such things can and do occur under certain conditions). First, as discussed in Chapter 6, the United States is supposedly experiencing a critical teacher shortage in many subject areas and many geographic regions. If teachers were instantaneously replaceable, we would neither have this teacher shortage, nor would we certify teachers through crisis-oriented methods.

Second, we need to consider the continuity of a classroom. Imagine a schoolchild whose teacher was terminated after the first week of classes. For better or worse, this teacher just spent a week establishing some initial level of rapport with the students, and vice versa for the students. Now a new teacher comes in for the second week. The process begins anew. Yes, there are circumstances where teachers need to be replaced during a school year (e.g., illness, death, pregnancy, resignation, or necessary termination), but schools either plan for these circumstances or try to best minimize their occurrence.

During my high school teaching career, I worked in two different schools that experienced "musical biology teachers." In each case, students encountered four different biology teachers during one school year. In most cases, the changes were made at the end of marking periods or semesters. However, for one school, during a four-week period (approximately half of a marking period), students encountered three new teachers after their original teacher resigned at the end of the first semester. The first new teacher began the third marking period and new semester but, less than two weeks later, was offered a very lucrative job with a biomedical company and immediately resigned. Certainly, this teacher was not particularly committed to being a teacher and may very well have been filling in time between jobs. The second teacher came on board, but the students were so angry over losing two teachers within less than a month that they rebelled against teacher number 3. This apparently was stressful for the teacher, for he died of a heart attack after only six days on the job. Needless to say, when teacher number 4 finally arrived, her job was very difficult, for she not only needed to deal with the subject matter and the students, she had to bring stability to a classroom in turmoil.

The probationary period for schoolteachers is influenced by three factors: (1) supply and demand, (2) classroom continuity, and (3) the developmental curve for teachers. This third factor reflects two premises. The first is that teachers need at least three years to develop their classroom skills. The second is that many teachers leave the profession within three years. This contributes to a common policy of granting teachers tenure after three years of service.

What is tenure? Tenure's roots began in the late 1800s at the university level (e.g., Tierney 1997). The original premise of tenure somewhat resembles the arrangement Laban the Syrian made with Jacob in biblical times: Jacob wanted to marry Laban's younger daughter, Rachel, and he agreed to seven years of servitude in order to earn her hand in matrimony. Of course, as we remember, Laban tricked Jacob by giving away his elder daughter, Leah, forcing Jacob to labor yet another seven years for his second, and most beloved, wife. But the number seven, ever since biblical days, has been significant in terms of servitude and reward (e.g., sabbaticals or freedom). In fact, the first system of tenure reflected a seven-year period of service (today, it can also reflect three or five years).

This still leads us back to the question, however, of what tenure is. Tenure is essentially an institutional reward for a period of service. The reward is guaranteed employment for life. That is right. Unless a teacher does something criminal or immoral, he or she is essentially protected from termination after a given number of years of service (in schools, it is typically three).

Why should we have tenure? Of what value is it for teachers, schools, and communities? There are pros and cons to the concept of tenure. In fact, tenure is under attack in American education, especially for professors in higher education (e.g., Tierney 1997). However, as President George W. Bush's educational agenda gathers momentum, tenure for schoolteachers will come under increasing scrutiny nationwide.

What are some pros of tenure? First, tenure ensures protection for teachers, especially those who are considered misfits or who are somewhat removed from the mainstream viewpoint of their school. Second, tenure provides economic security for teachers. This is important, considering the specialized roles and professional skills teachers spend many years developing. Salaries are not particularly high compared to those of other professions; the ability to provide for oneself and one's family is not only critical for adults in general (e.g., Knowles 1970, 1980) but very important to teachers (e.g., Lanier and Little 1986). Third, tenure helps ensure continuity and stability within a school. If a school has a high turnover rate among teachers, it becomes increasingly difficult to develop a sense of community within and beyond that school.

What are some cons of tenure? First, although tenure provides some protection for academic freedom and from persecution, we must wonder whether guaranteed permanent employment makes sense in our present economy of budget deficits (e.g., Tierney 1997). If there are many tenured teachers at a school, they may consume a great deal of a school's fiscal budget, thus limiting employment opportunities for younger teachers.

Second, tenure may give carte blanche to veteran teachers to do whatever they want, possibly to the detriment of students, the school culture, and the community at large. For example, suppose a teacher is tenured and protected from persecution for his or her political views. What if this teacher advocates homophobia, racism, or anti-Semitism? Although free speech is protected by the First Amendment of the U.S. Constitution, there is a limit to how far a teacher may exercise free speech and still be a community role model.

Third, critics of tenure are concerned that if tenure guarantees employment for the remainder of a career, a faculty will lack any incentive to care and grow together. Although tenure brings protection, it also potentially brings privilege and power. Perhaps it brings hegemony, in which tenured teachers, for the sake of their own selfish agendas, suppress the development of untenured teachers. Consequently, young teachers are forced to conform to the dominant political view for self-preservation. To go against the old guard could trigger retaliation.

However, the most significant con about tenure relates to inertia. The more tenured teachers in a school, perhaps the more complacent they become, regardless of politics. Critics of tenure fear that teachers and their schools will become stale, unmotivated, and unproductive. Worse, tenure potentially protects incompetent teachers who have survived long enough to put in their time yet do not contribute positively to meaningful learning.

As is the case in various industries, especially professional sports, debate has focused on alternatives to tenure, such as variable contracts in short-term, long-term, and renewable forms (e.g., Tierney 1997). Merit pay and restructured salaries with incentives (akin to commissions) have also been discussed but have met with considerable opposition. At the present time, there appears to be no easy alternative. Tenure is a loaded issue, for it preserves the viability of the teaching profession yet potentially causes schools' effectiveness to stagnate.

TEACHING EXPECTATIONS

Teachers want to be evaluated fairly by people who understand the context of the teaching environment and subject matter. There needs to be some genuine due process involved, where teachers are held to high yet relatively equal standards. New teachers (as discussed in Chapter 4) do not appreciate being dumped into classroom environments without any guidance or support network. It takes time for new teachers to grow into their professionalism and become part of school communities and cultures. As new teachers are evaluated for contract renewal and tenure, the concept of professional growth needs to be foremost in our consideration.

Unfortunately, this is not always the case. Teachers are often evaluated not on the basis of their effectiveness or competence but on the basis of how well they conform to or comply with the dominant paradigm of teaching in a school (e.g., Kincheloe and Steinberg 1998). As noted in Chapter 1, we live in an impatient, "want it now" society. Consequently, those evaluating and guiding new teachers often place their own pragmatic agendas ahead of teacher development; this often alienates new teachers and contributes to a very short teaching career.

Needless to say, what new teachers' expectations are differ considerably from what expectations of them are. Not too long ago in one of my newspapers, I saw a cartoon whose caption read, "The role of a teacher." The picture showed a teacher standing over a seated student whose head was opened as if his skull was the lid of a box. The teacher poured something from a bucket labeled "curriculum" into the student's head, saying, "We have lots to give today. . . . we're getting ready for accountability testing." In many respects, achievement on accountability tests is all that schools seem to expect of new teachers. They are expected to cover the course content or adopted curriculum as quickly as possible to be ready for standardized testing. Never mind innovative pedagogical techniques or meaningful learning. Teachers need to "deliver the goods" (e.g., Jenkins 2001; Pushkin 2001) as efficiently as possible, verify their delivery, and hope for validating results.

Teaching is a multidimensional, multitask job. However, as states move closer and closer toward technocratic, inflexible, and unforgiving outcomes-based curricula, teaching (as a consequence of crisis mode policy) becomes one-dimensional. As long as the bottom line of accountability testing is met to a school's satisfaction, all other sins can be forgiven. As discussed earlier in this chapter, some relatively incompetent teachers manage to survive long enough at a school to gain tenure and are thus protected from termination, regardless of their classroom effectiveness.

Perhaps "effectiveness" has multiple meanings. Perhaps it can only be defined in terms of test scores. What is the implication? A teacher who perhaps does not demonstrate good pedagogical practice (according to our ever-evolving theories), does not have good rapport with the students, or does not advocate critical thinking and meaningful learning yet who manages to produce high test scores every year may very well be viewed as an excellent teacher. Conversely, a teacher who does demonstrate, promote, and advocate the good things theorists envision may very well find him- or herself unemployed if test scores are not living up to school standards and expectations.

Case in point: Consider a former student teacher I supervised in New York City. This particular student teacher was assigned to a Regents-level biology class in a large high school. All students would be required to pass the state Regents Exam at the end of the year in order to be promoted to the next year of science (typically chemistry) and to be on-pace for graduation. The stakes are high (we should not forget what happened to Biff Loman, in *Death of a Salesman;* he failed his algebra Regents Exam, and this led to his path of being a journeyman). This teacher's student teaching experience was not much different from what was described in Chapter 4. He was thrown into an overcrowded classroom to teach an outcomes-based curriculum during the middle of the school year. His mentor was a second-year teacher, so the guidance he received came with little experience behind it.

This student teacher was very thoughtful of the content, his students, and the classroom environment (he had graduated from this high school four years earlier). He tried to ask probing questions, stimulate genuine critical thinking, and promote genuine learning. Granted, he showed signs of inexperience, primarily in terms of how he prepared materials for lessons and answered questions, but these were things he would outgrow. His potential to be a wonderful biology teacher was clearly evident. Consequently, all of my feedback was given within the context of "when you become a little older and wiser." I did not want him to dramatically change his teaching style or expectations; I wanted him to evolve naturally and grow more conscious of himself as an educator.

Unfortunately, this was not how his mentor saw things. With each passing week, she continuously reminded him that developing his teaching skills and promoting critical thinking were all well and good, but *the Regents was coming! The Regents was coming!* There was still so much to cover of the curriculum before the class began reviewing for the exam. Her advice was that he needed to teach faster; to not worry about the depth of the content but just to cover the high points of it; to not waste time asking questions but to tell the students what they needed to know. Considering that her job depended on those exam scores, his certification suddenly depended on them too. What if he could not do as expected? The implications are scary. The students do not "learn" everything they are supposed to (to what degree any of this is related to learning is still a mystery). They do poorly on the Regents Exam, and their teacher's job is in jeopardy. She gives the student teacher a bad evaluation, he possibly fails to receive his certificate and is potentially unemployable as an incompetent teacher.

ADMINISTRATIVE EXPECTATIONS

Administrators face difficult dilemmas, in part because of the various (and potentially competing) demands on them. However, the paradigm they were indoctrinated into also plays a role (see Chapter 9). School administrators, as noted in Chapters 1, 6, and 10, are often forced to run their schools in crisis mode. Will every classroom have a teacher by the first day of a school year? How many teachers will be certified, and how many will be teaching out of field? How many teachers will be lost from the following year, and how many new hires are needed? These are some of the pragmatic questions administrators deal with on an annual basis.

We can add issues of accountability testing, school safety, and professional and ethical standards on top of this; even these issues do not
present the full scope of the challenges facing administrators.

In many respects, administrators have very fundamental questions in mind when evaluating a new teacher during the probationary
period. Can the teacher do the job? This is the overarching question, but
it has multiple dimensions. For example, the teacher needs to provide a
conducive learning environment for students. This may or may not simply come down to test scores and grades. There may be issues of pedagogical style to consider. There may be issues of rapport with students.
There may be issues of how the teacher relates to his or her departmental and schoolwide colleagues. Good classroom practice may or may not
translate to good political or public relations.

Administrators, perhaps because of their environmental and paradigmatic context, do not always appear to have time to help new teachers develop or veteran teachers evolve. Development and evolution are
long-term processes and quite individual. Administrators do not always
take this into account.

Consider the discussion of the "Seven Step Lesson Plan" developed in the 1970s (see Chapter 2). Allegedly, Madeline Hunter recommended a prescribed set of features that lesson units should ideally
have. However, as discussed in Chapter 2, school administrators and
teacher supervisors drastically truncated this notion from lesson units
to individual lessons. Who has time to observe the evolution of perhaps
a month or semester-long lesson unit when an individual lesson may
only require 30 to 50 minutes? Consequently, rather than being able to
demonstrate all seven lesson features over an extended period of time,
teachers are forced to demonstrate them within a single lesson.

What are the potential implications? Administrators, who may
only observe/evaluate a new teacher less than a handful of times during
a school year, enter classrooms armed with a rubric. There is no time, in
their minds, to contextualize the teacher, the subject area, the subject
matter, the grade level, or the time of day, week, or year. The observa-
tion/evaluation needs to be efficient, consistent, and unambiguous.

Yes, we would like the process to be fair, equitable, and consistent. We would not want administrators prejudicing themselves against
science teachers because science is viewed not as positively as social
studies or English (or vice versa). However, we cannot afford to make the
process so generic that administrators expect science teachers to teach
exactly like English teachers and social studies teachers to teach exactly
like mathematics teachers. We also cannot afford administrators to presume that pedagogical approaches appropriate for elementary class-

rooms serve just as well for secondary or middle school classrooms. Unfortunately, this is what rubricized observation/evaluation approaches imply: that teachers are generic, teaching is generic, and administrators are forced to decontextualize classrooms in order to do their jobs efficiently. Sadly, this forces teachers to comply with a rubric in order to be deemed competent. The practice of observing/evaluating teaching becomes contrived.

Case in point: When I taught high school chemistry and physics, my administrators would not observe me during laboratory activities. Why not? They presumed that no real teaching or learning was taking place (which leads one to wonder why anyone advocates hands-on learning). What they really intended was that the rubric they used to observe/evaluate my teaching was inappropriate for laboratory settings. In fact, it was inappropriate for cooperative group activities, not to mention constructivist-guided activities or any activity where students were actively engaged with the subject matter. The rubric intended students to be passively seated in rows, following the teacher's lead in the lesson. The teacher talks or presents, asks questions, calls on students, listens to replies, provides reinforcement and feedback, and continues until closure at the end of the lesson.

We teachers referred to this observation/evaluation experience as the "dog and pony show." We all despised it, but my administrators felt morally bound to it, for their superiors (e.g., district superintendents or state education leaders/politicians) imposed it on them. It was their duty. They did not care about my teaching (although they worried about complaints from students and parents); they only cared on the days when we had to be collectively accountable. It was a struggle. Conformity and compliance were, and still are to some degree, contrary to my nature. Somehow, I forced myself to conform to the rubric as best I could without compromising my principles and beliefs too much. However, those days led me to seriously question my reasons for being an educator and often caused me to loathe myself as an educator. No one was really fulfilled on those days, not I, not my students, and not my administrators; only the rubric itself would be fulfilled, and it was an inanimate piece of paper.

But what can administrators do? They advance into their professional level guided by a technocratic efficiency paradigm, and somehow they need to oversee entire schools with a diversity of educators and learning contexts, some of which may be completely outside their experience. Although administrators are generally sensitive to the distinctions between various grade levels and subject areas, they are not yet armed with the genuine means to observe/evaluate educators contextually. They are essentially caught between the expectations of theory and the realities of practice (e.g., Clark and Clark 1996). This will be discussed further in Chapter 9.

COMMUNITY EXPECTATIONS

Community expectations can be simultaneously simplistic and complex, as we gradually sensed back in Chapter 1. On one hand, parents want schools to be safe and their children to be respected, properly taught, and successful. Parents also want their teachers and administrators to be competent (if not the very best), their schools to be academically accountable, and their concerns to be taken seriously, especially when their children's futures are at stake.

On the other hand, taxpayers, who may or may not have children in school (or children at all), want schools to be cost-effective, efficient, and fiscally justifiable. Local politicians and other community leaders share similar concerns. As we discovered in both Chapters 1 and 6, communities do not enjoy knowing their schools may be the worst in their state. The United States is a rank-oriented nation; being number one is of high priority. No one particularly enjoys being last.

It is generally accepted in American society that education is a key to our societal future. Whether discussing John Dewey at the dawn of the twentieth century, educational leaders in the wake of Sputnik, or our presidents since *A Nation at Risk* was published, the United States continually looks to its public schools for the next generation of societal leaders and contributors. That being said, the expectations placed on public schools are extremely high, and the scrutiny placed on teachers continues to increase. Although schools have their own probationary mechanisms for new teachers, we must be mindful in this era of hyper-accountability and politically laced rhetoric that society sees *all* teachers as being on probation, not just new ones. It remains to be seen how secure *any* teacher, regardless of tenure, feels in the profession. Professional policy and union practices notwithstanding, expendability is becoming more and more the reality.

DISCUSSION

So what is the "take-home" lesson about tenure? Tenure provides a means of professional protection and security for educators. Tenure helps bring stability to schools and community. However, tenure is also viewed as archaic, evil (perhaps "detrimental" is a better word), and out of step with the corporate and capitalist paradigm driving the United States and other nations. Tenure is branded as one of the key causes of educational decline, and yet we are still flailing away at what the specific causes of educational decline are, what characterizes this decline, and when this decline definitively began.

We cannot deny that teachers are under some level of heightened suspicion and scrutiny. Professional security is caught amid the battle lines between politicians, teachers' unions, communities, and financially strapped school districts. Everyone wants results yesterday, and heads are expected to roll if results are not as desired. No new teacher needs to be put in such a conflict, yet this is the current climate of the profession.

Perhaps the one overarching issue in this chapter is that of compliance (or conformity). With all the complex and competing demands that politicians, community leaders, and educational leaders place on schools today, administrators appear to seek the path of least resistance regarding how their schools function. Perhaps they know no better; perhaps they have no other choice. From their perspective, perhaps it is much more effective (or at least efficient) to run a school (or manage school reform) uniformly. To what degree does individualism contradict the "company line"? This is perhaps a critical question.

It is interesting that in an era of looking at learners as individuals, we do not apply the same perspective to teachers (e.g., Rhine 1998). Just recently, in a conversation, I likened learners to snowflakes; no two are supposed to be identical. Upon reflection, I wondered if the same could be true about teachers. Teachers are individual and unique. They have a specific context within education (e.g., content related, pedagogy related, geography related, or school/grade related). And yet they are often evaluated according to a generic rubric, and their professionalism is decontextualized. One could argue that the probationary period is a relatively short time in which one plays the game, keeps one's nose clean, and does as the Romans do in order to achieve tenure and security. In many respects, this is the ultimate in multiplicity (e.g., Perry 1970). However, such chameleon-like behavior could ultimately become cognitive capitulation (Pushkin 2001).

As a parting thought, please consider the following vignette:

> *It's funny. . . . when I first joined the faculty, the dean asked me to submit my personal philosophy of teaching and learning. I struggled for hours, sitting in front of a blank computer screen, trying to figure out what my philosophy was and how to put it in writing. I thought I had a vision of*

what my lecture classes should look like, but writing about it wasn't easy. One of the senior faculty [Dr. A] came by my office, and handed me a two-page thing, and said "You don't need to worry about that stuff; here's your philosophy of teaching and learning." It was basically the same thing everyone used when they first got here. I thought it was weird, but these are the guys who will determine my tenure. Hey, five years isn't so long. . . . eventually I'll get my tenure, and can develop my own way of teaching General Chemistry. The only problem is it's five years later, and I can't remember what I wanted to do anymore. Oh well; at least I have a routine down pat. (Pushkin 2001)

What can we infer from these thoughts? Here was a new professor in a university chemistry department whose superiors dictated what his teaching philosophy and practice should be. Recognizing the potential reward for conformity, he adopted this departmental philosophy. After winning his reward (i.e., tenure), he sought to regain his own individualism; ultimately, he failed to do so. This is why tenure is criticized, whether at the K–12 or college/university levels. The reward and punishment system is based not on competence or merit but on the replication of an existing paradigm. Although tenure is supposed to protect those who subscribe to nonmainstream practices, one can only wonder how many actually gain tenure if their practices are nonmainstream during the probationary period. In an obscene way, although tenure allows us to be ourselves, we cannot expect to gain tenure by being ourselves.

REFERENCES

Clark, D. C., and S. N. Clark. 1996. "Better Preparation of Educational Leaders." *Educational Researcher* 25, no. 8: 18–20.

Jenkins, E. W. 2001. "Research in Science Education in Europe: Retrospect and Perspective." Pp. 17–26 in *Research in Science Education: Past, Present, and Future*. Edited by H. Behrendt et al. Dordrecht, The Netherlands: Kluwer Academic Publishers.

Kincheloe, J. L. 1999. "Trouble Ahead, Trouble Behind: Grounding the Post-Formal Critique of Educational Psychology." Pp. 1–54 in *The Post-Formal Reader: Cognition and Education*. Edited by J. Kincheloe, S. Steinberg, and P. H. Hinchey. New York: Garland Publishers.

———. 1995. *Toil and Trouble: Good Work, Smart Workers, and the Integration of Academic and Vocational Education.* New York: Peter Lang.

Kincheloe, J. L., and S. R. Steinberg. 1998. "Lesson Plans from the Outer Limits: Unauthorized Methods." Pp. 1–23 in *Unauthorized Methods: Strategies for Critical Teaching.* Edited by J. Kincheloe and S. Steinberg. New York: Routledge.

Knowles, M. S. 1980. *The Modern Practice of Adult Education.* Englewood Cliffs, NJ: Prentice Hall Regents.

——. 1970. *The Modern Practice of Adult Education: Andragogy versus Pedagogy.* New York: Association Press.

Lanier, J. E., and J. W. Little. 1986. "Research on Teacher Education." Pp. 527–569 in *Handbook of Research on Teaching,* 3rd ed. Edited by M. C. Wittrock. New York: Macmillan.

McLaren, P., and R. Farahmandpur. 2001. "Teaching against Globalization and the New Imperialism: Toward a Revolutionary Pedagogy." *Journal of Teacher Education* 52, no. 2: 136–150.

——. 2000. "Reconsidering Marx in Post-Marxist Times." *Educational Researcher* 29, no. 3: 25–33.

Perry, W. G. 1970. *Forms of Intellectual and Ethical Development in the College Years: A Scheme.* New York: Holt, Rinehart, and Winston.

Pushkin, D. B. 2001. "Cookbook Classrooms; Cognitive Capitulation." In *(Post) Modern Science (Education).* Edited by J. Weaver, P. Appelbaum, and M. Morris. New York: Peter Lang. In press.

Rhine, S. 1998. "The Role of Research and Teachers' Knowledge Base in Professional Development." *Educational Researcher* 27, no. 5: 27–31.

Senge, P. 1990. *The Fifth Discipline: The Art and Practice of the Learning Organization.* New York: Doubleday.

Tierney, W. G. 1997. "Tenure and Community in Academe." *Educational Researcher* 26, no. 8: 17–23.

Chapter Nine

❧ Professional Development

The purpose of this chapter is to discuss professional development in terms of graduate education and professional advancement. As academic credential requirements increase for classroom teachers, school-administrator and district-administrator certification and master's and doctoral degree programs become a more prevalent part of teachers' professional lives. Although these degrees represent credentials and opportunities for advancement, we might be better off viewing them in terms of professional enhancement, that is, as an enhancement of intellectual foundations or an opportunity for intellectual growth.

The reason I take such a tepid view of graduate programs is multidimensional. To begin with, several states now require a master's degree for permanent classroom certification, giving the mistaken impression that such a degree is no longer as valuable as it once was. Second, as noted by Lanier and Little (1986) and touched upon in Chapter 3, many master's degree programs are either added onto bachelor's degree programs or serve as alternative-certification programs for change-of-career professionals. Such programs are primarily aimed at the acquisition and mastery of competency skills rather than at presenting intellectual perspectives on teaching and learning.

Years ago, a master's degree had special significance for teachers. It represented an intellectual endeavor beyond minimal education. Teachers were nicely rewarded for this degree in terms of increased salary and opportunity within their school systems. But if every teacher were required to have a master's degree, it would no longer seem special or unique, for it would represent a minimal credential. Therefore, we need to reflect on what the ultimate purpose of graduate-level teacher education might be.

GRADUATE EDUCATION'S INFLUENCE

According to Lanier and Little (1986), the image of teachers' and teacher educators' family and academic backgrounds is less than flattering. For instance, teachers are typically thought to come from unskilled or skilled-laboring families, possibly being the first members of the family to go to college. This perceived lower-middle-class socioeconomic background included the notion that teachers attended local colleges (rather than large universities far away) for their training and consequently brought with them very localized perspectives about the world and the education profession.

Because of their families' vocational backgrounds, these prospective teachers expected their teacher education programs to focus primarily on job-skills mastery and task completion (Lanier and Little 1986). In other words, such prospective teachers view teaching as an occupation rather than a profession. To paraphrase a dictionary definition, an *occupation* is an activity that engages much of one's time. On the other hand, a *profession* is a vocation requiring advanced education and involving intellectual skills. As a result, such prospective teachers consider education courses well grounded in theory irrelevant to their adult goals, for there is not enough concreteness for them (Lanier and Little 1986).

Local teacher education programs more than accommodate the localized and concrete perspectives of prospective teachers. As noted in Chapter 3, these prospective teachers are trained according to a prescriptive and programmatic curriculum in which methods and skills-mastery courses are more dominant than intellectually focused theory and practice and foundations courses. Consequently, the intellectual norms of teacher education programs are viewed as being considerably lower than such norms for universities as a whole (e.g., Lanier and Little 1986). This localized, prescriptive, conservative occupational training effectively denies prospective teachers an opportunity to encounter alternative views or to develop breadth of perspective, tolerance of non-conformity, and intellectual flexibility. The dualism and cognitive stunting of classroom teachers is not necessarily their fault, for this is how higher education has prepared them for the professional world (Kincheloe and Steinberg 1998). However, there is not much resistance on the part of teachers regarding this practice (e.g., Kincheloe 1992, 1993).

So what happens after teachers earn initial bachelor's degrees and certification for the classroom? Perhaps they are "fortunate" enough to find a teaching position in the school district they were formally educated in and may even have student taught in. Perpetuating the localized perspective, teachers may seek to return to their *cocoon of familiarity*. In some cases, this may be the result of genuinely noble intentions, as in the case of young teachers seeking to give back to their communities. Nevertheless, returning to a former school may give new teachers a false security, attributable to the notion that they already know the terrain and, more importantly, know the routine. They may not feel there is anything new to be learned beyond an experiential apprenticeship. They spent many years observing how their teachers did things. In some respects, those teachers may have been their inspiration to become a teacher, possibly for altruistic reasons, possibly for misguided reasons.

Perhaps the new teachers struggle in the classroom and so perceive a need for further education, feeling as if maybe they did not master the job skills as well as they thought in college. As a profession, teaching has been socially, intellectually, and economically devalued (e.g., Feiman-Nemser and Floden 1986). Teachers may be female, already married and raising families, and very settled and vested within the community. Teachers are not necessarily the most mobile professionals; they tend to be "squatters," remaining within a school setting or system for many years, if not the entire length of a career. Changing districts or geographic locations may be traumatic for them, for it could mean uprooting family and breaking community ties. In other words, the cocoon of familiarity would be ruptured, resulting in profound instability.

Faced with the need to maintain stability, new teachers return to the local college and teacher education program for graduate courses and perhaps master's degrees in search of becoming better teachers. Again, just as in their undergraduate experiences, the academic experiences are localized, skills-mastery oriented, homogenized, and more focused on practical aspects of teaching and learning than on theoretical or intellectual aspects.

Inevitably time passes, and perhaps these teachers reach another crossroads. Maybe there is still a struggle within the classroom. Maybe there is a conflict with school and district administration. Maybe there is a desire to leave the classroom and escape to something higher in the system. Maybe a sense of identity, purpose, and direction has been lost. Feiman-Nemser and Floden ask, "What rewards do teachers get from teaching? How do they envision their career prospects?" (1986, 510–511). Do teachers look to external rewards, such as salary, status within the community, and power within the system (e.g., administrative versus classroom position), or are the internal rewards of student learning, collegial stimulation, and the process of teaching enough to sustain them?

> Often the tension between the job and the work of teaching is cast in terms of conflicting goals and standards. Many teachers want student learning to be based on individual needs, yet their schools expect them to improve standardized test scores, cover prescribed curricula at a set pace, and maintain an orderly classroom. (Feiman-Nemser and Floden 1986, 517)

Perhaps new teachers are motivated to return to school for additional graduate courses or another master's degree. However, a new trend in graduate education appears to be doctor of education (i.e., Ed.D.) programs, either in educational administration or educational leadership. One chief advocate of such programs is John Goodlad at the University of Washington in Seattle. A leading advocate for educational renewal (Goodlad 1994), Goodlad envisions teachers as lifelong learners and professional practitioners. He argues that physicians, dentists, and attorneys are doctorate-possessing professional practitioners and asks why classroom teachers should not attain the same professional status. In other words, the doctorate of education degree should hold the same professional legitimacy for educators as doctoral degrees hold for other professions.

Unfortunately, there are some fundamental differences between the profession of teaching and the professions of medicine, dentistry, and law. One cannot overlook the significant difference in salary for teachers compared to those of the other professionals, despite the number of years of professional experience teachers have before earning a doctorate. One also cannot overlook the intellectual norms of teacher education compared to those of medicine, dentistry, and law. Medical, dentistry, and law students generally matriculate from schools of arts and sciences, and whether true or not, the intellectual norms of schools of arts and sciences are considered higher than the norms for schools of education (e.g., Pushkin 1998a, 1998b, 1998c, 2000). And one cannot overlook the concrete job-skills expectations of teacher education students compared to those of medical, dental, and law school students. For the Ed.D. to be genuinely viewed as equivalent to M.D., D.D.S., and J.D. degrees, there needs to be a paradigm shift within the profession, and especially by the students pursuing such a degree and the faculty educating those students.

There is a prevailing notion that Ed.D. degrees are perhaps the quickest and easiest doctorates to obtain (e.g., Lanier and Little 1986). Interestingly, however, there is evidence that graduate students pursuing the Ed.D. are the least successful in terms of completion and quality (e.g., Pearson 1999). Beyond the intellectually limiting image of teacher education, we need to consider the anti-intellectual culture of schools and school systems and the intellectual limitations of doctoral program faculty.

Regarding the anti-intellectual culture Ed.D. students encounter, we must take into account that most teachers and administrators continue to work full-time during the day while attending classes at night. Aside from the general tiredness and stress related to such a routine, which also includes family responsibilities, there is a distinct difference in cultural climates to contend with. The school environment tends to be a custodial environment, where compliance and orderliness take priority over more intellectual goals. Because of this, the school environment itself is anti-intellectual, failing to stimulate deep critical discourse about the processes of teaching and learning.

This is the dominant environment for many Ed.D. students, and doctoral faculty who hope to cultivate intellectual discourse and paradigm shifts are at the mercy of this dominant culture. Unfortunately, limited time on campus away from the school environment exacerbates the situation; there are simply not enough opportunities to encourage cognitive dissonance. Consequently, many Ed.D. students struggle to change their thinking modes.

Perhaps the most alarming observation concerns the intellectual expectations of some Ed.D. students. Considering that they have already been acculturated into a paradigm of concrete-skills mastery, it should be no surprise if they carry this paradigm into doctoral courses. Unaware of the intellectual expectations of doctoral work (particularly in terms of writing assignments and dissertation research), some students approach each class expecting to learn something tangible to help them cope with their jobs the next day. As if they were expecting closure to each class (along the lines of the "Seven Step Lesson Plans" based on Madeline Hunter's "seven-step" pedagogical model; see Chapter 2) (e.g., Kincheloe and Steinberg 1998), they anticipate that at the end of a several-hours-long class they will have learned a new technique or skill. It is greatly disappointing for them to discover classes do not end with "and that's how you do it." It troubles them to be left with an abstract thought to ponder during their time away from class, perhaps with the expectation of reflection and prepared discussion for the next class.

Anecdotally, I have observed students approach problem-based activities, as well as their own dissertation studies, from their own localized perspectives. Students approach problems according to the way they do something in their districts, what their state curriculum guidelines say, what their test scores verify, how it works in their classrooms. However, besides their localized frames of reference, I observe very narrow lenses of observation. More often than not, they get bogged down in minute and local details and completely ignore the big picture of a situation.

It is somewhat disheartening to work with students interested in multicultural education who refuse to read the works of Paulo Freire, bell hooks, or Donaldo Macedo. It is disconcerting to hear students talk about constructivism yet be completely unfamiliar with the writings of Jean Piaget or Lev Vygotsky. Imagine students interested in curriculum issues who are nevertheless unaware of scholars like Elliot Eisner, Ivor Goodson, Bill Pinar, and Michael Apple. Sadly, I have even interviewed candidates for a doctoral program who did not know who John Dewey was.

It suffices to say that the greatest challenge to faculty is to get students to remove their cognitive blinders as they take classes and begin their dissertation studies. Students are sometimes dumbstruck at the amount of literature they encounter, and they often question its relevance. They consider it inconceivable that books and journal articles written by educational researchers from other countries pertain to their specific dissertation topic. They often need to refine their on-line searches for literature simply because they use a very limited scope of keywords and claim that little was found to assist them. Students need to be more savvy and cognizant of the scholarly literature beyond the books required for specific courses. This is certainly a monumental task for students who only read what their local districts and professional organizations publish.

In other words, many of the students recognize only one paradigm: their own. They only recognize one frame of reference: their own. They only recognize one perspective: their own. Why? It is what they are most familiar with, and quite possibly the only one they have been exposed to. Their dualism is entrenched. In fact, many students struggle to think multiplistically, even though they have been acculturated to defer to authority figures all of their adult lives.

The limiting factor in this cognitive progression is the education faculty member, for if a faculty member presents too contradictory a paradigm, students perceive it as too threatening to consider. To suddenly hear that the center of one's universe is not necessarily the real center (or that one's universe is not the entire universe) is frightening, for one is then forced to consider the walls of the cocoon of familiarity as temporary boundaries. This is especially frightening when the existence of one's universe is questioned only one or two nights a week while the universe within a school environment is reinforced daily and hourly.

To what extent can education faculty members extricate doctoral students from dualism? We first need to consider whether faculty members have even extricated themselves. There is a distinct possibility that faculty members are products of Ed.D. programs similar to the ones they teach in. Consequently, doctoral students are encountering credentialed versions of themselves. Their professors may have earned doctorates from local graduate schools and moved on up from the classroom to administrative positions (e.g., Lanier and Little 1986). After some time, perhaps many of these administrators had opportunities to move on up again into higher education, becoming professors of teacher education, with the premise of passing on their wisdom to new generations. Unfortunately, this raises the question of whether these new professors' records of professional success and advancement merely create opportunities to perpetuate the status quo within local school districts, an educational inbreeding of sorts.

My earlier anecdotal observation is hardly fiction. For the past two years, I taught in such a doctoral program, a Doctorate of Educational Innovation and Leadership Program in Delaware; it offers the Ed.D. degree. Although there are several positive features to this program (to be discussed in the next section of this chapter), many of its negative aspects strongly reflect what Pearson (1999), Lanier and Little (1986), and Feiman-Nemser and Floden (1986) describe. The program is very localized in its perspective. Many of the faculty (specifically the adjunct members) are products of this program. Not only is the intellectual rigor less than that required in other doctoral programs, the program celebrates the fact.

However, the greatest flaw in this program lies with its conceptualization. In the early 1990s, as various school districts experienced turnover at the superintendent level, the pool of qualified candidates for superintendent was apparently limited. This coincided with a newly initiated state requirement that a superintendent hold a doctoral degree. At the time, only one university in the state offered such a degree program (e.g., Educational Leadership/Administration), and only a limited number of candidates successfully completed the program.

Another institution in Delaware, a smaller, private college, saw an opportunity for itself. Several educators were interested in district-level administrative positions but not interested in pursuing their doctorate at the large university. Reflective of our "want it now, gain no pain" society, they wanted a doctoral program that would provide a means to their desired ends. This particular college was more than eager to oblige. Collaborating with the state Department of Education, this college designed a doctoral degree program that appeared progressive and flexible. However, every course offered toward the degree exactly matched the course requirements for superintendent certification. After ten years, although this program continues to thrive and admit a large number of students, the degree is hardly more than a credential; professional advancement and intellectual growth are not always synonymous.

THE LURE OF ADMINISTRATION

Why do teachers wish to leave teaching and "move up" to administrative positions? Is it the money? Is it a sense of power? Is it to escape the classroom environment? The answer is a combination of all three. It is no secret that administrators make more money than teachers do. It is no secret that administrators rarely teach. It is no secret that administrators are believed to hold more power than classroom teachers do. After all, to the victor go the spoils. But to what degree are aspiring administrators up to this new challenge? The one on top calls the shots, but in many respects the buck stops there too. Power has its benefits and its disadvantages.

We need to keep in mind that administrators are caught between two roles, management and leadership. One view of management is that its purpose is to make sure *things get done right*. On the other hand, leadership is sometimes viewed as *doing the right thing*. Is there a fundamental difference? There certainly is, and there is also a commonality.

If we reflect on some of the issues discussed in Chapters 6 and 8, we realize that administrators are supposed to avert crises in their schools. These crises can manifest as classrooms without teachers, teachers' union strikes, school violence, and poor results on outcomes-based assessment tests. A crisis implies something is wrong; administrators cannot afford to have things go wrong in their schools. Therefore, making sure things get done right translates to making sure there are teachers in classrooms, schools are busy and safe, and students get good test scores.

However, does this mean administrators are doing the right thing? Are children genuinely learning? Are teachers growing intellectually and making a positive impact on children's lives and their school communities? Do the schools reflect democratic learning communities? Schools can be very efficient on a bureaucratic level and yet be very dysfunctional on an educational and humanity level.

Where is the commonality? If "doing the right thing" means leading schools holistically, that is, giving novice teachers extensive support in developing their classroom skills, encouraging children to be genuinely critical thinkers, and making schools an integral part of communities, then perhaps things will go right. Educational leaders and politicians constantly argue that better teachers translate to better learning and better schools. However, it remains to be seen what they actually mean by "better teachers"; in the meantime, the linear progression of improvement appears to be discontinuous.

I often wonder why anyone wants to be a leader or manager of others. While interviewing several candidates for the doctoral program I taught in, I observed many who simply wanted to be "the boss." They were tired of taking orders from others and wanted to be the one in charge, the disseminator of orders, the supreme authority. Rarely did they have any vision of what a school should be, what good teaching was, or what learning genuinely meant. They thought everything in their school worked wonderfully, but they wanted to be in a position of power and influence. But what would they influence? Part of innovation and leadership involves being an agent of change and helping one's school become more progressive.

Why would teachers who are convinced everything in their school works wonderfully want to leave the classroom? Are they dissatisfied as teachers? There seems to be a counterlogic at play. On one hand, they think the system works wonderfully, yet on the other hand, they wish to become the leader by means of a program that allegedly advocates changing the status quo. It seems contradictory to simply move into a leadership role to maintain things. It is essentially educational inbreeding. It reflects what Alice Kramden (played by Audrey Meadows) once called Ralph (played by Jackie Gleason) during one of many arguments in *The Honeymooners:* "Yeah, the King of Nothin'!"

According to Donald C. Clark and Sally N. Clark (1996), we must wonder how genuinely (and adequately) prepared for leadership school administrators are. The problems and issues facing schools and administrators at the dawn of this new century are very different from what was faced a few decades ago. Clark and Clark point out that leadership needs to be "transformational." Leaders cannot simply maintain the status quo, even if the status quo is pretty good. Leaders need to strive toward better means of enabling and supporting teachers' success. Leaders need to effectively manage reform, not as the boss but as a facilitator. Leaders need to foster stronger relationships between schools and communities. Leaders need to create environments of trust and openness. In other words, what Freire (1985) and Giroux (1988) tell us about transformative intellectualism applies to what Clark and Clark (1996) call transformational leadership. Teachers need to create nurturing and constructivist environments for students, so they can develop intellectually for a democratic society. Teachers also need to be in nurturing and constructivist environments, so they too can develop intellectually for a democratic society. School leaders (i.e., administrators) carry a heavy responsibility to safeguard such development.

DISCUSSION

So what should we think about regarding professional development? First, we need to appreciate that professional development is as important for educators as it is for physicians, attorneys, and other professionals. Graduation from medical school, law school, or any other professional school does not imply that learning ceases. Most professions require continuous education and training as fields change and knowledge bases evolve. Why should we expect education to be any different? Education is indeed a *profession*, just as medicine, dentistry, and the law are.

However, there are those who attack the notion of professional development for teachers. For example, New York City Mayor Rudy Giuliani questioned why the city school system scheduled six professional development days during the school year (*New York Times*, December 8, 2000). Such days, albeit helpful for educators, were viewed as economically wasteful. Children would not be in school on those days, yet teachers would still be paid for "not working." The mayor frankly could not understand why teachers needed so many days at the expense of the fiscal budget.

Keep in mind that this is a mayor who has routinely questioned the competence of teachers. On one hand, he does not consider them qualified enough to teach children at a satisfactory level, yet on the other hand, he does not think their professional development should be his fiscal responsibility. The mayor felt teachers should do their own staff development on their own time. This in a city where a considerable number of teachers are already taking night classes toward initial certification, permanent certification, or a graduate degree. The mayor seems to think teachers have an unlimited amount of personal time in which to develop themselves into the kind of teachers he will not be embarrassed by.

What is the consequence? According to Steve Rhine (1998), reform-minded teachers are hungry for continuing education and professional development. Unfortunately, they encounter many activity-based contexts for students (i.e., "how to do a new teaching approach," as if the approach applies to anything) that decontextualize the subject matter, grade level, or learning environment. In many respects, this decontextualization reflects the genericism of the seven-step lesson plans; it seems to say that teaching is a universal practice applicable to any teacher.

Decontextualization also reinforces the perspective of Mayor Giuliani; decontextualized activities keep children busy and out of trouble. Theoretically, according to the mayor, not having professional development days keeps children in school more often, keeps them busy, and keeps them out of trouble. My, how schools have evolved since the days of Horace Mann and those 1830s public schools! Here we are, approximately 170 years later, and we still let the cliché "Idle hands make the Devil's work" drive our educational practices.

Needless to say, some professional development interventions actually *de-professionalize*. Busy children are mistaken for learning children, and teachers unwittingly grab the newest magic bullet, hoping for empowerment, but end up disarmed and disabled. Rhine (1998) talks about the way teacher-development packages are presented in "teacher friendly" language. How different is this from what Macedo (1994) calls *stupidification?* Just as we wonder to what extent cognitive development is genuinely considered in outcomes-based assessment, we are left to wonder to what extent, if at all, it is considered in professional development of teachers.

This does not paint a pleasant picture about teachers, and it only makes attracting quality people to the profession more and more difficult, despite many creative and passionate efforts (e.g., Scott 1998). As stated earlier, educational leaders correlate teaching effectiveness with assessment results. However, we continue to struggle to understand the extent to which teaching effectiveness depends on pedagogical content knowledge (Rhine 1998).

We consider it a form of professional development if teachers leave the classroom but not the school system. But are we developing them within the same profession, especially in light of the fact that administrators do so little classroom teaching? Is there a threshold point at which educators stop being educators?

That being said, how do we prepare administrators for the new century (and millennium) when they were not necessarily prepared for the challenges of education as teachers? Clark and Clark (1996) make several recommendations for how universities can better prepare administrators:

1. There needs to be a strong sense of purpose and vision, both for the university program and for graduating administrators.
2. There needs to be a healthy connection between educational theory and school practice.
3. There needs to be a healthy balance of coverage on psychosocial and academic issues.

4. There needs to be a genuine focus on problem-based learning activities.
5. There needs to be a commitment to authentic assessment, and individualism.

The fourth and fifth recommendations can be very problematic for aspiring administrators who only subscribe to outcomes-based assessment. The inability to view learners and educators as individuals (see Chapter 8) precludes any chance of having genuine vision. Consequently, this leads to disjointed, or *antiholistic,* leadership. There is no opportunity for transformation, and the status quo remains. Teachers and students alike are expected to comply and conform. The administrator's role is to ensure things are predictable, consistent, and efficient. The administrator becomes the boss, the storekeeper, a caretaker, the "King of Nothin'." He or she is simply expected to keeps the ship steady and afloat.

In many respects, this should not shock us; however, it should sadden us. If we reflect back on the inbreeding of education that Lanier and Little (1986) allude to, we should realize many administrators are rewarded for being loyal teachers. Many were good soldiers, kept their politics in the mainstream, and followed their marching orders. When the time came for a change in leadership, consideration was given toward loyal soldiers; it was time for their promotion, their *stars and stripes.*

One does not hire a new administrator without consideration for preservation. As Michael Fullan (1993) notes, schools are conservative systems and continuously tend back toward the status quo. If a school system wants to maintain its hierarchical structure of power and influence, it is highly unlikely to hire administrators who threaten the status quo. Agents of change need not apply.

Professional development, whether for teachers seeking to remain in the classroom or for aspiring administrators, needs to have some intellectual purpose and vision for genuine change. To simply offer professional development courses or to require additional academic training for training's sake seems counterproductive. Furthermore, there needs to be a better connection to the intellectual growth of students and educators. To organize professional development around efficiency models also seems counterproductive and undermines the process of knowledge.

Unfortunately, we are a long way from reaching the ideal for professional development. There are still workshops designed to increase students' busyness level. There are still development requirements geared toward helping teachers achieve better mastery on outcomes-based assessment tests. There are still graduate degree programs in educational leadership eschewing a community of visionaries in favor of mass-produced supervisors.

"Development" is synonymous with "growth," "maturation," "progress," "evolution," and "improvement." Unfortunately, it is also synonymous with "advancement," "enlargement," and "addition." What do these words suggest? An inherent conflict. On one hand, there is a picture of development that advocates making schools better and encouraging teachers to have unlimited potential. On the other hand, there is a picture of development that lacks any vision; it simply sees teachers as new cogs into a preexisting paradigmatic machinery.

REFERENCES

Clark, D. C., and S. N. Clark. 1996. "Better Preparation of Educational Leaders." *Educational Researcher* 25, no. 8: 18–20.

Feiman-Nemser, S., and R. E. Floden. 1986. "The Cultures of Teaching." Pp. 505–526 in *Handbook of Research on Teaching*, 3rd ed. Edited by M. C. Wittrock. New York: Macmillan.

Freire, P. 1985. *The Politics of Education: Culture, Power, and Liberation.* New York: Bergin and Garvey.

Fullan, M. 1993. *Change Forces: Probing the Depths of Educational Reform.* London: Falmer Press.

Giroux, H. 1988. *Teachers as Intellectuals: Toward a Critical Pedagogy of Learning.* Boston: Bergin and Garvey.

Goodlad, J. I. 1994. *Educational Renewal: Better Teachers, Better Schools.* San Francisco: Josey-Bass.

Kincheloe, J. L. 1993. *Toward a Critical Politics of Teacher Thinking: Mapping the Postmodern.* Westport, CT: Bergin and Garvey.

———. 1992. "Education Reform: What Have Been the Effects of the Attempts to Improve Education over the Last Decade?" Pp. 227–232 in *Thirteen Questions: Reframing Education's Conversation.* Edited by J. L. Kincheloe and S. R. Steinberg. New York: Peter Lang.

Kincheloe, J. L., and S. R. Steinberg. 1998. "Lesson Plans from the Outer Limits: Unauthorized Methods." Pp. 1–23 in *Unauthorized Methods: Strategies for Critical Teaching.* Edited by J. L. Kincheloe and S. R. Steinberg. New York: Routledge.

Lanier, J. E., and J. W. Little. 1986. "Research on Teacher Education." Pp. 527–569 in *Handbook of Research on Teaching*, 3rd ed. Edited by M. C. Wittrock. New York: Macmillan.

Macedo, D. 1994. *Literacies of Power: What Americans Are Not Allowed To Know.* Boulder, CO: Westview Press.

Pearson, M. 1999. "The Changing Environment for Doctoral Education in Australia: Implications for Quality Management, Improvement, and Innovation." *Higher Education Research and Development* 18, no. 3: 269–287.

Pushkin, D. B. 2000. "Critical Thinking in Science: How Do We Recognize It? Do We Foster It?" Pp. 211–220 in *Perspectives in Critical Thinking: Essays by Teachers in Theory and Practice.* Edited by D. Weil and H. K. Anderson. New York: Peter Lang.

———. 1998a. "Introductory Students, Conceptual Understanding, and Algorithmic Success." *Journal of Chemical Education* 75, no. 7: 809–810.

———. 1998b. "Is Learning Just a Matter of Tricks? So Why Are We Educating?" *Journal of College Science Teaching* 28, no. 2: 92–93.

———. 1998c. "Teacher Says; Simon Says: Dualism in Science Learning." Pp. 185–198 in *Unauthorized Methods: Strategies for Critical Teaching.* Edited by J. L. Kincheloe and S. R. Steinberg. New York: Routledge.

Rhine, S. 1998. "The Role of Research and Teachers' Knowledge Base in Professional Development." *Educational Researcher* 27, no. 5: 27–31.

Scott, C. H. 1998. "Albert Shanker's Advocacy Advertising." *Educational Researcher* 27, no. 5: 22–26.

Chapter Ten

◦ Professional Disillusionment

I would like to begin this chapter by sharing insights about a recent newspaper article. On December 11, 2000, *USA TODAY* presented a story on how parents deal with school discipline policies as they affect their children. Perhaps no one issue seems to challenge classroom educators more than discipline. Discipline problems are considered to disrupt teaching and learning, potentially contributing to students' underachievement in an era when high-stakes assessment dominates educational systems.

What struck me about this article was its beginning: "Contrite parents used to come to the principal's office and apologize if a child had broken school rules. . . . Now the scenario is dramatically different. . . . School officials—not the misbehaving kids—often . . . catch the brunt of parental fury." It somehow brought back memories of when I was a student and even of when I was a teacher. My, have the times changed, right before my very eyes. And yet, as conscious as I have been of this change, it still amazes me to some extent.

I remember the times my parents met with my teachers during my school years. Whenever the teacher raised concerns about my academics or conduct, my parents would listen intently, trust the experience and wisdom of the teacher, and respond. Sometimes my parents agreed with my teachers, and sometimes they disagreed; however, they always allowed the teachers to say their piece. My parents took the Old World, old-school view, in which the teachers were authority figures, and children were expected to respect and obey their elders. The teachers were trusted as experts, and more importantly, as adults; the word of an adult was more to be trusted than that of a child, especially if a conflict arose.

Those meetings, albeit rare, were very predictable. My parents would meet with my teachers and immediately ask, "What is the problem? Is David in trouble? What did he do wrong?" On at least two occasions during high school, my father opened up the dialogue by asking my teacher, "Now what did he do?" and then immediately looking at me and saying, "You have nothing to say yet."

I was always presumed guilty before any trial took place, but those were the good old days when parents still believed in the "Evil Eye." In fact, at back-to-school nights, my mother would always give teachers permission to give me what for if I was ever out of line. Granted, my mother, as well as some of my teachers, would have needed to stand on a stool to reach my head, but the mere threat was very real to me, and I respected it despite my mildly rebellious disposition. No one ever raised a hand to me (my parents only did so twice during my entire youth), but in those days one tried not to tempt fate.

When I became a high school teacher, only one parent ever came to me with such a blanket invitation. In 1989, the father of one of my best physics students introduced himself to me at back-to-school night and said, "Hey, if my son gives you any lip, just give him a smack." Interestingly enough, the father was old school, just like my parents, and my student, Nick, was nearly 18 and already taller than I was. I never had a problem with Nick; he was a very good student. However, it was somewhat comforting to hear a parent talk as mine had more than a decade earlier.

But Nick's father was a rarity; in fact, he was the *only* parent to ever make such an offer. So many of the parents I dealt with expected me to cater to their sons and daughters, to keep them happy, and never to overstep my bounds. In other words, their children could do no wrong, and Heaven help me if I dared to suggest such a thing, regardless of their behavior or academic flaws. Come to think of it, I even deal with this as a professor at the college and university level, regardless of whether I deal with undergraduate or graduate students.

BATTLES AND CONFRONTATIONS

The issue of discipline is not of primary importance for this chapter, even though it provides the context for reflection. What that *USA TODAY* article stimulated was a reflection on how parents deal with schools and how teachers deal with parents, and on the fact that student accountability and responsibility seem to be the crux of both. It was interesting to read that parents would immediately enter schools and confront teachers and administrators with threats of litigation before finding out what the circumstances of their child's behavior exactly were. Also new to the debate is the influence of learning disabilities; if misbehavior is due to a disability, is a child legally protected from disciplinary action? This is an issue too complicated to debate within a few pages of a book chapter.

The issues of confrontation and litigation threats are troubling yet fascinating. Keeping in mind the trend toward high-stakes accountability testing in our schools and the increased competitiveness for opportunities for higher education, schools, students, and parents increasingly sense less and less margin for error. Do we worry that a less-than-excellent assessment in third-grade math may eventually keep a child from a Harvard education ten years later? Some might consider this a ridiculous question; others might consider it genuinely real and life determining. In light of this, parental hyper-reactivity, whether excusable or not, may have a context.

Perhaps parents have developed shorter fuses and thinner skins in this new era of education. However, I sense that this phenomenon is not necessarily new; I dealt with confrontational parents when I began teaching in the mid-1980s—in public schools, private schools, and at the university level. There were parents who would come to school and curse at me face-to-face or make derogatory comments to me. There were parents who would never contact me but would directly contact my principal or school board instead. There were even parents who contacted my university department chairperson, dean, or provost. More often than not, the issue revolved around grades and my expectations and standards for students.

My first experience with this occurred while I was a graduate student and teacher in a university chemistry department. I was teaching a one-credit freshman laboratory course, and one of my students earned a D. She happened to be a pre-med major, and such a grade was not good if medical school was her goal. Sometime after the course concluded and grades were determined and mailed to students, this student and her father (an attorney) flew from Washington, D.C., to Tampa, Florida, demanding that her grade be changed or heads would roll. They went directly to my department chairperson, who patiently listened to the father's ranting and raving and threats of litigation. After the father said his piece, the chairperson showed him his daughter's final exam, my grade book, and politely told him to go back to Washington. Case closed. Her grade was never changed, and I never heard anything about it again.

Approximately two years later, I was teaching high school chemistry and physics in a private school. Most of my students were very good; some were not strong. Rarely did I encounter parental complaints, and I often dealt with very supportive and understanding parents who just wanted their sons and daughters to do the best they could and earn a respectable grade. However, I also encountered parents who could not settle for anything less than an A on report cards. In fact, one parent bluntly told me at back-to-school night, "I don't pay several thousands of dollars in tuition for my kid to get a B; do we understand each other?"

That was not the last time I encountered such a parent. Sometimes, I was harangued by parent and child together with "but B is *bad,* Mr. Pushkin! You're ruining my life!" Parents would tell me I was not fit to teach their child. If their child did not get the grade they wanted, threats of school board hearings and lawsuits were bandied about. It was almost as if I were a police officer and the parents were local citizens threatening, "We'll have your badge!"

My syllabi, tests, and grade books were presumed to be too demanding and abusive of their children's well-being. Imagine the furor raised when I caught students cheating on tests or plagiarizing in written reports. All I ever expected was their best, honest, effort; apparently I failed to comprehend that they unconditionally wanted my best reward possible, as if it was constitutionally guaranteed, an inalienable right.

Even as a professor, students have cursed at me, and parents have threatened lawsuits, because my expectations and standards are perceived to be too unrealistic and unfair, making it too tough for students to achieve what they think they deserve. In other words, my students (and their parents) automatically expected exemplary grades for every course they took, and it was my job to ensure this happened. If the desired outcome did not happen (i.e., the reward was not given), it must have been *my* fault. I apparently did something dastardly, permanently scarring these students by expecting them to *earn* their grades. One might wonder if students can even achieve academically on their own anymore.

Interestingly, during one semester in the mid-1990s while I was a physics professor, the majority of my students were freshmen (their very first semester of college). For some unknown reason, the college administered course evaluations to students during the midterm of the fall semester, rather than toward the end (which was the case during the spring semester). Naturally, the majority of the students lashed out at me on these evaluations. After all, they were barely through their first seven or eight weeks of college, experiencing expectations much different from and more demanding than what they had been used to in high school. From the perspective of students' intellectual growth—their sense of themselves and their experience in higher education—it was a shame these same students were unable to submit evaluations again at the end of the semester, for their perspectives did change. In fact, many of their views had dramatically changed by the end of the second-semester course, after having a full year of new experiences to reflect upon.

However, what was most intriguing about their comments (to both multiple-choice and open-ended questions) was how they charac-

terized themselves. The freshmen all noted that they were in the first semester of college, and yet all responded that their GPAs were a perfect
4.0 (A). They then noted an expected grade of F in my course. After seven
or eight weeks of college! Looking back at my old syllabus, barely one-
third of their grade contribution would have been known at that point,
and yet course and cumulative grades were very concrete to them. I
could only wonder how they responded to evaluations for their other
courses; final grades were probably no more concrete there.

Believe it or not, I even experience this with graduate students.
Master's students have complained that I gave them a B for a paper they
thought was "long enough," despite its flaws (as if quantity mattered
more than quality). Even doctoral students have complained that I have
destroyed their self-esteem by correcting their grammar on research
proposals or questioning the soundness of their theoretical premises.
Apparently, I must be the first professor they have ever encountered
who did not confirm they were perfect. Interestingly enough, graduate
students rarely bring such complaints directly to me; they typically go
over my head to an administrator. Even more interesting is that some of
these very same students experience similar treatment in the schools
they teach. Somehow, no one seems to be learning a lesson or observing
a recurrent pattern from this.

Everyone complains in one form or another (including me), and
I really have no qualms with students complaining. However, it is troubling that many do not complain directly to me; they immediately take
it to a higher level. Schools constantly direct students and parents to follow a chain of command if there is a disagreement over something. Colleges and universities follow a similar policy. Yet students and parents
fail to follow such policies. Why?

Perhaps students and parents sense a feeling of power by going
over teachers' heads to administrators. Perhaps they do not respect
teachers in the first place. Perhaps they fear the harsh truth and hope
going to another level might muddy the waters regarding a teacher's position in a disagreement. Perhaps they want automatic absolution free
of consequences. Perhaps they believe making enough threats will result in immediate placation. Perhaps they presume a teacher's mind
cannot be changed without an administrative edict or threat. Regardless
of the reason, educators are clearly compromised, undermined, and *de-
powered* when such actions are taken.

As I mentioned in Chapter 1, we live in a "want it now" society,
and when students and parents are upset or dissatisfied with outcomes,
they apparently expect satisfaction *now*. It is almost like a screaming
baby: give it a bottle, a toy, a pacifier, something to immediately please

it. We have become impatient with education, its structure, and its processes. We no longer want to take the time to think things out or challenge ourselves. We almost want education to function like a microwave oven: cook the final dish, not prepare it from scratch.

What these students and parents fail to realize is that their actions sometimes backfire. Although some complaints are real and justified, some complaints may be made for selfish and unfounded reasons. Perhaps some students and parents fail to comprehend or appreciate the grand scheme, the big picture, of education. Sadly, when administrators act hastily to quell complaints, as if complaints represented bad business, they potentially reinforce the myopic impatience that underlies many of the conflicts between students and educators.

Just as misbehavior detracts from the teaching and learning process, so do confrontations and litigious threats. Are teachers really trained to deal with such situations? Should they need to be trained for such situations? Again, going back to Chapter 1, we could only wonder what university administrators like Arthur Levine and Leon Botstein would say. I cannot help but wonder what Ann, the teacher Acel Moore introduced us to in Chapter 1, would say.

However, the issue still comes back to accountability and responsibility; this goes well beyond grades and test scores. Educators and educational systems are expected to hold students to high standards and expectations. However, students need to demonstrate their own accountability. Apparently, society seems to be saying, students do not need to take responsibility for failing to meet expectations or standards. Apparently they are not accountable for their lack of accountability. Someone else must bear the responsibility, most likely, teachers; after all, how much trust do they receive (Eisner 2001)?

Theoretically, state tests determine whether or not a student graduates; this is the supposed bottom line of outcomes-based education. However, some states have a two-tiered diploma system: If students pass the state tests, they earn certified diplomas; if they do not pass, they earn regular diplomas. Unless future employment or admission to higher education is at stake, of what consequence is testing? If students graduate regardless of testing, where is the accountability? Even educational systems have a mechanism in place to provide absolution and protection for students.

To shed further light on this, consider this comment from my sister, who has left the teaching profession to return to journalism. She describes a community college student who is taking classes on a part-time basis:

Right now I am waiting [at my community college office] to see if any students show up for grades. One student already showed up and he was not happy to hear he failed. In addition, his mom is going to show up, but I will not discuss his grade with her because that is the law. This kid is 15 and being home schooled. He doesn't belong here. Ironically, I taught this kid in elementary school and know his mom—I am not looking forward to the encounter.

Well the mother didn't come before I left, but she did show up to talk to the Program Director today. Suddenly, her son has a medical condition and wants an incomplete. I told the director about the situation before she showed up. I told her more [information] after she told me about the incomplete. I told her I don't think he should get one, but I will do whatever she wants. I obviously don't really care anymore. I am so tired of this nonsense. Nobody wants to take responsibility. That is why I am leaving the field. It is a pretty thankless job.

We are apparently passing the buck, avoiding taking any stand. In fact, it appears we take the path of least resistance, fearing the consequences if we stick to our principles. But what are our principles? When we treat education as a business, we view students as our customers. Customers deserve a quality product. Unfortunately, this has been taken to an extreme, for the customer is always right, regardless of the circumstances, and the product has yet to be defined.

But the customer knows what quality is: essentially whatever makes the customer happy. So rather than define what a "quality product" is, education now aims to pacify its customers. Give the students what they want, minimize the complaints, and pray they go away without costing the school any business. Reflect back on Chapters 6 and 9; administrators approach school leadership in crisis mode.

There is always an excuse for underachievement, and we are expected to reward students regardless of performance. It makes no difference if we are talking about misbehavior, poor test scores, poor grades, grade inflation, social promotion, or truancy. Somehow, students have an "out"; the system provides a mulligan (in golf, a "free shot").

Even when educators take a stand for standards and accountability, they may get only shaky, or completely nonexistent, administrative support. Do administrators fear legal retribution? Do they fear fiscal retribution? Do they fear never achieving blue-ribbon status? Professional tennis player Andre Agassi once said, "Image is everything"; perhaps he inadvertently made a key point about education. Education is image conscious, as are all its stakeholders. We want the image of being smarter than everyone else, more important than everyone else, and simply better than everyone else. Our national pride is based on thinking ourselves better than others. In our "want it now" society, everyone wants to feel good about education. However, we can only wonder how much credibility has been sacrificed in the process.

The issue is not really discipline or assessment; it is more related to expectations. We have always had expectations for ourselves, children, teachers, and schools. Somehow all those expectations changed, and they are no longer consistent among us. We collectively (and metaphorically) want education to be thin and beautiful again, but we want the result from miracle diet pills; we do not want to sacrifice cheesecake for celery. We no longer want to exercise; we expect everything to simply happen. In essence, education and its stakeholders have become sedentary, waiting for a painless solution to a painful problem that we all fear confronting. We want gain, with no pain. Seeking the easy way makes us impatient; our impatience makes us confrontational. We *want it now.* We want to *have it our way.* Or else!

IT IS NOT WHAT WE EXPECTED

It rarely is. We go through teacher education programs, student teaching, the hiring process, and then are suddenly in our own classrooms. I liken this to playing quarterback in football. No matter how many practice repetitions there are, confronting an enemy defense under real-game conditions is dramatically different. Things seem much quicker and stressful; the luxury of thinking time shrinks, as players go into reaction mode.

Perhaps one of the biggest shocks for new teachers, according to my former students, is realizing how much more energy is required to teach full-time in their own classrooms. When they student teach, they are often in a controlled environment. Mentor teachers are the authorities; responsibilities are delegated slowly, sparingly, and gradually, so the student teachers become more comfortable and accustomed to the classroom. More often than not, the student teachers eventually assume only half or less of the teaching duties; rarely is total responsibility given to "visiting novices."

So student teaching seems relatively easy, albeit more challenging than mere course work. However, since they have yet to feel the full brunt of teaching, new teachers can hit the wall quickly when the entire classroom is theirs. Perhaps they may be teaching twice as many classes as before, not to mention twice as many students. Responsibilities once given on a limited basis now multiply. Everything takes much longer than anticipated. Time is no longer as free as it used to be. Writing detailed lesson plans competes with writing student progress reports, disciplining, holding parent-teacher conferences, ordering supplies, developing and reproducing handout materials, grading papers, and doing bus, hall, or cafeteria duty. And we have not even considered extracurricular activities and obligations.

New teachers work later, stay up later, and wake up earlier than they did as student teachers. Time for sleep decreases. Meals are no longer as balanced or elaborate. Suddenly, they are exercising less and less, are constantly tired, and feel more run down. They may think they are falling apart, but in reality, they are putting their bodies and minds in unfamiliar situations. There is some level of culture shock involved, especially if a vastly different geographical context is involved (e.g., Guglielmi and Tatrow 1998).

It should not be too surprising to know that teachers are notoriously susceptible to urinary tract disorders, digestion problems, poor nutrition, and being overweight. According to R. Sergio Guglielmi and Kristin Tatrow (1998), many teachers suffer from physical, psychological, and physiological disorders (e.g., headaches, depression, and diabetes).

Considering what teachers put themselves through everyday to get their jobs done, it is a wonder they are not in worse physical condition! Add to the mix a society that thinks teachers have an easy life, since summers are supposedly work-free, and you have the beginnings of teacher stress and burn out. Two of my former students, Jane and Carol (pseudonyms), are still trying to wonder what hit them during their first semester of teaching. They are exhausted, both physically and mentally (Carol cannot even find the energy to read a book or watch PBS).

Everything is a shock to new teachers. I wonder if teachers eventually leave the profession when the shock reaches a saturation point, or when things no longer shock them. They are affected by what students say and do, how parents react, and how administrators respond. There are so many things we prepare them for during their formal training, but we unfortunately cannot prepare them for everything during the limited time allotted for teacher education programs. In many respects, they are thrown into the fire without the frying pan.

Another of my former students, Gerry, told me his students did not even know his name; they would simply yell, "Hey Mister!" No matter how many times he would write his name on the board, he was still "Hey Mister!" He also told me of his naiveté dealing with classroom chemistry. Students, regardless of age, can form alliances, banding together to either cooperate with new teachers or run them from the classroom. Students form social cliques, sometimes so exclusive that individuals become social outcasts within a classroom. Teachers need to deal with this. Teachers also need to deal with students' fighting, students' crying, and even students' attempts at suicide.

Yet another former student, Daisy, expressed frustration over her department chairperson, the school resources, and the curriculum. She felt her chairperson was too critical and negative. She thought the books were outdated. She felt bad about the layout of the school and classroom space, for it physically isolated her from the rest of her departmental colleagues.

Student teachers are assigned mentors, with whom they have relatively close relationships. This may not necessarily be the case when they are hired as full-time teachers. Everyone has so many responsibilities, not everyone has the time or inclination to check up on them or help out (unless required by the school system). During teacher education studies, we often tell students how liberating it will be to have their own classrooms. We encourage them to be creative and be independent. And yet, when they close that door for the first time, they wonder why they have been left all by themselves, as if the safety net was snatched away. They are focusing on survival, striving to steady their feet, and hoping to eventually become the teachers they dreamed of being.

And yet not everyone within a school shares the same dreams and visions as new teachers. Veteran teachers may chastise them for being too vocal or progressive. They may be viewed as troublemakers who have not paid their dues or who do not know their place. They encounter veteran teachers who are apathetic, petty, small-minded, inertial, vindictive, and paranoid. We send them out into the world of education with new energy and ideas, and sometimes they end up stifled and muzzled by the system.

Whenever I would discuss challenging paradigms within education, a couple of my former master's students would say, "See . . . it's talk like that that'll prevent you from ever becoming an administrator!" I found it very intriguing and humorous to hear this and asked them to elaborate. Basically, their explanation boiled down to a matter of following the party line; anyone who wants to advance in the system has to honor the status quo. So much for having one's own belief system when no one likes making waves. Needless to say, these students were not happy about their positions within the school system, and one of them, after ten years, is finally considering leaving teaching to "find himself." He simply had enough.

Simply having had enough—a recurring theme from Chapter 1. When people finally decide to leave education, it is not just because of one thing; it is usually because of a culmination of things: students, parents, administrators, policies, control, and integrity. We get tired of the nonsense. We get tired of the arguments, the confrontations, and dysfunction. The stress gets to us—the long hours, the demanding and tedious duties, the physical strains, the tiredness, the financial burdens, and the personal sacrifices. Somehow, the luster has been lost for us.

DISCUSSION

Teaching is a stressful profession; I will not deny or sugarcoat this. Yes, it is rewarding and challenging, but it takes its toll, physically, mentally, and emotionally. Everyone has a threshold limit. Many new teachers are said to leave the profession within the first three to five years. Some last longer than this; some are able to last an entire lifetime.

Guglielmi and Tatrow (1998) note that increasing scrutiny and attacks on education (and particularly teachers) obscure the rewards of teaching. Although Charlotte H. Scott (1998) wonders how we can attract quality people to teaching and promote our profession as honorable, Guglielmi and Tatrow (1998) point to accountability testing, outcomes-based objectives, and bloated curricula as considerable negatives. Many professions have glamorous and ugly sides; unfortunately, the ugly side of teaching seems more and more dominant.

Despite many intervention programs at the local, state, and university levels, teachers keep leaving the profession very quickly. Unlike the teachers described in Chapter 9 who seek to move into administrative positions, the teachers Guglielmi and Tatrow refer to are leaving education completely. Guglielmi and Tatrow wonder how well teachers fit into their environments. For example, how much control or autonomy do they have within their own classrooms? Schools (and education, in many respects) potentially *depower* teachers (e.g., Kincheloe 1993). Perhaps an overwhelming sense of powerlessness motivates some teachers to flee the profession.

Guglielmi and Tatrow (1998) also consider effort and reward issues, issues that affect why people choose or do not choose certain professions. Consider what my sister said earlier in this chapter: "It is a pretty thankless job." There comes a time when everyone asks, "Why am I knocking myself out? What am I getting out of this?"

Guglielmi and Tatrow (1998) also consider issues of teachers' dysfunctional lifestyles. Teachers often suffer the strain from financial woes, damaged personal relationships, and difficult home situations. Bankruptcy, divorce, and domestic violence are indeed prevalent among teachers. How do they cope with the stress and strain? Smoking, poor eating habits (overeating, anorexia, and bulimia), alcoholism, and drug addiction are unhealthy, yet they are common defense mechanisms among teachers.

Most intriguingly, Guglielmi and Tatrow (1998) wonder if there is a certain physical, psychological, personality, or demographic profile of a successful teacher for specific school environments. In other words, what qualities does a teacher need in order to survive an entire career in a school? Many teachers have the intellectual abilities and academic credentials to be successful, yet they flounder and leave. How does this relate to transformative intellectualism and transformational leadership (see Chapter 9)? Perhaps it really does matter who the teacher is and which school environment he or she is employed to teach in. Perhaps, on a more drastic level, certain people are simply not meant to be teachers. If that is the case, this suggests that intelligence and academic background might not be the best indicators of a good teacher.

Guglielmi and Tatrow (1998) suspect a key indicator might be how well teachers and school environments conform or adapt to each other. For example, some teachers may be certified or academically prepared to teach one subject yet be better suited to teach another. In Chapter 7, Rebecca Fabiano told us of her college training in English and her desire to teach health education. I myself was originally a biochemist, yet I felt more at home teaching physics. Daisy, mentioned in the previous section, was trained as a chemical engineer and teaches chemistry. However, she is also working toward secondary certification in Spanish because she prefers teaching her native language and finds it more liberating than teaching chemistry.

Perhaps the grade level one teaches in matters. Some teachers find elementary schools a much better environment than high schools, and vice versa. Some teachers prefer the middle school environment. Some teachers are simply not meant to work with young children; conversely, some teachers are not meant to work with adolescents.

Perhaps the geography and community context matters. For example, some teachers are overwhelmed by teaching in large, urban schools. Some thrive on the urban context and suffer tremendously in smaller, rural schools. Some teachers are meant to work in culturally diverse environments; others, perhaps, are not.

Something many do not take into account (yet Guglielmi and Tatrow [1998] did) is religion (as well as ethnicity). As discussed in Chapter 6, many school systems make concerted efforts to recruit and hire ethnic minorities in order to have a more diverse workforce and serve the needs of a diverse clientele of students. But what if ethnic minorities do not wish to teach in certain environments? For example, would

African Americans enjoy teaching in a school district that has a strong alliance with the Ku Klux Klan?

Among important religious factors, Guglielmi and Tatrow (1998) point to Judaism and Islam. For example, how observant can teachers of either religion be in their school districts? Devout Muslims pray five times a day; might non-Muslim students, teachers, and administrators view this as a "disruption" to the school routine? In this era of multicultural diversity and sensitivity, one wonders if a school system might nevertheless use Ramadan (a month in the Islamic calendar during which Muslims fast during daylight hours) as an excuse to dismiss a teacher.

The same could be said for Jewish holidays. Having taught in the south (Florida and Delaware) for a good part of my career, I have been subjected to criticism by students and administrators for taking too many "frivolous" days off. Just this past year, one of my doctoral students criticized me on my course evaluation for canceling class on Yom Kippur, the Day of Atonement. Apparently this student was greatly offended by this disruption of his education.

And yet in this era of multicultural diversity and sensitivity, there are plenty of geographic regions in the United States with high levels of racism, xenophobia, and anti-Semitism. Schools are choreographed to function according to their own calendars, not to those of individuals. The Hebrew calendar, the Muslim/Islamic calendar, and the Chinese calendar all offer contradictions to the typical school calendar.

And we have only scratched the surface! For example, Friday happens to be the Muslim Sabbath. The Sabbath for Jews begins sundown Friday night. What does an observant Jew do during the winter months, when sundown comes early, perhaps as the school day is ending? The U.S. Senate is able to accommodate and respect the observance level of Senator Joseph Lieberman of Connecticut. It seems doubtful that a school system is as tolerant.

What is a school system to do? Stop hiring Jews, Muslims, Hindus, and Buddhists? Force them to convert to the mainstream religion in order to ensure conformity and a smooth-running ship?

What are Jewish teachers to do? Teach only in regions with large Jewish communities? There is merit to this practice. Having grown up in New York and having briefly taught in the CUNY system, I was very spoiled by an academic calendar that coincided well with the Jewish calendar. Schools were closed on the major Jewish holidays, and spring break always coincided with Passover, when kosher dietary restrictions become a logistical nightmare for school cafeterias. After two years in isolation in Delaware, I am considering moving to Canada and a region with a significant Jewish population, in part for these very reasons.

We should keep in mind the potential dangers of broaching this discussion. The United States is already a nation very polarized over race, ethnicity, and religion (not to mention sexual orientation and gender). To design school systems exclusively to serve one segment of our population drastically undermines the premise of democratic, public education in a pluralistic society and potentially gives ammunition to those advocating resegregation. And yet, in so many respects, the majority of our school systems fail to adequately serve the needs of any segment of our population.

As was discussed in Chapter 8, to succeed in this profession means a great deal of conformity and compliance. However, by no means should this imply a surrender of one's individual values and sense of cultural identity. Guglielmi and Tatrow (1998) wonder how well teachers and schools conform or adapt to each other. However, unless there is a dominant ethnic population with considerable influence, it appears that teachers are expected to do the bulk of the conforming and adapting. This can be incredibly stressful to teachers, as well as potentially alienating. To maintain their sense of cultural identity, they must "disrupt" the school environment; to maintain employment, they must "disrupt" their own set of cultural values. The consequence, sadly, is personal strain, which affects teachers' work, homes, psyches, and spirits. They are placed between a rock and a hard place, and something eventually gives.

Leaving the teaching profession can be attributed to a variety of factors, for rarely does one single factor lead one to leave. However, as discussed in this chapter, teaching takes its toll in many regards. Unfortunately, the one common theme somehow reflects our need for individualism and sense of self-identity. As I will discuss in Chapter 11, we are finally coming back full-circle to Chapter 1 and the notion of teachers being a dime a dozen. We are not supposed to be, but somehow the system leads us to think otherwise.

REFERENCES

Eisner, J. 2001. "Why Are Teachers Undervalued?" *Philadelphia Inquirer,* April 8, E1, E4.

Guglielmi, R. S., and K. Tatrow. 1998. "Occupational Stress, Burnout, and Health in Teachers: A Methodological and Theoretical Analysis." *Review of Educational Research* 68, no. 1: 61–99.

Kincheloe, J. L. 1993. *Toward a Critical Politics of Teacher Thinking: Mapping the Postmodern.* Westport, CT: Bergin and Garvey.

Scott, C. H. 1998. "Albert Shanker's Advocacy Advertising." *Educational Researcher* 27, no. 5: 22–26.

Chapter Eleven

⊷ Looking beyond the Current Horizon: In Retrospect

We return to the question broached in Chapter 1: Are teachers a dime a dozen? My answer has not changed since that chapter: No, I do not think teachers are a dime a dozen. However, as we have traveled the journey through this book, I do believe we are left with the gnawing feeling that my answer may be out of the mainstream.

In Chapters 8–10, I noted that teachers should be viewed as snowflakes: individually, for no two are alike. Teachers have their own individual contexts (e.g., grade level or subject area specializations), and we need to consider their academic and (especially) professional development with respect to their intellectual baselines. However, as discussed in Chapters 3–6, this is not necessarily what happens.

American education is guilty of rubricizing itself and teachers. Why? Simply put, it is more efficient. As discussed in Chapters 6, 8, and 9, administrators want a smoothly running ship. They do not want to deal with problems, primarily because problems turn into crises; administrators are trained to perpetually respond in crisis mode.

There appears to be a universal need for predictability, as if efficient education is something one can set a clock or calendar by: If it is noon, it must be lunchtime. If it is Tuesday, it must be meat loaf day. If it is April, it must be high-stakes assessment time. School calendars are orchestrated to the last moments of time management, as if punch cards will be thoroughly audited at the end of each fiscal year. School calendars, as well as curricula, leave little flexibility for the unexpected. Consider school districts with built-in snow days on the calendar. Despite all the preplanning, we still hear threats to eliminate holiday breaks and encroach on summer vacation if too many days are affected by inclement weather. Essentially, the efficiency of schools becomes an issue in control, even control of the uncontrollable.

Notice that I used the term "fiscal" above. Why did I not use the term "academic"? Because schools (and education) are becoming less academic and more fiscal in nature. Case in point: As McLaren and

Farahmandpur (2000, 2001) note, education, in terms of pedagogical and curricular practices, is becoming ever-more corporatized in our era of globalization. The corporatization of education is hardly a trivial concern. Globalization has not only technological implications but economic and intellectual implications as well (McLaren and Farahmandpur 2001). As our accessibility to each other expands, through telecommunications and through participation in world-market economies, one cannot help but wonder to what extent our freedom of individual thought will be limited.

This corporatization of education is perhaps a manifestation of what some call "neo-positivism," or "neo-functionalism" (e.g., Weil 2001). To give a sense of what I mean, perhaps I should define "positivism" (or "modernism"). Positivists, or modernists, view the world in terms of a linear, cause-and-effect rationality. Every question has a specific answer; every hypothesis is valid. Kincheloe (1993) refers to this mode of thought in terms of a "Cartesian-Newtonian paradigm" (i.e., a paradigm that sees modern science as an outgrowth of natural philosophy). In other words, the world is predictable, and all its variables can be controlled. In terms of education, assessment is considered a valid measure of learning for all students, regardless of context, and how students perform on achievement tests is considered an indicator of quality teaching, regardless of context. Consequently, as described in Chapter 2, functionalism views individuals in terms of their relative normalcy and usefulness toward society as a whole. The more compliant an individual is with the norms of society, the more productive he or she will be.

Putting these two thoughts together, positivism and functionalism essentially view individuals as raw data points to be analyzed statistically and dispassionately (i.e., objectively). This would presume an a priori notion of what a typical learner and a typical teacher should be; this is the standard reference for normalization or acceptability. When learners and teachers deviate from the norm, positivists and functionalists are able to predict how unsuccessful they will ultimately be; in this context, "norm" is not a statistical term, so deviation is rarely analyzed for future success. The implication is that deviance translates to lack of success, which translates to lack of productivity, which translates to marginalization in society.

In Chapter 1, I discussed my postmodern stance regarding epistemologies and ontologies. I take the stance that an epistemology is a philosophical perspective about the process of knowledge (e.g., teaching and learning), and an ontology is a philosophical perspective about knowledge itself (e.g., curriculum). This counters the modernist/positivist stance that sees epistemologies as representing philosophies about knowledge and ontologies as representing philosophies about reality.

What does this mean? Those who subscribe to a modernist/ positivist/functionalist paradigm hold very distinct and absolute views of what constitutes knowledge and what is reality. In many cases, these views are arbitrary, nonnegotiable, intolerant, and oppressive. In other words, these views are considered the norm for acceptability. Those who do not share these views (or at least comply with them) are considered deviant and will be marginalized by the dominating societal view. In the teaching profession, such marginalization could affect hiring practices, licensure, tenure, and professional advancement. If the ship of education is to be kept running smoothly, all teachers need to preach the "company line." Compliant teachers are good employees, thus making the school or organization productive and efficient. In our ever-expanding capitalist society, this implies education is a for-profit institution, in which schools are supposed to be cost-effective, and educators and learners alike are supposed to be viable commodities.

So what does "postmodernism" (or "post-positivism") mean? Whereas modernists/positivists/functionalists see the world in terms of arbitrary, decontextualized norms of reality, where deviance incurs marginalization, postmodernists see the world in terms of context, where knowledge and reality are contextual. If knowledge and reality have context, then the norms of teaching and learning also have context. Consequently, postmodernists view the world in terms of the marginalized masses of society, the deviants of technical rationalism.

Who are these deviants? First, there are women. As Sue Jackson (2000) notes, women feel compelled to "think like men" in order to succeed. Why? Men originally established the norms that all are compared to, men analyze others for deviance, and men, therefore, marginalize women who do not comply with these norms.

Second, there are racial, ethnic, and religious minorities (e.g., African Americans and Hispanic Americans). As bell hooks (1994) notes, America is a white, patriarchal society. So when we speak of the men who establish the norms of society, we must appreciate that these are white men, and more specifically, white, English-speaking, Anglo-Saxon, Protestant men. As noted in Chapter 10, professional stress is not related just to gender, race, ethnicity, or language proficiency; one's religious beliefs and practices are also subject to marginalization.

Third, there are sexual-orientation minorities. As Jackie M. Blount (2000) notes, for the better part of two centuries, American education has continued to seek out and destroy gays and lesbians, both by restricting their access to licensure and hiring and by promoting noninclusive curricula. Educators are supposed to be role models for children and communities, but only insofar as they model the norms of society's dominant culture.

So when we speak of postmodernism and marginalization, we speak of a paradigm that takes into account all the members of our society who are alienated and disenfranchised by American education and its dominant culture. Postmodernists view the world as having multiple contexts and realities. This translates to multiple forms of teaching and learning. This translates to multiple forms of curricula. This translates to multiple forms of assessment. The one-size-fits-all approach of modernism cannot suffice. Just as Albert Einstein showed in his theory of general relativity, new questions require new answers, but these answers require a newer, more contextual, and more flexible process of generation (Kincheloe, Steinberg, and Tippins 1999).

So what is neo-positivism? It is, simply put, a renewal of positivism, a return to the days of decontextualization and standardized norms. Ever since the publication of *A Nation at Risk,* there has been a renewed fervor for standards, accountability testing, and evaluating schools, teachers, and students according to the bottom line.

"The bottom line," "the profit margin," "the efficiency ratio," "the ratings index"—all are catchphrases indicating a desire for tangible results. What do educational leaders consider a legitimate outcome? In our "want it now, gain no pain" society, American education, its leaders, and its power brokers are not inclined to invest considerable time or patience waiting for genuine change and intellectual growth. Instead, the call is for immediate results, *any results,* to instantly gratify us, no matter how contrived these results may be. Neo-positivists do not wish to know about contextualizing factors, mitigating circumstances, or confounding variables. They do not wish to know about Vygotsky's zone of proximal development or Shulman's pedagogical content knowledge.

Neo-positivists wish to see "good schools," schools that maintain excellent scores on standardized tests, which in turn translate to "good" neighborhoods and communities. In a perverse way, according to G. Collins (2001), community leaders and politicians actually see a direct correlation between test scores and property values. This implies a class war between affluent suburban school districts and "poorer" urban school districts, further feeding the frenzied debate over school choice, school vouchers, and charter schools. We begin to see the essence of marginalization.

However, neo-positivists do not see themselves as advocates of marginalization; they see themselves as defenders of individual freedom and education reflective of Jeffersonian democracy. Thomas Jefferson, our nation's third president and author of the Declaration of Independence, advocated an equitable education for all. The neo-positivists have an interesting adaptation of this. President George W. Bush advocates a program for public education that would "leave no child behind," and yet the question remains as to whether any child will ever get ahead (see Chapter 2). To guarantee every child receives the same equitable level of education, the Bush agenda would need to take contextualizing factors, mitigating circumstances, or confounding variables into account. This is not what neo-positivists do. What the Bush agenda (essentially a third-generation Reagan agenda) advocates is *equivalent* education for all children. In other words, every child, regardless of contextualizing factors, mitigating circumstances, or confounding variables, would receive the same bare-bones education and be assessed according to that curriculum. Schools and children are assessed as if every school starts from the same point and every child has the same foundation, even if it is not the case. In the eyes of the Bush administration, if everyone receives the same quantity of education, then everyone should be able to achieve accordingly and become productive members of the adult workforce. This is as flawed a theory as is the theory of revenue sharing in major league baseball. As long as the New York Yankees maintain their original economic foundation, small-market teams will never really catch up and compete on a level field.

But the issue is not quantity, it is *quality*. Offering an equivalent amount of curriculum to all schools presumes that "poor" urban (and rural, according to Williams 2000) schools are able to provide supplemental resources, just as affluent suburban schools are. If these schools cannot supplement the bare-bones curriculum, the Bush agenda nevertheless absolves the government from any responsibility for their insufficiencies, for the federal government did its part. When "poor" urban and rural schools cannot offer more than the basics, the neo-positivists see this inability as an individual freedom. However, if these schools are labeled as failures, neo-positivists see no philosophical conflict with closing them down and reopening them under some corporate watch. Corporations also have individual freedom, the freedom to make money. Sometimes we forget these words from the Declaration of Independence: "all men . . . are endowed by their Creator with certain unalienable Rights, that among these are Life, Liberty and the pursuit of Happiness." Making money is a form of happiness in the realm of neo-positivism. Failing schools do not make money; therefore, they do not result in happiness. Neo-positivistic logic dictates that the pursuit of happiness trumps the pursuit of mediocrity, even if mediocrity is the intellectual standard for schools and its children.

Intellectual standards are not the concern of the neo-positivists;

standards for normalcy, consistency, and efficiency are. Neo-positivists are concerned with the logic of supply and demand, especially in terms of meeting their ultimate demands in the pursuit of happiness. Neo-positivists want *their* kind of people: those who do whatever it takes to satisfy the demands and expectations of the dominant, to get ahead in life. Those who do not get ahead obviously failed to satisfy expectations; their failure is their own fault, not the neo-positivists'. Neo-positivists lower the bar for everyone, akin to giving all players their minimal allotment of Monopoly money before the game begins. Aggressive players are free to pillage their opponents at will, for winning is the name of the game. Those who cry foul are reminded life is not fair, and nice guys finish last. As long as everyone got an equal share at the beginning, anything that follows is simply fair play in terms of the laws of nature. Neo-positivism sets the stage for an educational version of Darwinism.

What this really sets the stage for is a polarized society of haves and have-nots. With an educational bar set so low, neo-positivists can point to the have-nots and attribute their failure to inherent factors rather than to the game board. "Poor" schools do not fail because of the rules; "poor" schools fail because they perpetuate failure (see Chapter 1, regarding the CUNY system). Failure is their fault; failure is in their genetic code. Neo-positivists hold up these schools as poster children of failure, to be ridiculed, despised, and feared by all of American society. Not by design but by coincidence, the neo-positivists say, these failures are "poor," urban, and racially, ethnically, and linguistically diverse. And yet the neo-positivists hold up these failures as if they are societal bogeymen, the educational version of the elder President Bush's Willie Horton.

But the demographic profile of failure *is* by design. Neo-positivism represents the New Right, a neo-conservative, capitalistic, technical rationalist, racist, misogynist, homophobic, and Anglocentric cultural paradigm that presumes others to be deviants and failures (e.g., Kincheloe 1993; Kincheloe and Steinberg 1998; Pinar 1998). Neo-positivists polarize society into *us* and *them.* However, *us* is a terribly narrow and exclusive group; *them* is a perversely expanding group whose members have little chance of ever joining *us.* Neo-positivists continuously chant the theme of systemic reform (e.g., Boyd 2000), demanding rapid improvement while wielding the threat of corporate takeover (see Chapter 6, regarding Edison Schools). But genuine reform is not their desire, for it weakens their threat. Genuine reform is not their desire, for it potentially depolarizes society. Genuine reform is not their desire, for it gives them one less thing to chant about. Neo-positivists do not want reform (despite their chants and rhetoric); they want a socially and politically divisive mechanism that perpetually marginalizes and depowers those who see beyond the boundaries. A perpetually polarized society supports the Darwinist agenda of neo-positivistic education; it validates the dichotomy between normalcy and deviance and the premise that certain people are simply not destined to succeed.

There seems to be an increasing trend in school systems to take a greater interest in the neo-positivistic view, especially in terms of applying corporate principles. Why? Corporations work, they succeed, they are cost-effective, they are efficient, and they are predictable. We rarely see the media attack corporate America the way education is attacked. We rarely hear of failing corporations the way we hear of failing schools. If corporations fail, they simply disappear; failing schools are said to last forever.

Somehow schools are willing to abdicate their sense of power and autonomy for the sake of a panacea, a shining knight on a white horse. Schools seem so desperate to improve, according to the indices established by neo-positivists, that they are willing to capitulate. It is simpler to allow an external authority to tell them what to do, as if they no longer bear any direct responsibility for education.

All this translates to tremendous stress for classroom educators and teacher educators (e.g., Guglielmi and Tatrow 1998; Troman and Woods 2000). When external authorities assume control and power over the process of knowledge, what does this mean for the individualism of teaching? Sadly, it implies teachers cannot be individuals; they are cogs within a giant machine, pressured to produce highly skilled human widgets for the job market. Of course, it remains to be debated what exactly "highly skilled" (e.g., Boyd 2000) and "human" ultimately mean.

Educators are forced to contend with the expectations of capitalism and industrialism. The corporate world still looks at schools, at all levels, as factories. I have heard colleagues say that everyone, at different points in life, eventually goes to work. This implies that the primary mission of education, above everything else, is to prepare everyone for a life of work (i.e., gainful employment). Never mind intellectual growth; some attack this as elitist, something only for the privileged few. In some respects, those attackers fail to realize how such logic supports neo-positivist contentions that certain people are inherently unable to grow intellectually. By keeping expectations low enough to ensure minimal knowledge for everyone, neo-positivists and their unwitting supporters ensure a glass ceiling for the vast majority of our society.

So in our industrialist, corporatized schools, knowledge and its consumers and producers (i.e., teachers and students, on both counts) are viewed simultaneously as raw materials and products (e.g., Anderson 2001; Aronowitz 2000; McLaren and Farahmandpur 2001). Not only is this dehumanizing, but it also dictates our worth and viability, not according to our merits, but according to society's catalog. If for some reason, we are viewed as unmarketable, as products with low sales volume, we could be discontinued, pulled from the shelves. We would not be marginalized according to our beliefs; we would be marginalized according to our lack of usefulness in the eyes of our consuming society.

What does this say about professional development? Based on what neo-positivism dictates, professional development is only genuine if it is useful to the neo-positivists. For example, it would be useless to neo-positivists for teachers to attend in-service workshops on children's conceptions about the nature of science. For neo-positivists, there is nothing to be gained or debated; the nature of science is the correct answer to items on accountability tests. The purpose of professional development should not be the individual intellectual growth of teachers or students; it should be improved classroom efficiency and achievement proficiency.

The same can be said for professional advancement. Unless one can demonstrate to neo-positivists that a teacher who wants to move up will be of ultimate use and value, neo-positivist leaders have no reason to promote him or her. As noted in Chapter 9, many teachers view administration as an avenue toward power and influence. In reality, there is no power or influence; administration is merely an artificial reward for satisfying the expectations of neo-positivism. Teachers who are promoted to new levels of responsibility must still meet the same expectations: the expectations of neo-positivism.

Is it any wonder that so many teachers escape the profession after only a few years? Teachers do not necessarily leave the profession because of their competence (or lack thereof); perhaps they leave in order to rescue their souls as individual, intelligent, and empathetic human beings. There was a time, a few decades ago, when teachers committed themselves to staying. Granted, many left the profession in search of better economic opportunities, but I rarely recall hearing about teachers like Ann, the teacher from West Philadelphia we encountered in Chapter 1. Yes, we can say that teacher salaries are still low compared to those of the private sector, but salaries are much better than they were a few decades ago. Considering that school systems are offering signing bonuses and other financial incentives to attract new teachers, can we really say money is a major issue? There are many more issues to consider besides money. Schools have changed. Communities have changed. Curricula have changed. Assessment has taken on greater prominence. The politics of education have changed. In short, the whole perspective about education has changed, and not for the better. Since the publication of *A Nation at Risk,* things have become testier, nastier, and edgier. Everyone is under suspicion; everyone is fighting for survival and respect. Now, more than ever before, educators are forced to constantly defend themselves; we have essentially entered an era of academic McCarthyism. No one enjoys being branded. Why not leave the profession and salvage one's dignity?

I seem to be painting a very bleak picture for American education and teacher education. I cannot help it. We have entered an era of education in which the word "education" is gradually disappearing from our discourse. Why? Again, we see the dominance of neo-positivism. We are no longer working in a paradigm that equates education with intellectualism. We work in a paradigm of feeding a capitalistic, corporatized society.

As much as I hate to say it, consider the title of this book, *Teacher Training*. Why are we using the term "training"? It has very corporate implications. Worse, it has very behavioristic implications. According to Dewey (1916), *training* is what we do with animals in order to illicit desired behaviors; on the other hand, *education* can result in mental and emotional disposition changes. *Education* seems more academic, more intellectual. I was recently criticized by academic colleagues who asked me, "What were you thinking when you penned the title?!" In their eyes, no matter what is written between the covers of this book, the title already de-legitimizes me a tad as a scholar of education, for it does not sound very scholarly.

The choice of wording for this book title was predetermined by business people. Business people are *bottom line* people; they function in a world of tangible results. "Training" sounds like a tangible term; "training" sounds like something that produces results. Business people want results; they *love* results. Educational leaders want and love results too. Unfortunately, education is not exactly a business, even though, as already mentioned, schools are looking toward business principles for organizational guidance.

Perhaps, in response to this changing view, publishers sense a hook within the economic market. Educational leaders are looking for books that tell them what they want to hear. Just as educational leaders streamlined the intentions of the unit-lesson-plan models of the 1970s, perhaps now they go about looking for books that utilize a similar protocol. The search is merely an extension of the quest for greater efficiency.

Publishing books is big business. Publishing companies do not make money unless they sell books; books, therefore, need to be sellable. What makes a book sellable? Perhaps its title. For example, people searching for books that will help them quit smoking for the rest of their lives will naturally look for books with the word "smoking" in the title.

How much time will they invest looking at a book titled *Happiness for You?* Do they really want to take the time to read through the book until they come across a small section on quitting smoking, assuming the author wrote about it? Granted, one may need to quit smoking in order to be happy, but unless the book is titled *Smoking and Your Unhappiness*, they will probably put the book back on the shelf and continue looking for what immediately meets their criteria.

Why should we expect anything different from educational leaders or anyone else searching for a book about the teaching profession? What if this book was titled *A New Perspective on Education?* Nope, too broad—next! What if it was titled *Philosophical Trends and the Classroom Practitioner?* Nope, too esoteric—next! What if it was titled *How To Make Teachers More Competent in Five Easy Steps?* Hey, a winner! Let's buy the book! Never mind what the book says on the inside; the title offered magic words, and the reader has been hooked for a sale.

In our "want it now, gain no pain" and "quick tidy fix" society, purchasers of books want solutions to the ultimate problem and answers to the ultimate question. Think of all the self-help books on the market today, promising to make us healthy, wealthy, sexually satisfied, physically fit, and eternally happy. These are all manifestations of our immediate-gratification era. Consumers of such books seek a written Holy Grail, and publishers want to convince them they have found it in their books. Everyone wins. The buyer finds Utopia, and publishers make profits.

This is not to say I am a communist (although I do see considerable merit to Karl Marx's socialism theory). I do appreciate my livelihood, the purchasing power of currency, and the comforts of a roof over my head, food on my table, and clothes on my body. However, I do not view currency as if it were a golden calf. It is not the be all and end all, nor is it the symbol of democracy. As discussed earlier in this chapter, the ideal of democracy, as proposed by Thomas Jefferson more than two centuries ago, is vastly different from what neo-positivists advocate. Somehow, education needs to represent more than profit for power brokers, the polarizing of society, and survival of the fittest. As the reductionists of approximately a century ago noted, societal growth needs to include individual growth in order to be completely meaningful and successful. This is lost on neo-positivists.

So have you found Utopia yet? If you recall the first few pages of this book, I promised neither solutions to the ultimate problem, nor answers to the ultimate question. Approximately 200 pages later, I still offer neither. It was never my intention to provide either. That is not my role as an educator, and that is not what education is about, at least from my perspective.

Education is a little like the cliché "You can lead a horse to water, but you can't make it drink." In this book, I have introduced the terms "transformative intellectualism" and "transformational leadership." What exactly are these terms supposed to mean? These terms mean change, on a simplistic level; on a more abstract level, the meaning is more profound. In my prior existence as a chemistry and physics professor, I was (and I still am) incredibly fascinated by the concept of *entropy*, for it has multiple contextual meanings (Pushkin 1997). However, for this discussion, we should be aware that "entropy," on a historical level, is essentially the Greek word for "transformation" (Baierlein 1992). A transformation essentially means a "significant change." To transform as a leader, one needs to advocate significant changes in schools. To transform as an educator, one needs to advocate significant changes in knowledge, thinking, and learning. To transform as a learner, one needs to advocate significant changes within one's own mind.

But many scientists define entropy in terms of disorder, or randomness (Baierlein 1992; Pushkin 1997). To them, transformations bring about some level of chaos. In terms of scientific processes, this chaos is good, for it encourages new possibilities. In terms of education and systemic educational reform, this chaos is considered bad, for it interferes with predictability (scientifically speaking, no it does not), uniformity, and efficiency (scientifically speaking, yes it can). In other words, "to transform" means to perturb a system, the entire system, not merely a small segment of it.

One cannot reform learners without reforming teachers. One cannot reform teachers without reforming leaders. Reform has many dimensions; all dimensions need to reform simultaneously. This, of course, is counterlogical to neo-positivists, who approach reform in a piecemeal linear progression. It is akin to Dewey's (1916) observation that the unexpected suddenly interferes with routine maintenance; entropy destabilizes the system, thus the system ceases to properly function. However, this functionality only works in dichotomous fashion; the system appears to be inherently incapable of accommodating new possibilities. As Dewey wrote, "Mankind likes to think in terms of extreme opposites. It is given to formulating its beliefs in terms of *Either-Ors*, between which it recognizes no intermediate possibilities" (1938, 17).

Reform is somehow expected to obey and honor the way things are and to dismiss all other schemes; to question or challenge a conservative system is virtual heresy. To deviate from the norm of familiarity brings consequences, as if we threaten the ultimate truth and the safety of its guardians. Without this sense of truth, reality, and safety, people cannot handle challenge; it is too much of a perturbation.

To transform means to create a steady barrage of opportunities for people to dare to look themselves in a mirror and challenge their personal truths, realities, and sense of safety and comfort. It is not our job to make them look in the mirror or to bring the mirror to them; we are supposed to plant the seed in their minds for them to want to look in the mirror on their own. Reform by decree is ineffective (Kincheloe 1992); there needs to be an individual stake in it for all of us.

Perhaps people are too terrified, fearing the unknowns within themselves. Reform may be too much to ask of those who know no differently. For safety's sake and for self-preservation, we suppress these challenges, shroud the mirrors, and purge all perturbations. This is why reform seems interminably perpetual. Change is not the issue, for change never genuinely happens. Change is the mantra yet hardly the vehicle.

This book was presented to you not as a reference handbook but as a *point-of-reference* handbook. The point of reference presented to you is that of epistemologies and ontologies. There are underlying philosophical beliefs that shape education at all levels and for all learning contexts. The same can be said for teacher education, professional development, and the vocation of being an educator. Unfortunately, after nearly two centuries of public education in the United States, we have yet to completely come to terms with our own individual beliefs. Consequently, we continue to work from a model that fails to acknowledge the many different fabrics and flavors of the education profession. As we gradually enter our third century of public education, perhaps it is finally time we take a new, more open, and more individualized look at this profession and at those who continue to honor it.

REFERENCES

Anderson, M. S. 2001. "The Complex Relations between the Academy and Industry." *Journal of Higher Education* 72, no. 2: 226–246.

Aronowitz, S. 2000. *The Knowledge Factory: Dismantling the Corporate University and Creating True Higher Learning.* Boston: Beacon.

Baierlein, R. 1992. "How Entropy Got Its Name." *American Journal of Physics* 60: 1151.

Blount, J. M. 2000. "Spinsters, Bachelors, and Other Gender Transgressors in School Employment, 1850–1990." *Review of Educational Research* 70, no. 1: 83–101.

Boyd, W. L. 2000. "The 'R's of School Reform' and the Politics of Reforming or Replacing Public Schools." *Journal of Educational Change* 1, no. 3: 225–252.

Collins, G. 2001. "Those Who Can't, Test." *New York Times,* April 17, A25.

Dewey, J. 1938. *Experience and Education.* New York: Macmillan.

———. 1916. *Democracy and Education: An Introduction to the Philosophy of Education.* New York: Macmillan.

Guglielmi, R. S., and K. Tatrow. 1998. "Occupational Stress, Burnout, and Health in Teachers: A Methodological and Theoretical Analysis." *Review of Educational Research* 68, no. 1: 61–99.

hooks, b. 1994. *Teaching to Transgress: Education as the Practice of Freedom.* London: Routledge.

Jackson, S. 2000. "Differently Academic? Constructions of 'Academic' in Higher Education." *Higher Education Research and Development* 19, no. 3: 279–296.

Kincheloe, J. L. 1993. *Toward a Critical Politics of Teacher Thinking: Mapping the Postmodern.* Westport, CT: Bergin and Garvey.

———. 1992. "Education Reform: What Have Been the Effects of the Attempts To Improve Education over the Last Decade?" Pp. 227–232 in *Thirteen Questions: Reframing Education's Conversation.* Edited by J. L. Kincheloe and S. R. Steinberg. New York: Peter Lang.

Kincheloe, J. L., and S. R. Steinberg, eds. 1998. *Unauthorized Methods: Strategies for Critical Teaching.* New York: Routledge.

Kincheloe, J. L., S. R. Steinberg, and D. J. Tippins. 1999. *The Stigma of Genius: Einstein, Consciousness, and Education.* New York: Peter Lang.

McLaren, P., and Farahmandpur, R. 2001. "Teaching against Globalization and the New Imperialism: Toward a Revolutionary Pedagogy." *Journal of Teacher Education* 52, no. 2: 136–150.

———. 2000. "Reconsidering Marx in Post-Marxist Times." *Educational Researcher* 29, no. 3: 25–33.

Pinar, W. F., ed. 1998. *Curriculum: Toward New Identities.* New York: Garland Publishers.

Pushkin, D. B. 1997. "Can Thermistor Probes Illustrate Entropy?" *Physics Essays* 10, no. 1: 50–54.

Troman, G., and P. Woods. 2000. "Careers under Stress: Teachers' Adaptations at a Time of Intensive Reform." *Journal of Educational Change* 1, no. 3: 253–275.

Weil, D. 2001. "From Functionalism to Neo-Functionalism and Neo-Liberalism: Developing a Dialectical Understanding of the Standards Debate through Historical Awareness." In *The Encyclopedia of Educational Standards.* Edited by J. L. Kincheloe and D. Weil. Santa Barbara, CA: ABC-CLIO Publishers. In press.

Williams, H. E. 2000. "A Descriptive Study: African-American Adolescent Males, Absenteeism, Mentoring, and Alienation in Rural Public Schools." Ed.D. diss., Wilmington College of Delaware.

Chapter Twelve

✎ Organizations, Associations, and Government Agencies

RECOMMENDED PROFESSIONAL ORGANIZATIONS

American Association of Colleges for Teacher Education

1307 New York Avenue, NW, Suite 300
Washington, DC 20005-4701
Telephone: (202) 293-2450; fax: (202) 457-8095
www.aacte.org

This organization is a national, voluntary association of colleges and universities, primarily concerned with the preparation of professional educators. One of its major publications is the *Journal of Teacher Education.*

American Educational Research Association

1230 17th Street, NW
Washington, DC 20036-3078
Telephone: (202) 223-9485; fax: (202) 775-1824
www.aera.net

This organization is primarily concerned with improving education by means of scholarly research. Among its publications are *Educational Researcher* and *Review of Educational Research.*

American Federation of Teachers

555 New Jersey Avenue, NW
Washington, DC 20001
Telephone: (202) 879-4400, (800) 238-1133; fax: (202) 879-4545
www.aft.org

This organization is one of the largest and most active teachers' unions in the United States. It is primarily concerned with the professional status and working conditions for classroom teachers at all levels of education.

Association for the Study of Higher Education
University of Missouri–Columbia
202 Hill Hall
Columbia, MO 65211-2190
Telephone: (573) 882-9645; fax: (573) 884-2197
http://www.ashe.missouri.edu

This organization concerns itself with the policies and practices of colleges and universities, including issues of pedagogy and curriculum. Among its publications is *The Review of Higher Education.*

National Education Association
1201 16th Street, NW
Washington, DC 20036-3290
Telephone: (202) 833-4000; fax: (202) 822-7974
www.nea.org

This organization is the oldest and largest organization committed to advancing the cause of public education in the United States. Founded in 1857, it has more than 2.5 million members from every level of public education.

National Society for the Study of Education
5835 Kimbark Avenue
Chicago, IL 60637

This organization, founded in 1901, annually explores specific topics of concern to educators, researchers, and administrators, through its series of yearbooks. Numerous scholars and practitioners write these yearbooks.

STATE DEPARTMENTS OF EDUCATION

Information follows for all the state teacher certification offices in the United States, including the District of Columbia. The following listing is based on the one provided by the National Teachers Clearinghouse of Boston, Massachusetts, during the 1998–1999 academic year. The University of Kentucky College of Education also maintains a Web page with links to pages showing each state's certification requirements: *http://www.uky.edu/Education/TEP/usacert.html.* For all requirements for teacher certification, administrator certification, and guidance counselor certification, please contact the most relevant office.

Teacher Certification Section
Alabama Department of Education
P.O. Box 302101
Montgomery, AL 36130
Telephone: (334) 242-9977; fax: (224) 242-0498
http://www.alsde.edu

Alaska Department of Education Certification
801 W. 10th Street, Suite 200
Juneau, AK 99801-1894
Telephone: (907) 465-2831; fax: (907) 465-2441
http://www.educ.state.ak.us

Teacher Certification
Arizona Department of Education
1535 W. Jefferson
Phoenix, AZ 85007
Telephone: (602) 542-4367; fax: (602) 542-1141
http://ade.state.az.us

Teacher Education and Licensure
Arkansas Department of Education
4 State Capitol Mall
Little Rock, AR 72201-1071
Telephone: (501) 682-4342; fax: (501) 682-1079
http://arkedu.state.ar.us/teacher.htm

California Commission on Teacher Credentialing
1812 9th Street
P.O. Box 944270
Sacramento, CA 94244-2700
Telephone: (916) 445-7254; fax: (916) 327-3166
http://www.ctc.ca.gov/default.html

Educator Licensing
Colorado Department of Education
201 E. Colfax Avenue
Denver, CO 80203-1799
Telephone: (303) 866-6628; fax: (303) 866-6968
http://www.cde.state.co.us

Bureau of Certification and Professional Development
Connecticut Department of Education
P.O. Box 2219
Hartford, CT 06145-2219
Telephone: (203) 566-5201; fax: (203) 566-8289
http://www.state.ct.us/sde/dtl/cert/index.htm

Professional Standards and Certification
Delaware Department of Public Instruction
P.O. Box 1402
Dover, DE 19903-1402
Telephone: (302) 739-4686, (800) 433-5292; fax: (302) 739-4654
http://www.doe.state.de.us

District of Columbia Public Schools
Logan Administration Building, Room 101A
215 G Street, NE
Washington, DC 20002
Telephone: (202) 724-4249, (800) 443-3277; fax: (202) 724-8784
http://www.k12.dc.us

Bureau of Teacher Certification
Florida Department of Education
The Florida Education Center, Room 203
325 W. Gaines Street
Tallahassee, FL 32399-0400
Telephone: (904) 488-2317; fax: (904) 488-3352
http://www.firn.edu/doe/index.html

Certification Section
Georgia Professional Standards Commission
1452 Twin Towers E
Atlanta, GA 30334
Telephone: (404) 657-9000, (800) 869-7775; fax: (404) 651-9185
http://www.doe.k12.ga.us

Personnel Certification and Development Section
Hawaii Department of Education
P.O. Box 2360
Honolulu, HI 96804
Telephone: (808) 586-3276; fax: (808) 586-3419
http://www.k12.hi.us

Office of Teacher Education and Certification
Idaho Department of Education
P.O. Box 83720
Boise, ID 83720-0027
Telephone: (208) 334-3475; fax: (208) 334-2228
http://www.sde.state.id.us

Teacher Education and Certification
Illinois Board of Education
100 N. 1st Street
Springfield, IL 62777-0001
Telephone: (217) 782-2805; fax: (217) 524-1289
http://www.isbe.state.il.us

Teacher Certification
Indiana Professional Standards Board
251 E. Ohio Street, Suite 201
Indianapolis, IN 46204-2133
Telephone: (317) 232-9010; fax: (317) 232-9023
http://www.doe.state.in.us

Board of Educational Examiners
Iowa Department of Education
Grimes State Office Building
Des Moines, IA 50319-0147
Telephone: (515) 281-3245; fax: (515) 281-4122
http://www.state.ia.us/educate

Certification and Teacher Education
Kansas Board of Education
120 S.E. 10th Street
Topeka, KS 66612-1182
Telephone: (913) 296-2288; fax: (913) 296-7933
http://www.ksbe.state.ks.us

Division of Certification
Kentucky Department of Education
Capital Plaza Tower
500 Metro Street
Frankfort, KY 40601
Telephone: (502) 564-4606; fax: (502) 564-6470
http://www.kde.state.ky.us

Bureau of Higher Education and Teacher Certification
Louisiana Department of Education
P.O. Box 94064
Baton Rouge, LA 70804-9064
Telephone: (504) 342-3490; fax: (504) 342-3499
http://www.doe.state.la.us

Division of Certification and Placement
Maine Department of Education
State House Station 23
Augusta, ME 04333
Telephone: (207) 287-5944; fax: (207) 287-5900
http://www.state.me.us/education/homepage.htm

Teacher Education and Certification Branch
Maryland Department of Education
200 W. Baltimore Street
Baltimore, MD 21201-2595
Telephone: (410) 767-0100; fax: (410) 333-8963
http://www.msde.state.md.us

Bureau of Teacher Certification
Massachusetts Department of Education
350 Main Street
P.O. Box 9140
Malden, MA 02148-9140
Telephone: (617) 388-3380; fax: (617) 388-3396
http://www.doe.mass.edu

Teacher/Administration Preparation and Certification
Michigan Department of Education
P.O. Box 30008
Lansing, MI 48909
Telephone: (517) 373-3310; fax: (517) 373-0542
http://www.mde.state.mi.us

Personnel Licensing Team
Minnesota Department of Education
616 Capitol Square Building
550 Cedar Street
St. Paul, MN 55101
Telephone: (612) 296-2046; fax: (612) 282-5892
http://www.educ.state.mn.us

Teacher Certification
Mississippi Department of Education
P.O. Box 771
Jackson, MS 39205
Telephone: (601) 359-3483; fax: (601) 359-3242
http://www.mde.k12.ms.us

Teacher Education and Certification
Missouri Department of Elementary and
Secondary Education
P.O. Box 480
Jefferson City, MO 65102
Telephone: (314) 751-3486; fax: (314) 751-1179
http://services.dese.state.mo.us

Division of Certification and Teacher Education
Montana Office of Public Instruction
P.O. Box 202501
Helena, MT 59620-2501
Telephone: (406) 444-3150; fax: (406) 444-2893
http://www.metnet.state.mt.us/

Teacher Education and Certification
Nebraska Department of Education
P.O. Box 94987
Lincoln, NE 68509-4987
Telephone: (800) 371-4642; fax: (402) 471-0117
http://www.nde.state.ne.us

Nevada Department of Education
1850 E. Sahara, Suite 207, State Mail Room
Las Vegas, NV 89158
Telephone: (702) 486-6455; fax: (702) 796-3475
http://www.nde.state.nv.us/

New Hampshire Bureau of Credentialing
Division of Program Support
Department of Education
101 Pleasant Street
Concord, NH 03301
Telephone: (603) 271-2407; fax: (603) 271-1953
http://www.ed.state.nh.us

Office of Licensing and Academic Credentials
New Jersey Department of Education
CN 500
Trenton, NJ 08625-0500
Telephone: (609) 292-2070; fax: (609) 292-3768
http://www.state.nj.us/education

Professional Licensure Unit
New Mexico Department of Education
300 Don Gaspar Avenue
Santa Fe, NM 87501-2786
Telephone: (505) 827-6587; fax: (505) 827-6696
http://sde.state.nm.us

Office of Teaching
New York Department of Education
Cultural Education Center, Room 5A-11
Albany, NY 12230
Telephone: (518) 474-3901; fax: (518) 473-0271
http://www.nysed.gov

Licensure Section
North Carolina Department of Public Instruction
301 N. Wilmington Street
Raleigh, NC 27601-2825
Telephone: (919) 733-4125; fax: (919) 715-1094
http://www.dpi.state.nc.us

North Dakota Education Standards and Practices Board
600 E. Boulevard Avenue
Bismarck, ND 58505-0440
Telephone: (701) 328-2264; fax: (701) 328-2461
http://www.state.nd.us/espb

Teacher Education and Certification
Ohio Department of Education
65 S. Front Street, Room 416
Columbus, OH 43215-4183
Telephone: (614) 466-3593; fax: (614) 466-1999
http://www.ode.state.oh.us

Professional Standards Section
Oklahoma Department of Education
Hodge Education Building, Room 211
Oklahoma City, OK 73105
Telephone: (405) 521-3337; fax: (405) 521-6205
http://sde.state.ok.us

Oregon Teacher Standards and Practices Commission
Public Service Building
255 Capitol Street NE, Suite 105
Salem, OR 97310-1332
Telephone: (503) 378-3586; fax: (503) 378-4448
http://www.ode.state.or.us

Bureau of Teacher Preparations and Certification
Pennsylvania Department of Education
333 Market Street
Harrisburg, PA 17126-0333
Telephone: (717) 787-2967; fax: (717) 783-6736
http://www.pde.psu.edu

Office of Teacher Education and Certification
Rhode Island Department of Education
22 Hayes Street
Providence, RI 02908
Telephone: (401) 277-2675; fax: (401) 277-2048
http://www.ric.edu/sehd/information_students/riteachercert.html

Office of Education Professions
South Carolina Department of Education
Rutledge Building, Room 702
1429 Senate Street
Columbia, SC 29201
Telephone: (803) 734-8317; fax: (803) 734-6225
http://www.sde.state.sc.us

Teacher Education and Certification
South Dakota Department of Education and Cultural Affairs
700 Governors Drive
Pierre, SD 57501-2291
Telephone: (605) 773-3553; fax: (605) 773-6139
http://www.state.sd.us/deca

Office of Teacher Licensing
Career Ladder Certification
Tennessee Department of Education
5th Floor Gateway Plaza
710 James Robertson Parkway
Nashville, TN 37243-0377
Telephone: (615) 532-4885; fax: (615) 741-6236
http://www.state.tn.us/education

Division of Educator Preparation
Texas Education Agency
1701 N. Congress Avenue
Austin, TX 78701
Telephone: (512) 463-9734; fax: (512) 463-6299
http://www.tea.state.tx.us

Teacher Certification
Utah Board of Education
250 E. 500 S
Salt Lake City, UT 84111
Telephone: (801) 538-7740; fax: (801) 538-7769
http://www.usoe.k12.ut.us

Licensing Office
Vermont Department of Education
120 State Street
Montpelier, VT 05620
Telephone: (802) 828-2445; fax: (802) 828-3140
http://www.state.vt.us/educ

Office for Teacher Education and Licensure
Division for Compliance Coordination
Virginia Department of Education
P.O. Box 2120
Richmond, VA 23216-2120
Telephone: (804) 225-2022; fax: (804) 225-2831
http://www.pen.k12.va.us/VDOE/newvdoe/teached.html

Professional Education and Certification
Washington Department of Education
Old Capitol Building
P.O. Box 47200
Olympia, WA 98504-7200
Telephone: (360) 753-6773; fax: (360) 586-0145
http://www.k12.wa.us/cert

Office of Professional Preparation
West Virginia Department of Education
Building 6, Room 337
Capitol Complex
Charleston, WV 25305-0330
Telephone: (304) 558-7010, (800) 982-2378; fax: (304) 558-0459
http://wvde.state.wv.us

Licensing Team, Teacher Education Team
Wisconsin Department of Public Instruction
125 S. Webster Street
P.O. Box 7841
Madison, WI 53707-7841
Telephone: (608) 266-1027; fax: (608) 264-9558
http://www.dpi.state.wi.us

Professional Teaching Standards Board
Wyoming Department of Education
Hathaway Building, 2nd Floor
2300 Capitol Avenue
Cheyenne, WY 82002
Telephone: (307) 777-6261; fax: (307) 777-6234
http://www.k12.wy.us/wdehome.html

Chapter Thirteen

✷ Selected Print and Nonprint Resources

PRINT RESOURCES

Journal Articles

Adams, P. E., and G. H. Krockover. 1999. **"Stimulating Constructivist Teaching Styles through Use of an Observation Rubric."** *Journal of Research in Science Teaching* 36, no. 8: 955–971.

This article discusses interventions with novice high school science teachers to promote student-centered instruction.

Aikenhead, G. S., and O. J. Jegede. 1999. **"Cross-Cultural Science Education: A Cognitive Explanation of a Cultural Phenomenon."** *Journal of Research in Science Teaching* 36, no. 3: 269–287.

This article discusses science-for-all curricula and taking cultural life and world experience into account.

Akatugba, A. H., and J. Wallace. 1999. **"Sociocultural Influences on Physics Students' Use of Proportional Reasoning in a Non-Western Country."** *Journal of Research in Science Teaching* 36, no. 3: 305–320.

This article discusses how social and cultural contexts influence the way certain mathematics skills are applied by physics students in Nigeria.

Akerson, V. L., F. Abd-El-Khalick, and N. G. Lederman. 2000. **"Influence of a Reflective Explicit Activity-Based Approach on Elementary Teachers' Conceptions of Nature of Science."** *Journal of Research in Science Teaching* 37, no. 4: 295–317.

This article discusses how a university science-teaching-methods course explicitly focuses on developing conceptions of the nature of science.

Allen, N. J., and F. E. Crawley. 1998. **"Voices from the Bridge: Worldview Conflicts of Kickapoo Students of Science."** *Journal of Research in Science Teaching* 35, no. 2: 111–132.

This article discusses the contrast between Native American children's worldviews and the views of traditional science curricula.

Arora, A. G., E. Kean, and J. L. Anthony. 2000. **"An Interpretive Study of a Teacher's Evolving Practice of Elementary School Science."** *Journal of Science Teacher Education* 11, no. 2: 155–172.

This article discusses how elementary school teachers change their teaching practices in the face of reforms in science education.

Ashton, P. T. 1996. **"Improving the Preparation of Teachers."** *Educational Researcher* 25, no. 9: 21–22, 35.

This article discusses reform for teacher-certification programs.

Atwater, M. M. 1996. **"Social Constructivism: Infusion into the Multicultural Science Education Research Agenda."** *Journal of Research in Science Teaching* 33, no. 8: 821–837.

This article discusses the potential impact of incorporating social constructivism and multiculturalism into science curricular and pedagogical practices.

Bailey, B. L., K. C. Scantlebury, and E. M. Johnson. 1999. **"Encouraging the Beginning of Equitable Science Teaching Practice: Collaboration Is the Key."** *Journal of Science Teacher Education* 10, no. 3: 159–173.

This article discusses preparing prospective science teachers to promote gender equity in classrooms despite their own inequitable school experiences.

Bencze, L., and D. Hodson. 1999. **"Changing Practice by Changing Practice: Toward More Authentic Science and Science Curriculum Development."** *Journal of Research in Science Teaching* 36, no. 5: 521–539.

This article discusses the role of teachers' beliefs about and practices in science teaching in the face of reform in Ontario.

Blount, J. M. 2000. **"Spinsters, Bachelors, and Other Gender Transgressors in School Employment, 1850–1990."** *Review of Educational Research* 70, no. 1: 83–101.

This article discusses the historical context of gender roles and the teaching profession.

BouJaoude, S. 2000. **"Conceptions of Science Teaching Revealed by Metaphors and by Answers to Open-Ended Questions."** *Journal of Science Teacher Education* 11, no. 2: 173–186.

This article discusses how prospective science teachers in Lebanon develop their conceptions about science.

Bryan, L. A., and S. K. Abell. 1999. **"Development of Professional Knowledge in Learning To Teach Elementary Science."** *Journal of Research in Science Teaching* 36, no. 2: 121–139.

This article discusses how a novice elementary school teacher sought to balance her science content knowledge with her pedagogical knowledge.

Crawford, B. A. 1999. **"Is It Realistic To Expect a Preservice Teacher To Create an Inquiry-Based Classroom?"** *Journal of Science Teacher Education* 10, no. 3: 175–194.

This article discusses the challenges facing new teachers who are asked to teach inquiry-based science despite having no inquiry experience as students.

Czerniak, C. M., A. T. Lumpe, and J. J. Haney. 1999. **"Science Teachers' Beliefs and Intentions To Implement Thematic Units."** *Journal of Science Teacher Education* 10, no. 2: 123–145.

This article discusses the compatibility between teachers' beliefs about science content and their inclusion of science in thematic teaching units.

Donato, R., and M. Lazerson. 2000. **"New Directions in American Educational History: Problems and Prospects."** *Educational Researcher* 29, no. 8: 4–15.

This article discusses educational reform during the 1960s and 1970s.

Geddis, A. N., and D. A. Roberts. 1998. **"As Science Students Become Science Teachers: A Perspective on Learning Orientation."** *Journal of Science Teacher Education* 9, no. 4: 271–292.

This article discusses the influence of learning experiences on future teaching practices.

Grunau, H., E. Pedretti, E. Wolfe, and D. Galbraith. 2000. **"Collaborative Professional Development for Science Educators: Locating Reflection in Practice through a Science Methods Course."** *Journal of Science Teacher Education* 11, no. 1: 47–61.

This article discusses how education faculty and prospective teachers can collaborate together to help promote more reflective practice.

Hanrahan, M. 1999. **"Rethinking Scientific Literacy: Enhancing Communication and Participation in School Science through Affirmational Dialogue Journal Writing."** *Journal of Research in Science Teaching* 36, no. 6: 699–717.

This article discusses how incorporating student experiences into science instruction could make learning more meaningful.

Harding, P., and W. Hare. 2000. **"Portraying Science Accurately in Classrooms: Emphasizing Open-Mindedness Rather Than Relativism."** *Journal of Research in Science Teaching* 37, no. 3: 225–236.

This article discusses the relative compatibility between the views of science education and the views of science.

Hogan, K., and A. R. Berkowitz. 2000. **"Teachers as Inquiry Learners."** *Journal of Science Teacher Education* 11, no. 1: 1–25.

This article points out that teachers need to become inquiry-oriented learners before they can teach such learning in their classrooms.

Koballa, T. R., W. Gräber, D. Coleman, and A. C. Kemp. 1999. **"Prospective Teachers' Conceptions of the Knowledge Base for Teaching Chemistry at the German Gymnasium."** *Journal of Science Teacher Education* 10, no. 4: 269–286.

This article discusses the content knowledge base expected of high school chemistry teachers in Germany.

Korthagen, F. A. J., and J. P. A. M. Kessels. 1999. **"Linking Theory and Practice: Changing the Pedagogy of Teacher Education."** *Educational Researcher* 28, no. 4: 4–17.

This article discusses a more realistic, pragmatic approach to the role of theory in teacher education.

Lederman, N. G. 1999. **"Teachers' Understanding of the Nature of Science and Classroom Practice: Factors That Facilitate or Impede the Relationship."** *Journal of Research in Science Teaching* 36, no. 8: 916–929.

This article discusses the relationship between teachers' conceptions about science and their classroom practice.

Loewenberg-Ball, D., and D. K. Cohen. 1996. **"Reform by the Book: What Is—or Might Be—the Role of Curriculum Materials in Teacher**

Learning and Instructional Reform?" *Educational Researcher* 25, no. 9: 6–8, 14.

This article discusses the influence of curriculum packages on school reform.

Luft, J. A. 1999. **"Teachers' Salient Beliefs about a Problem-Solving Demonstration Classroom In-Service Program."** *Journal of Research in Science Teaching* 36, no. 2: 141–158.

This article discusses the relationship between practicing teachers' beliefs regarding problem solving in science and their classroom practices.

Lumpe, A. T., J. J. Haney, and C. M. Czerniak. 2000. **"Assessing Teachers' Beliefs about Their Science Teaching Context."** *Journal of Research in Science Teaching* 37, no. 3: 275–292.

This article discusses the relationship between teachers' school environments and their teaching practices.

McLoughlin, A. S., and T. M. Dana. 1999. **"Making Science Relevant: The Experiences of Prospective Elementary School Teachers in an Innovative Science Content Course."** *Journal of Science Teacher Education* 10, no. 2: 69–91.

This article discusses the preparation of prospective elementary school teachers in the face of science-education reform.

Naylor, S., and B. Keogh. 1999. **"Constructivism in Classroom: Theory into Practice."** *Journal of Science Teacher Education* 10, no. 2: 93–106.

This article discusses the influence of constructivism in teacher education courses promoting constructivist classroom teaching practice.

Pedersen, J. E., and R. K. Yerrick. 2000. **"Technology in Science Teacher Education: Survey of Current Uses and Desired Knowledge among Science Educators."** *Journal of Science Teacher Education* 11, no. 2: 131–153.

This article discusses the expectations of incorporating technology (e.g., desktop computers, the Internet) in science teaching and technological literacy among science teachers.

Putnam, R. T., and H. Borko. 2000. **"What Do New Views of Knowledge and Thinking Have To Say about Research on Teacher Learning?"** *Educational Researcher* 29, no. 1: 4–15.

This article discusses the role of cognitive theory in teacher education.

Sánchez, G., and M. V. Valcárcel. 1999. **"Science Teachers' Views and Practices in Planning for Teaching."** *Journal of Research in Science Teaching* 36, no. 4: 493–513.

This article discusses science teachers' views about and practices in lesson planning in Spain.

Schriver, M., and C. M. Czerniak. 1999. **"A Comparison of Middle and Junior High Science Teachers' Levels of Efficacy and Knowledge of Developmentally Appropriate Curriculum and Instruction."** *Journal of Science Teacher Education* 10, no. 1: 21–42.

This article discusses the role of teachers' confidence in their ability to teach science content as well as their competence to teach science content.

Shepard, L. A. 2000. **"The Role of Assessment in a Learning Culture."** *Educational Researcher* 29, no. 7: 4–14.

This article discusses the historical role of assessment in improving teaching and learning during the twentieth century.

Shumba, O. 1999. **"Relationship between Secondary Science Teachers' Orientation to Traditional Culture and Beliefs Concerning Science Instructional Ideology."** *Journal of Research in Science Teaching* 36, 3: 333–355.

This article discusses how high school science teachers in Zimbabwe balance traditional culture with their beliefs about science teaching.

Simmons, P. E., et al. 1999. **"Beginning Teachers: Beliefs and Classroom Actions."** *Journal of Research in Science Teaching* 36, no. 8: 930–954.

This article discusses systemic reform in science education and the role of science teachers' beliefs in their classroom practice.

Smylie, M. A. 1996. **"From Bureaucratic Control to Building Human Capital: The Importance of Teacher Learning in Educational Reform."** *Educational Researcher* 25, no. 9: 9–11.

This article discusses the role of teacher learning and education (versus student learning and curriculum standards) in educational reform.

Spencer, D. A. 1996. **"Teachers and Educational Reform."** *Educational Researcher* 25, no. 9: 15–17, 40.

This article discusses teachers' professional role and image as they relate to educational reform.

Stahl, S. A. 1999. **"Why Innovations Come and Go (and Mostly Go): The Case of Whole Language."** *Educational Researcher* 28, no. 8: 13–22.

This article discusses the wide historical variation in reading education during the twentieth century.

Thair, M., and D. F. Treagust. 1999. **"Teacher Training Reforms in Indonesian Secondary Science: The Importance of Practical Work in Physics."** *Journal of Research in Science Teaching* 36, no. 3: 357–371.

This article discusses the constraints on the reform of science teaching in Indonesia.

Tobin, K., C. McRobbie, and D. Anderson. 1997. **"Dialectical Constraints to the Discursive Practices of a High School Physics Community."** *Journal of Research in Science Teaching* 34, no. 5: 491–507.

This article discusses the role of dialogue in classroom learning situations.

Waldrip, B. G., and P. C. Taylor. 1999. **"Permeability of Students' Worldviews to Their School Views in a Non-Western Developing Country."** *Journal of Research in Science Teaching* 36, no. 3: 289–303.

This article discusses the compatibility between children's non-Western worldviews with school science instruction advocating a Western worldview.

Zeichner, K. 1999. **"The New Scholarship in Teacher Education."** *Educational Researcher* 28, no. 9: 4–15.

This article discusses research on teacher education in the United States since the late 1970s.

Books

Apple, M. W., and J. A. Beane, eds. 1995. ***Democratic Schools.*** Alexandria, VA: Association for Supervision and Curriculum Development.

This book discusses the goal of a democratic ideal in education for public schools and concludes that schools should reflect shared interests, freedom in interaction, participation, and social relationships.

Ayers, W., ed. 1995 ***To Become a Teacher: Making a Difference in Children's Lives.*** New York: Teachers College Press.

This book discusses the ways in which teaching is a professional calling, an intellectual challenge, and a profoundly human enterprise.

Bell, B., and J. Gilbert. 1996. *Teacher Development: A Model from Science Education.* London: Falmer Press.

This book discusses a teacher development process that took place for a group of science teachers in New Zealand.

Beyer, L. E., and M. W. Apple, eds. 1988. *The Curriculum: Problems, Politics, and Possibilities.* Albany, NY: SUNY Press.

This book discusses six major areas of theory and practice relevant to curriculum: historical dimensions, planning and organization, selecting appropriate content, pedagogy, technology, and evaluation.

Bruner, J. 1996. *The Culture of Education.* Cambridge, MA: Harvard University Press.

This book discusses the fact that education can usher children into their societal culture as complete participants but often fails to do so.

Conrad, C. F., and J. Grant-Haworth, eds. 1995. *Revisioning Curriculum in Higher Education.* Needham Heights, MA: Simon and Schuster.

This book discusses how curricula have evolved at the college and university level.

Cuban, L. 1999. *How Scholars Trumped Teachers: Change without Reform in University Curriculum, Teaching, and Research, 1890–1990.* New York: Teachers College Press.

This book discusses the historical roles of teaching, research, and curricula at Stanford University.

DeBoer, G. E. 1991. *A History of Ideas in Science Education: Implications for Practice.* New York: Teachers College Press.

This book discusses the historical evolution of science education in the United States.

Dewey, J. 1938. *Experience and Education.* New York: Macmillan.

———. 1916. *Democracy and Education: An Introduction to the Philosophy of Education.* New York: Macmillan.

These classic books discuss the role of education as a means of advancement for individuals and society. Together, these two books laid the foundation for a new and progressive movement in U.S. education.

Elliott, J. 1998. *The Curriculum Experiment: Meeting the Challenge of Social Change.* Buckingham, UK: Open University Press.

This book discusses the interface between curriculum policy and practice, on one hand, and social change within technologically driven advanced societies on the other.

Freire, P. 1998a. *Pedagogy of Freedom: Ethics, Democracy, and Civic Courage.* New York: Rowman and Littlefield.

———. 1998b. *Teachers as Cultural Workers: Letter to Those Who Dare Teach.* Boulder, CO: Westview Press.

———. 1992. *Pedagogy of Hope.* New York: Continuum.

———. 1985. *The Politics of Education: Culture, Power, and Liberation.* New York: Bergin and Garvey.

———. 1973. *Education for Critical Consciousness.* New York: Continuum.

———. 1970. *Pedagogy of the Oppressed.* New York: Continuum.

These books collectively present Paulo Freire's lifelong efforts to advocate adult literacy, democratic society, and civic participation within a Third World context. Education and the passionate, caring pedagogy of teachers are viewed as the vehicles that will transform and promote meaningfulness in society and life.

Fullan, M. 1993. *Change Forces: Probing the Depths of Educational Reform.* London: Falmer Press.

This book discusses the nature of educational reform, its complexity, and the inherent systematic forces that conspire to undermine it.

Giroux, H. 1988. *Teachers as Intellectuals: Toward a Critical Pedagogy of Learning.* Boston: Bergin and Garvey.

This book discusses the new role teachers need to assume in order to produce a new generation of learners as intellectual leaders.

Giroux, H. A., and P. McLaren, eds. 1989. *Critical Pedagogy, the State, and Cultural Struggle.* Albany, NY: SUNY Press.

This book discusses a theory of schooling that takes teaching, learning, and cultural dynamics, collectively, into account.

Good, T. L., ed. 2000. *American Education: Yesterday, Today, and Tomorrow.* Chicago: University of Chicago Press.

This book is the ninety-ninth yearbook of the National Society for the Study of Education. It primarily discusses the evolution of educational beliefs, curriculum content, classroom practices, and the profession of teaching during the twentieth century.

Goodchild, L. F., and H. S. Wechsler, eds. 1997. *The History of Higher Education,* 2nd ed. Boston: Pearson Custom Publishing.

This book discusses the historical evolution of colleges and universities in the United States since the colonial era.

Goodlad, J. I. 1994. *Educational Renewal: Better Teachers, Better Schools.* San Francisco: Josey-Bass.

This book discusses how "centers of pedagogy" can bring schools and teacher education programs together to form a mutually renewing relationship.

Goodson, I. 1993. *School Subjects and Curriculum Change.* London: Falmer Press.

This book discusses the political implications of school curricula from a sociohistorical perspective.

Grimmett, P., and G. L. Erickson, eds. 1988. *Reflection in Teacher Education.* Vancouver, BC: Pacific Educational Press.

This book discusses the role of instructional supervision in teacher education and professional development.

Jackson, P. W., ed. 1996. *Handbook of Research on Curriculum.* New York: Macmillan.

This book discusses the theoretical and philosophical principles of curriculum development and the relevant role of research on curriculum policy and practice.

Kincheloe, J. L. 1993. *Toward a Critical Politics of Teacher Thinking: Mapping the Postmodern.* Westport, CT: Bergin and Garvey.

This book argues that teacher education needs to take a new direction in order to empower teachers to be self-directed professionals.

Kincheloe, J. L., and S. R. Steinberg, eds. 1998. *Unauthorized Methods: Strategies for Critical Teaching.* New York: Routledge.

———. 1992. *Thirteen Questions: Reframing Education's Conversation.* New York: Peter Lang.

These books discuss the current state of education and teaching and seek to reinvigorate school systems and classroom practice with a new, progressive application of pedagogical theory.

Kincheloe, J. L., S. R. Steinberg, and P. H. Hinchey, eds. 1999. *The Post-Formal Reader: Cognition and Education.* New York: Falmer Press.

This book discusses general psychology and educational psychology from a postmodern and critical perspective. Specifically discussed are topics of normalcy, learning, intelligence, and critical thinking.

Kincheloe, J. L., S. R. Steinberg, and D. J. Tippins. 1992. *The Stigma of Genius: Einstein and beyond Modern Education.* Boulder, CO: Hollowbrook Publishing.

This book discusses the ways that the U.S. educational system has deadened the consciousness and intellectual creativity of teachers, children, and schools.

Lambert, L., et al., eds. 1995. *The Constructivist Leader.* New York: Teachers College Press.

This book discusses the role of constructivism as a means to a new conceptualization of school leadership and school as a learning community.

Maeroff, G. I. 1988. *The Empowerment of Teachers: Overcoming the Crisis of Confidence.* New York: Teachers College Press.

This book argues that teachers need more autonomy and recognition in our American school systems and that without these, the teaching profession is in peril.

McLaren, P. 1998. *Life in Schools: An Introduction to Critical Pedagogy in the Foundations of Education.* New York: Longman.

This book discusses how children's lives play a critical role in schooling and argues that schools need to consider this role more diligently in order for education to transform itself and the lives of its students.

McLaren, P., and P. Leonard. 1993. *Paulo Freire: A Critical Encounter.* New York: Routledge.

This book critically analyzes the work of Paulo Freire. It specifically looks to Freire's work within a Third World context and considers its potential application to First World countries (e.g., the United States).

McNeil, J. D. 1990. *Curriculum: A Comprehensive Introduction.* 4th ed. New York: HarperCollins.

This book provides a general overview of curriculum theories, reform movements, and implications for teaching.

Novak, J. M., ed. 1994. *Democratic Teacher Education: Programs, Processes, Problems, and Prospects.* Albany, NY: SUNY Press.

This book discusses the creative efforts of teacher educators who advocate democracy in their own teaching and for the prospective teachers they train.

Pinar, W. F., ed. 1998. *Curriculum: Toward New Identities.* New York: Garland Publishers.

This book discusses how postmodern pedagogical practice helps reconceptualize curriculum.

Russell, Y., and H. Munby, eds. 1992. *Teachers and Teaching: From Classroom to Reflection.* London: Falmer Press.

This book discusses the role of self-reflection in teacher education and how it can be translated into classroom practice.

Seale, C., ed. 1998. *Researching Society and Culture.* London: Sage Publications.

This book discusses research methods relevant to the social sciences. Such research deals with social and cultural dynamics and is thus applicable to classrooms and schools, which teachers need to be aware of.

Shor, I., and P. Freire. 1987. *A Pedagogy for Liberation.* Westport, CT: Bergin and Garvey.

This book discusses how teachers, in both First and Third World contexts, can transform classrooms and in turn empower students to be critical thinkers and transform themselves and society.

Tabachnich, B. R., and K. Zeichner, eds. 1991. *Issues and Practices in Inquiry-Oriented Teacher Education.* London: Falmer Press.

This book discusses how self-reflection can be promoted in teacher education programs.

Weil, D., and H. K. Anderson, eds. 2000. *Perspectives in Critical Thinking: Essays by Teachers in Theory and Practice.* New York: Peter Lang.

This book discusses the theoretical applications relevant to critical thinking and shows how teaching practices promote critical thinking in various domains of education.

Wittrock, M. C., ed. 1986. *Handbook of Research on Teaching.* 3rd ed. New York: Macmillan.

This book discusses the theoretical and philosophical principles of teaching and the role of research on the profession.

Doctoral Dissertations

Davis, S. J. H. 2000. **"A Survey of Public School Educators on the Needs of Home-Schooled Students Entering the Public School at the Secondary Level."** Ed.D. diss., Wilmington College, Delaware.

This dissertation explores the perceptions public school teachers have about home-schooling curricula and pedagogy, as well as about children who have matriculated to public schools from the home-schooling environment.

Hallock, S. 2000. **"A Transition Intervention Program for At-Risk Students in a Rural Public High School."** Ed.D. diss., Wilmington College, Delaware.

This dissertation explores the impact of an intervention program on the academic success of ninth graders in terms of achievement, attendance, and behavior.

Kerbin, D. L. 2000. **"Project Outreach Extended-Day Program: A Formative Evaluation of Implementation."** Ed.D. diss., Wilmington College, Delaware.

This dissertation explores the efficacy of an after-school program's implementation aimed at improving achievement by African American children on state accountability testing.

Reinard Stock, D. 2000. **"A Qualitative Examination of the Processes of Racial and Gender Identity Development in Female Multicultural Facilitators."** Ed.D. diss., Wilmington College, Delaware.

This dissertation explores the ways that teachers become advocates of multicultural education in their schools.

Shiels, K. 2001. **"A Qualitative Analysis of the Factors Influencing Stress and Second Language Acquisition in Immigrant Students."** Ed.D. diss., Wilmington College, Delaware.

This dissertation explores the role of enculturation as it relates to children receiving ESL education.

Sole, D. G. 2000. **"Evaluating the Impact of the Intensive Scheduling Model at a Rural High School: The Student and Teacher Behavior Changes."** Ed.D. diss., Wilmington College, Delaware.

This dissertation explores the impact of "block" scheduling on student achievement, classroom climate, and teaching practices.

Thurber, T. 2001. **"The Impact of the Academic Programs for Excellence on Promoting Academic Rigor at Easton High School."** Ed.D. diss., Wilmington College, Delaware.

This dissertation explores the impact of a new curriculum on student achievement.

Williams, H. E. 2000. **"A Descriptive Study: African-American Adolescent Males, Absenteeism, Mentoring, and Alienation in Rural Public Schools."** Ed.D. diss., Wilmington College, Delaware.

This dissertation explores the impact of a mentoring program on African American male high school students demonstrating high absenteeism.

Recommended Journals for Further Reading

Educational Researcher

This journal publishes articles that report, synthesize, review, or analyze research and development work in education. It also publishes book reviews and commentaries regarding trends, policies, and practices in education. It is a major publication of the American Educational Research Association (AERA).

Educational Studies

This journal publishes a broad array of articles related to educational foundations. It particularly endorses interdisciplinary scholarship and is a publication of the American Educational Studies Association.

Higher Education Research and Development

This journal publishes a broad array of articles to serve the needs and interests of those working in institutions of higher education.

Journal of Teacher Education

This journal publishes articles on scholarship relevant to the academic preparation of classroom educators. It is a publication of the American Association of Colleges for Teacher Education (AACTE).

Reviews in Educational Research

This journal, another AERA publication, publishes integrative reviews and interpretations of educational research literature, in terms of both theoretical principles and methodologies.

Review of Higher Education

This journal publishes a broad array of articles related to theory, policy, and practice in higher-education institutions. It is the journal of the Association for the Study of Higher Education (ASHE).

NONPRINT RESOURCES

Current Issues in Education (CIE)

This electronic journal is published by Arizona State University and primarily seeks to advance scholarly thought with articles promoting dialogue, research, practice, and policy with regards to education.
http://cie.ed.asu.edu

Education Policy Analysis Archives (EPAA)

This electronic journal is published by Arizona State University and primarily examines historical aspects of educational policies, practices, and reforms.
http://epaa.asu.edu

Education Review

This electronic journal is published by Arizona State University and primarily provides reviews of books written about education.
http://coe.asu.edu/edrev

International Electronic Journal for Leadership in Learning (IEJLL)

This electronic journal is published by the University of Calgary and primarily promotes the study and discussion of substantive leadership issues as they relate to educational communities, especially as they impact life in schools.
http://www.ucalgary.ca/~iejll

International Journal: Continuous Improvement Monitor (The CIM Journal)

This electronic journal (a member of the International Consortium for Advanced Academic Publications) publishes articles by researchers and practitioners on issues pertaining to the continuous improvement of quality in education (for K–12 and college/university levels).
http://llanes.panam.edu/

Journal of Educational Thought (JET)

This electronic journal is published by the University of Calgary and promotes speculative, critical, and historical research concerning educational theory and practice relevant to many different aspects of education (e.g., administration, curriculum, and pedagogy).
http://external.educ.ucalgary.ca/jet/jet.html

Practical Assessment, Research, and Evaluation (PARE)

This electronic journal is published jointly by the ERIC Clearinghouse on Assessment and Evaluation (ERIC/AE) and the Department of Measurement, Statistics, and Evaluation at the University of Maryland, College Park. It primarily provides articles aiming to make a positive impact on assessment, research, evaluation, and teaching practice, especially at the local education agency level.
http://ericae.net/pare

•◦ Index

➌ About the Author

Dr. Pushkin was a high school and community college chemistry and physics teacher in the Tampa Bay, Florida, region from 1985 to 1993 before moving on to Penn State University, where he earned his Ph.D. in Curriculum and Instruction in 1995. From 1995 to 1998, he was a chemistry and physics professor at the university level in Pennsylvania and New Jersey. Since 1999, he has served as an education professor in New York City, New Jersey, and Delaware, working with both prospective and veteran teachers and teaching courses related to science instruction, curriculum theory, and educational research. He has worked with students pursuing their bachelor's, master's, and doctoral degrees.

Since 1986, he has published numerous articles related to teaching, learning, and curriculum issues in K–12 and university-level science education and has made several presentations on these issues at professional conferences in the United States (e.g., American Educational Research Association, 1998; National Association for Research in Science Teaching, 1999; Gender and Science Education Association, 1999), Canada (e.g., Science Teachers Association of Ontario, 1996; Canadian History of Education Association, 1998), Mexico (New Trends in Physics Teaching, 1997), China (International Cultural Research Network, 2000), and Europe (e.g., European Science Education Research Association, 1997, 1999, and 2001; Gender and Science and Technology Association, 2001). Dr. Pushkin is also currently writing other books based on his ongoing work on teaching and curriculum in higher education. He is a member of several professional organizations related to science education, teacher education, and educational research, and he serves as a reviewer or editorial board member for the following professional journals: *History of Intellectual Culture, Journal of College Science Teaching,* and *Journal of Research in Science Teaching.*